Implementing Electronic Document and Record Management Systems

Implementing Electronic Document and Record Management Systems

BY

AMELIA THOMPSON

KNOWLEDGE BAKERS

ISBN: 978-93-9001-373-9 (HB)

Published by : **Knowledge Bakers**
Pune, India
Email: info@knowledgebakers.com

PREFACE

In the digital age, the efficient management of electronic documents and records is paramount for organizations striving to enhance productivity, compliance, and information governance. Electronic Document and Record Management Systems (EDRMS) offer a comprehensive solution for organizing, storing, retrieving, and securing digital documents and records throughout their lifecycle. As organizations transition from paper-based processes to digital workflows, the successful implementation of EDRMS becomes essential for optimizing operational efficiency, ensuring regulatory compliance, and facilitating collaboration and knowledge sharing. As we embark on this exploration of implementing electronic document and record management systems, we delve into a realm where technology, information management, and organizational change converge, uncovering the principles, strategies, challenges, and best practices that define successful EDRMS initiatives.

This book, titled "Implementing Electronic Document and Record Management Systems," is crafted to provide a comprehensive guide to the planning, implementation, and optimization of EDRMS within organizations. Through collaboration with leading experts, practitioners, and consultants in information management and technology, we aim to offer readers a multidimensional and insightful journey through the complexities of EDRMS implementation.

As editors of this volume, we have curated a collection of chapters that cover a wide range of topics in implementing EDRMS, including project planning, stakeholder engagement, system selection, customization, data migration, training, change management, and ongoing maintenance. Each chapter is structured to provide practical guidance, real-world examples, case studies, and lessons learned to help organizations navigate the challenges and complexities of EDRMS implementation.

Furthermore, this book seeks to highlight the strategic importance of EDRMS in the digital transformation journey of organizations and its impact on operational efficiency, risk management, and organizational performance. By showcasing examples of successful EDRMS implementations across various industries and sectors, we aim to inspire readers to adopt innovative approaches and collaborative strategies to maximize the value and benefits of EDRMS within their organizations.

As we embark on this enlightening journey through the world of implementing electronic document and record management systems, we extend our gratitude to the contributors whose expertise and dedication have enriched this book. We hope that "Implementing Electronic Document and Record Management Systems" serves as a valuable resource for professionals, managers, and executives involved in information management, technology, compliance, and organizational change, empowering them to successfully navigate the complexities of EDRMS implementation and unlock the full potential of digital transformation.

Amelia Thompson

CONTENTS

1

INTRODUCTION

Electronic document and records management system (EDRMS) is a type of content management system and refers to the combined technologies of document management and records management systems as an integrated system.

USE

Electronic document and records management is used by organizations to manage documents and records throughout the document life-cycle, from creation to destruction. Typically, systems consider a document or file to be a work-in-progress until it has undergone review, approval, lock-down, and (potentially) publication, where it will wait to be used. The version of the form that is saved containing user content will become a formal record within the organization.

Once a document achieves the status of a record, the organization may apply best-practice or legally enforced retention policies which state how the second half of the record life-cycle will progress. This typically involves retention (and protection from change), until some events occur which relate to the record and which trigger the final disposition schedule to apply to the record. Eventually, typically at a set time after these events, the record undergoes destruction.

EDRMS software

A range of software vendors offer these systems at an enterprise level (i.e. targeted at managing all documents and records within an enterprise). These vendors have historically provided electronic document management systems and have acquired smaller records management system companies. The seamlessness of the integration and the original intention of the records-management component to manage electronic records typically sets the complexity of deploying and potentially of using the final system. The

IRMS (Information and Records Management Society) (formerly known as the Records Management Society) was founded in 1983 as the main professional body for records managers in Great Britain and Ireland. Its objectives are to strive to further knowledge of good governance in the management of information and records created during the course of the business activities of any organisation, whatever their media, and to promote fellowship and co-operation amongst individuals working in the field.

All those in any country concerned with records and information, regardless of their professional or organisational status or qualifications, can join the society, which currently has over 1100 members from 30 countries. There are specific interest groups for the public sector, third sector, SharePoint, property, financial and higher and further education, as well as geographical groups in Ireland, Scotland and Wales and the North, Midlands, London, and South West of England.

The society organises meetings and an annual conference, publishes the bi-monthly Record Management Bulletin containing comment, analysis, case studies and news from the UK and international information and records management scene, produces information guides on issues such as records retention and information technology, and runs training courses for members and non-members.

The society changed its name to the Information and Records Management Society in 2010. The society changed its name to the IRMS in 2014 along with its strap line from "The Home of Information and Records Management" to The Interactive Hub of the Information World.

National Archives and Records Administration

The National Archives and Records Administration (NARA) is an independent agency of the United States government charged with preserving and documenting government and historical records and with increasing public access to those documents, which comprise the National Archives. NARA is officially responsible for maintaining and publishing the legally authentic and authoritative copies of acts of Congress, presidential directives, and federal regulations. The NARA also transmits votes of the Electoral College to Congress.

The Archivist of the United States is the chief official overseeing the operation of the National Archives and Records Administration. The Archivist not only maintains the official documentation of the passage of amendments to the U.S. Constitution by state legislatures, but has the authority to declare when the constitutional threshold for passage has been reached, and therefore when an act has become an amendment.

The Office of the Federal Register publishes the Federal Register, Code of Federal Regulations, and United States Statutes at Large, among others. It also administers the Electoral College.

The National Historical Publications and Records Commission (NHPRC)-the agency's grant-making arm-awards funds to state and local governments, public and private archives, colleges and universities, and other nonprofit organizations to preserve and publish historical records. Since 1964, the NHPRC has awarded some 4,500 grants.

The Office of Government Information Services (OGIS) is a Freedom of Information Act (FOIA) resource for the public and the government. Congress has charged NARA with reviewing FOIA policies, procedures and compliance of Federal agencies and to recommend changes to FOIA. NARA's mission also includes resolving FOIA disputes between Federal agencies and requesters.

Rotunda of the National Archives Building

Originally, each branch and agency of the U.S. government was responsible for maintaining its own documents, which often resulted in the loss and destruction of records. Congress established the National Archives Establishment in 1934 to centralize federal record keeping, with the Archivist of the United States as chief administrator. The National Archives was incorporated with GSA in 1949; in 1985 it became an independent agency as NARA (National Archives and Records Administration).

The first Archivist, R.D.W. Connor, began serving in 1934, when the National Archives was established by Congress. As a result of a first Hoover Commission recommendation, in 1949 the National Archives was placed within the newly formed General Services Administration (GSA). The Archivist served as a subordinate official to the GSA Administrator until the National Archives and Records Administration became an independent agency on April 1, 1985.

In March 2006, it was revealed by the Archivist of the United States in a public hearing that a memorandum of understanding between NARA and various government agencies existed to "reclassify", i.e., withdraw from public access, certain documents in the name of national security, and to do so in a manner such that researchers would not be likely to discover the process (the U.S. reclassification program). An audit indicated that more than one third withdrawn since 1999 did not contain sensitive information. The program was originally scheduled to end in 2007.

In 2010, Executive Order 13526 created the National Declassification Center to coordinate declassification practices across agencies, provide secure document services to other agencies, and review records in NARA custody for declassification.

Records

NARA's holdings are classed into "record groups" reflecting the governmental department or agency from which they originated. Records include paper documents, microfilm, still pictures, motion pictures, and electronic media.

Archival descriptions of the permanent holdings of the federal government in the custody of NARA are stored in the National Archives Catalog. The archival descriptions include information on traditional paper holdings, electronic records, and artifacts. As of December 2012, the catalog consisted of about 10 billion logical data records describing 527,000 artifacts and encompassing 81% of NARA's records. There are also 922,000 digital copies of already digitized materials.

Most records at NARA are in the public domain, as works of the federal government are excluded from copyright protection. However, records from other sources may still be protected by copyright or donor agreements. Executive Order 13526 directs originating agencies to declassify documents if possible before shipment to NARA for long-term storage, but NARA also stores some classified documents until they can be declassified. Its Information Security Oversight Office monitors and sets policy for the U.S. government's security classification system.

Many of NARA's most requested records are frequently used for genealogy research. This includes census records from 1790 to 1940, ships' passenger lists, and naturalization records.

Archival Recovery Teams

The most well known facility of the National Archives and Records Administration is the National Archives Building (informally known as "Archives I"), located north of the National Mall on Constitution Avenue in Washington, D.C.. A sister facility, known as the National Archives at College Park ("Archives II") was opened 1994 near the University of Maryland, College Park. The Washington National Records Center (WNRC), also located in the Washington, D.C., metropolitan area, is a large warehouse facility where federal records that are still under the control of the creating agency are stored. Federal government agencies pay a yearly fee for storage at the facility. In accordance with federal records schedules, documents at WNRC are transferred to the legal custody of the National Archives after a certain time; this usually involves a relocation of the records to College Park. Temporary records at WNRC are either retained for a fee or destroyed after retention times have elapsed. WNRC also offers research services and maintains a small research room.

Across the United States, the National Archives maintains both research facilities and additional federal records centers (FRCs). In many cases, the research rooms of regional archives are located at the same site as the federal records center, which are inaccessible to the public.

Public-private partnerships

In an effort to make its holdings more widely available and more easily accessible, the National Archives began entering into public-private partnerships in 2006. A joint venture with Google will digitize and offer NARA video online. When announcing the agreement, Archivist Allen Weinstein said that this pilot program is "... an important step for the National Archives to achieve its goal of becoming an archive without walls. Our new strategic plan emphasizes the importance of providing access to records anytime, anywhere. This is one of many initiatives that we are launching to make our goal a reality. For the first time, the public will be able to view this collection of rare and unusual films on the Internet."

On January 10, 2007, the National Archives and Fold3.com (formerly Footnote) launched a pilot project to digitize historic documents from the National Archives holdings. Allen Weinstein explained that this partnership would "allow much greater access to approximately 4.5 million pages of important documents that are currently available only in their original format or on microfilm" and "would also enhance NARA's efforts to preserve its original records."

In July 2007, the National Archives announced it would make copies of its collection of Universal Newsreels from 1929 to 1967 available for purchase through CreateSpace, an Amazon.com subsidiary. During the announcement, Weinstein noted that the agreement would "... reap major benefits for the public-at-large and for the National Archives." Adding, "While the public can come to our College Park, Maryland, research room to view films and even copy them at no charge, this new program will make our holdings much more accessible to millions of people who cannot travel to the Washington, D.C. area." The agreement also calls for CreateSpace partnership to provide the National Archives with digital reference and preservation copies of the films as part of NARA's preservation program.

In May 2008, the National Archives announced a five-year agreement to digitize selected records including the complete U.S. Federal Census Collection, 1790-1930, passenger lists from 1820 to 1960 and World War I and World War II draft registration cards. The partnership agreement allows for exclusive use of the digitized records by Ancestry.com for a 5-year embargo period whereupon the digital records will be turned over to the National Archives.

Social media

On June 18, 2009, the National Archives announced the launching of a YouTube channel "to showcase popular archived films, inform the public about upcoming events around the country, and bring National Archives exhibits to the people." Also in 2009, the National Archives launched a Flickr photostream to share portions of its photographic holdings with the general public. A new teaching-with-documents Web site premiered in 2010 and was developed by the education team. The site features 3,000 documents, images, and recordings from the holdings of the Archives. It also features lesson plans and tools for creating new classroom activities and lessons.

In 2011, the National Archives initiated a WikiProject on the English Wikipedia to expand collaboration in making its holdings widely available through Wikimedia.

Notable crimes

- In 1963, Robert Bradford Murphy and his wife, Elizabeth Irene Murphy were arrested and sentenced to ten years in prison for stealing documents from several federal depositories, including the National Archives.
- In 1987, Charles Merrill Mount was arrested and sentenced to five years in prison for stealing 400 documents from the National Archives.
- In 2002, Shawn Aubitz was arrested for stealing hundreds of documents and photographs from the National Archives; served 21 months in prison and paid $73,000 in restitution.
- In 2005, Sandy Berger was charged with an unauthorized removal of documents from the National Archives; sentenced to 100 hours of community service and fined $50,000.
- In 2005, Howard Harner was sentenced to two years in prison and fined $10,000 after stealing 100 documents from the National Archives.
- In 2006, Denning McTague was sentenced to 15 months in prison and fined $3,000 after stealing 164 documents from the National Archives.
- In 2011, Leslie Waffen was sentenced to 18 months in prison after stealing 955 recordings from the National Archives.
- In 2011, Thomas Lowry was permanently banned from the National Archives after he confessed to altering the date on a presidential pardon signed by Abraham Lincoln.
- In 2011, Barry Landau and Jason Savedoff were arrested and sentenced to seven-and-a-half years in prison for stealing ten thousand documents from the National Archives.

Records management taxonomy is the representation of data, upon which the classification of unstructured content is based, within an organization. It may manifest itself as metadata in structured database fields or in folder structures represented to end users from a user interface within a system. It is created to facilitate the correct records management policies within the organization, fulfilment of regulatory compliance, integration to operational and knowledge management systems and the search for information within the organization. It can be applied to physical and or electronic records.

Disciplines and or professions may create template taxonomies which are commonly used such as for Engineering and or Pharmaceutical Research. However, most organizations and or business functions within an organization may define taxonomies based on organizational requirements.

A records manager is the professional responsible for records management in an organization. This role has evolved over time and takes many forms, with many related areas of knowledge required for professional competency.

Records managers are found in all types of organizations, including business, government, and nonprofit sectors. Generally, dedicated (i.e., full-time) records managers are found in larger organizations.

History

Records management evolved from the development of archives in the United States government following World War II. With the explosion of paper records during that war, better systems of management were needed to retain and make the records available for current use. Records managers became specialists that bridged the gap between file clerks and archivists. The profession expanded into the corporate world in the 1950s.

Competencies

The records manager generally provides expertise in records management, constituting knowledge areas of:

- Records creation and use
- Active and inactive records systems
- Records appraisal, retention and disposition
- Vital records identification and protection
- Records and information management technology
- The Records Manager may also have subject matter expertise in:
- Law
- Privacy and data protection
- Information technology and electronic storage systems
- General business principles

Specialization

Records managers are present in virtually every type of organization. The role can range from one of a file clerk to the chief information officer of an organization. Records managers may focus on operational responsibilities, design strategies and policies for maintaining and utilizing information, or combine elements of those jobs.

The health care industry has a very specialized view of records management. Health information management involves not only maintaining patient files, but also coding the files to reflect the diagnoses of the conditions suffered by patients. The American Health Information Management Association (AHIMA) is the professional organization in this space.

Records managers in the pharmaceutical industry are responsible for maintaining laboratory research, clinical trials data, and manufacturing information.

Records managers in law firms often have responsibility for managing conflicts, as well as managing client matter files.

In the United States, records managers in nuclear power plants specialize in compliance with the Nuclear Regulatory Commission rules regarding the handling of nuclear materials. NIRMA is their local professional organization.

Records managers may have degrees in a wide variety of subjects in all disciplines, and few universities offer formal records management education. Graduate-level programs are often specialties within Library Science and Archival Science programs. Graduate-level Public History programs generally offer coursework in archives and records management. A recent addition to records management education in the United States is the MARA - the Master of Archives and Records Administration degree program - offered by the San Jose State University School of Information.

Professional and trade organizations offer continuing education conferences, seminars, and workshops. Governmental archives and records management departments such as the National Archives and Records Administration offer educational programs of interest to government records managers.

A professional certification, the Certified Records Manager credential, is offered by the Institute of Certified Records Managers. Other organizations may offer certificates reflecting completion of a course of studies, attendance at a seminar, or passing a subject matter test.

Disaster recovery and business continuity auditing

Given organizations' increasing dependency on information technology to run their operations, Business continuity planning covers the entire organization, and Disaster recovery focuses on IT.

Auditing of documents covering an organization's business continuity and disaster recovery plans provides a third-party validation to stakeholders that the documentation is complete and does not contain material misrepresentations. Lack of completeness can result in overlooking secondary effects, such as when vastly increased work-at-home overloads incoming recovery site telecommunications capacity, and the bi-weekly payroll that was not critical within the first 48 hours is now causing perceived problems in ever recovering, complicated by governmental and possibly union reaction. Often used together, the terms Business Continuity and Disaster Recovery are very different. Business Continuity refers to the ability of a business to continue critical functions and business processes after the occurrence of a disaster, whereas Disaster Recovery refers specifically to the Information Technology (IT) and data-centric functions of the business, and is a subset of Business Continuity.

Metrics

The primary objective is to protect the organization in the event that all or part of its operations and/or computer services are rendered partially or completely unusable. A DR plan illustrating the chronology of the RPO and the RTO with respect to the MI. Minimizing downtime and data loss during disaster recovery is measured in terms of two concepts:

- Recovery Time Objective (RTO), time until a system is completely up and running
- Recovery Point Objective (RPO), a measures of the ability to recover files by specifying a point in time restore of the backup copy.
- that the procedures stated in the BCP and DR plan are actually consistent with real practice
- that a specific individual within the organization, who may be referred to as the disaster recovery officer, the disaster recovery liaison, the DR coordinator, or some other similar title, has the technical skills, training, experience, and abilities to analyze the capabilities of the team members to complete assigned tasks
- that more than one individual is trained and capable of doing a particular function. Tests and inquiries of personnel can help achieve this objective.

Documentation

To maximize their effectiveness, disaster recovery plans are most effective when updated frequently, and should:

- be an integral part of all business analysis processes,
- be revisited at every major corporate acquisition, at every new product launch and at every new system development milestone.

Adequate records need to be retained by the organization. The auditor examines records, billings, and contracts to verify that records are being kept. One such record is a current list of the organization's hardware and software vendors. Such list is made and periodically updated to reflect changing business practice. Copies of it are stored on and off site and are made available or accessible to those who require them. An auditor tests the procedures used to meet this objective and determine their effectiveness.

Disaster recovery plan

A disaster recovery plan (DRP) is a documented process or set of procedures to execute an organization's disaster recovery processes and recover and protect a business IT infrastructure in the event of a disaster. It is "a comprehensive statement of consistent actions to be taken before, during and after a disaster". The disaster could be natural, environmental or man-made. Man-made disasters could be intentional (for example, an act of a terrorist) or unintentional (that is, accidental, such as the breakage of a man-made dam).

Types of plans

Although there is no one-size-fits-all plan, there are three basic strategies:

1. prevention, including proper backups, having surge protectors and generators
2. detection, a byproduct of routine inspections, which may discover new (potential) threats
3. correction

The latter may include securing proper insurance policies, and holding a "lessons learned" brainstorming session.

Relationship to the Business Continuity Plan

The Business Continuity Plan (BCP) is a comprehensive organizational plan that includes the disaster recovery plan, and it consists of five component plans:

- Business Resumption Plan
- Occupant Emergency Plan
- Continuity of Operations Plan
- Incident Management Plan
- Disaster Recovery Plan

The first three (Business Resumption, Occupant Emergency, and Continuity of Operations Plans) do not deal with the IT infrastructure. The Incident Management Plan (IMP) does deal with the IT infrastructure, but since it establishes structure and procedures to address cyber attacks against an organization's IT systems, it generally does not represent an agent for activating the Disaster Recovery Plan, leaving The Disaster Recovery Plan as the only BCP component of interest to IT.

Benefits

Like every insurance plan, there are benefits that can be obtained from proper planning, including:

- Minimizing risk of delays
- Guaranteeing the reliability of standby systems
- Providing a standard for testing the plan
- Minimizing decision-making during a disaster
- Reducing potential legal liabilities
- Lowering unnecessarily stressful work environment

Planning and testing methodology

According to Geoffrey H. Wold of the Disaster Recovery Journal, the entire process involved in developing a Disaster Recovery Plan consists of 10 steps:

- Performing a risk assessment: The planning committee prepares a risk analysis and a business impact analysis (BIA) that includes a range of possible disasters. Each functional area of the organization is analyzed to determine potential consequences. Traditionally, fire has posed the greatest threat. A thorough plan provides for "worst case" situations, such as destruction of the main building.
- Establishing priorities for processing and operations: Critical needs of each department are evaluated and prioritized. Written agreements for alternatives selected are prepared, with details specifying duration, termination conditions, system testing, cost, any special security procedures, procedure for the notification of system changes, hours of operation, the specific hardware and other equipment required for processing, personnel requirements, definition of the circumstances constituting an emergency, process to negotiate service extensions, guarantee of compatibility, availability, non-mainframe resource requirements, priorities, and other contractual issues.
- Collecting data: This includes various lists (employee backup position listing, critical telephone numbers list, master call list, master vendor list, notification checklist), inventories (communications equipment, documentation, office equipment, forms, insurance policies, workgroup and data center computer hardware, microcomputer hardware and software, office supply, off-site storage location equipment, telephones, etc.), distribution register, software and data files backup/retention schedules, temporary location specifications, any other such lists, materials, inventories, and documentation. Pre-formatted forms are often used to facilitate the data gathering process.

- Organizing and documenting a written plan
- Developing testing criteria and procedures: reasons for testing include
- Testing the plan: An initial "dry run" of the plan is performed by conducting a structured walk-through test. An actual test-run must be performed. Problems are corrected.

Initial testing can be plan is done in sections and after normal business hours to minimize disruptions. Subsequent tests occur during normal business hours.

Types of tests include: checklist tests, simulation tests, parallel tests, and full interruption tests.

Caveats/controversies

Due to high cost, various plans are not without critics. Dell has identified five "common mistakes" organizations often make related to BCP/DR planning:

- Lack of buy-in: When executive management sees DR planning as "just another fake earthquake drill" or CEOs fail to make DR planning and preparation a priority
- Incomplete RTOs and RPOs: Failure to include each and every important business process or a block of data. Ripples can extend a disaster's impact. Payroll may not initially be mission-critical, but left alone for several days, it can become more important than any of your initial problems.
- Systems myopia: A third point of failure involves focusing only on DR without considering the larger business continuity needs. Corporate office space lost to a disaster can result in an instant pool of teleworkers which, in turn, can overload a company's VPN overnight, overwork the IT support staff at the blink of an eye and cause serious bottlenecks and monopolies with the dial-in PBX system.
- Lax security: When there is a disaster, an organization's data and business processes become vulnerable. As such, security can be more important than the raw speed involved in a disaster recovery plan's RTO. The most critical consideration then becomes securing the new data pipelines: from new VPNs to the connection from offsite backup services.

Decisions and Strategies

- Site designation: hot site vs. cold site. A hot site is fully equipped to resume operations while a cold site does not have that capability. A warm site has the capability to resume some, but not all operations.

A cost-benefit analysis is needed.

- Occasional tests and trials verify the viability and effectiveness of the plan. An auditor looks into the probability that operations of the organization can be sustained at the level that is assumed in the plan, and the ability of the entity to actually establish operations at the site.
- The auditor can verify this through paper and paperless documentation and actual physical observation. The security of the storage site is also confirmed.
- Data backup: An audit of backup processes determines if (a) they are effective, and (b) if they are actually being implemented by the involved personnel.

The disaster recovery plan also includes information on how best to recover any data that has not been copied. Controls and protections are put in place to ensure that data is not damaged, altered, or destroyed during this process.

- Drills: Practice drills conducted periodically to determine how effective the plan is and to determine what changes may be necessary. The auditor's primary concern here is verifying that these drills are being conducted properly and that problems uncovered during these drills are addressed.
- Backup of key personnel - including periodic training and cross-training.

The auditor determines the adequacy of the company's insurance coverage (particularly property and casualty insurance) through a review of the company's insurance policies and other research.

Among the items that the auditor needs to verify are: the scope of the policy (including any stated exclusions), that the amount of coverage is sufficient to cover the organization's needs, and that the policy is current and in force. The auditor also ascertains, through a review of the ratings assigned by independent rating agencies, that the insurance company or companies providing the coverage have the financial viability to cover the losses in the event of a disaster.

Effective DR plans take into account the extent of a company's responsibilities to other entities and its ability to fulfill those commitments despite a major disaster. A good DR audit will include a review of existing MOA and contracts to ensure that the organization's legal liability for lack of performance in the event of disaster or any other unusual circumstance is minimized. Agreements pertaining to establishing support and assisting with recovery for the entity are also outlined. Techniques used for evaluating this area include an examination of the reasonableness of the plan, a determination of whether or not the plan takes all factors into account, and a verification of the contracts and agreements reasonableness through documentation and outside research.

Communication issues

The auditor must verify that planning ensures that both management and the recovery team have effective communication hardware, contact information for both internal communication and external issues, such as business partners and key customers.

Audit techniques include

- testing of procedures, interviewing employees, making comparison against the plans of other company and against industry standards,
- examining company manuals and other written procedures.
- direct observation that emergency telephone numbers are listed and easily accessible in the event of a disaster.

Emergency procedures

Procedures to sustain staff during a round-the clock disaster recovery effort are included in any good disaster recovery plan. Procedures for the stocking of food and water, capabilities of administering CPR/first aid, and dealing with family emergencies are clearly written and tested. This can generally be accomplished by the company through good training programs and a clear definition of job responsibilities. A review of the readiness capacity of a plan often includes tasks such as inquires of personnel, direct physical observation, and examination of training records and any certifications.

Environmental issues

The auditor must review procedures that take into account the possibility of power failures or other situations that are of a non-IT nature.

- Flashlights and candles may be needed.
- Safety procedures in case of gas leaks, fires or other such phenomena

MoReq2 is short for "Model Requirements for the Management of Electronic Records", second version. It consists of a formal requirements specification for a generic electronic records management system, accompanied by testing documentation and related information. Published in 2008 by the European Commission, it is intended for use across the European Union, but can be used elsewhere. MoReq2 is generally considered a de facto standard in Europe but it does not have any formal status as a standard.

Purpose

The MoReq2 specification is intended for users and suppliers of electronic records management systems and services, and educators. Its main intended usages are to serve as a basis for invitations to tender (also known as requests for proposal) and as a framework to guide development of new electronic records management systems. It can also be used to provide a basis for auditing existing electronic records management systems or services, and as a resource for academic or commercial trainers.

Availability

All the components of MoReq2, as well as translations and Chapters Zero (see below), are free to download from the official MoReq website. They are also available from several other websites. The requirements specification is also available in paper form from the European Commission as ISBN 978-92-79-09772-0.

History

The original MoReq was first conceived in the late 1990s by the DLM Forum (a European not-for-profit body), following the development and publication of US DoD 5015.2 by the United States Department of Defense. MoReq was intended to serve the same function as 5015.2, namely to describe a good electronic records management system; but whereas 5015.2 was designed specifically for the US defence community, MoReq was designed from the outset to be useful across the European Union and in any sector or industry. 5015.2 and MoReq therefore differ because the former is a standard that defines the mandatory behaviours of a system, whereas MoReq provides guidelines that define the capabilities of a good generic system - not all of which need be mandatory in a specific instance.

Development of the first version of MoReq was funded by the European Commission, and took place during 2000. MoReq was developed by a team of consultants supported by and Editorial Board of international experts. The resulting specification, frequently referred to (informally) as MoReq1, was published in 2001.

MoReq1 was received enthusiastically, being the subject of about a dozen translations and adaptations. However, its success was not accompanied by any form of governance or development; and there was no MoReq1 compliance testing programme. This prompted the DLM Forum to initiate the development of a major update, which was to become known as MoReq2.

Following the production of a scoping study report, the European Commission funded development of MoReq2. The development was once again performed by consultants, this time supported by panels of volunteer reviewers as well as by an Editorial Board of international experts. The panels were drawn from:

- suppliers of electronic records management system software;
- users and potential users of software;
- National Archives;
- professional bodies and trade associations.

Compliance testing

A compliance testing scheme was launched by the DLM Forum in Summer 2008. This scheme allows suppliers of electronic records management systems to submit their products for formal compliance testing. Suppliers can choose any testing centre accredited by the DLM Forum, and the results are applicable across Europe. Compliance testing requires that the core MoReq2 requirements are met; at the option of the supplier, requirements of any combination of 13 the optional modules. The first software product which has been MoReq2-certified is (Fabasoft Folio). It is at this time (June 2014) the only one worldwide.

Key features

MoReq2 is designed specifically to be an evolutionary upgrade of MoReq1. In addition to specifying functional requirements for a good, generic, electronic records management system it includes:

- Non-functional requirements.
- 13 "optional modules", each of which defines requirements for a set of features that are often required in tight integration to electronic records management, such as document management (thus providing the basis of a specification for an Electronic Document and Records Management System), fax, collaborative working environment, and content management.
- A metadata model that defines 345 metadata elements needed to support the functionality defined in the functional requirements.
- Testing documentation (test data, test conditions, expected results, instructions) to allow compliance testing.
- An xml schema consistent with the metadata model.
- Explanatory text, appendices and references.

In addition the MoReq2 structure allows for countries to develop country-specific, language-specific, or region-specific "Chapters Zero" that take account of linguistic differences, national and regional legislation, national standards etc.

Governance

The DLM Forum has established a MoReq Governance Board to guide the future development of MoReq. The Board is charged with:

- Managing ongoing development of MoReq.
- Managing the compliance testing process.
- Promoting the use of MoReq2.

- Validating translations and Chapters Zero.
- Ensuring the name and logo of MoReq2 are not inappropriately used.

The Institute of Certified Records Managers or ICRM is an international certifying organization of and for professional records and information managers. It is affiliated with ARMA International and the Nuclear Information and Records Management Association (NIRMA). It was incorporated in 1975 and is headquartered in Albany, New York.

The ICRM offers a six-part examination including sections focused on: Management Principles and the Records and Information (RIM) Program; Records and Information Creation and Use; Record Storage, Retrieval, Conversion, and Facilities; Records Appraisal, Retention, Protection and Disposition; and Technology. Part six (6) of the examination is a written exam consisting of case studies. Upon successful completion of which the applicant receives the designation of Certified Records Manager (CRM).

At the ARMA International Annual Conference and Expo in September 2016, the ICRM announced the creation of the Certified Records Analyst (CRA) designation. The CRA is a three-part examination including sections focused on: Records and Information Creation and Use; Record Storage, Retrieval, Conversion, and Facilities; and Records Appraisal, Retention, Protection and Disposition

Paperless office

A paperless office (or paper-free office) is a work environment in which the use of paper is eliminated or greatly reduced. This is done by converting documents and other papers into digital form, a process known as digitization. Proponents claim that "going paperless" can save money, boost productivity, save space, make documentation and information sharing easier, keep personal information more secure, and help the environment. The concept can be extended to communications outside the office as well.

Definition

The paperless world was a publicist's slogan, intended to describe the office of the future. It was facilitated by the popularization of video display computer terminals like the 1964 IBM 2260. An early prediction of the paperless office was made in a 1975 Business Week article. The idea was that office automation would make paper redundant for routine tasks such as record-keeping and bookkeeping, and it came to prominence with the introduction of the personal computer. While the prediction of a PC on every desk was remarkably prophetic, the "paperless office" was not. Improvements in printers and photocopiers have made it much easier to reproduce documents in bulk, causing the worldwide use of office paper to more than double from 1980 to 2000. This has been attributed to the increased ease of document production and widespread use of electronic communication, which has resulted in users receiving large numbers of documents that are often printed out. However, since about 2000, at least in the US, the use of office paper has leveled off and is now decreasing, which has been attributed to a generation shift; younger people are believed to be less inclined to print out documents, and more inclined to read them on a full-color interactive display screen. According to the United States Environmental Protection Agency, the average office worker generates approximately two pounds of paper and paperboard products each day.

The term "The Paperless Office" was first used in commerce by Micronet, Inc., an automated office equipment company, in 1978.

History

Traditional offices have paper-based filing systems, which may include filing cabinets, folders, shelves, microfiche systems, and drawing cabinets, all of which require maintenance, equipment, considerable space, and are resource-intensive. In contrast, a paperless office could simply have a desk, chair, and computer (with a modest amount of local or network storage), and all of the information would be stored in digital form. Speech recognition and speech synthesis could also be used to facilitate the storage of information digitally.

Once computer data is printed on paper, it becomes out-of-sync with computer database updates. Paper is difficult to search and arrange in multiple sort arrangements, and similar paper data stored in multiple locations is often difficult and costly to track and update. A paperless office would have a single-source collection point for distributed database updates, and a publish-subscribe system. Modern computer screens make reading less exhausting for the eyes; a laptop computer can be used on a couch or in bed. With tablet computers and smartphones, with many other low-cost value-added features like video animation, video clips, and full-length movies, many argue that paper is now obsolete to all but those who are resistant to technological change. eBooks are often free or low cost compared to hard-copy books.

Environmental impact of paper

Paper product manufacturing contributes significantly to deforestation and man-made climate change, and produces greenhouse gases. According to the American Forest & Paper Association, paper manufacturing is the third largest user of fossil fuels worldwide. Although measures such as recycling and using tree-free paper can help reduce the environmental impact of paper, most paper still ends up in landfills. Paper production also leads to air pollution, as paper manufacturing releases nitrogen dioxide (NO), sulfur dioxide (SO), and carbon dioxide (CO). Nitrogen dioxide and sulfur dioxide are major contributors to acid rain, whereas CO is a greenhouse gas responsible for climate change. Waste water discharged from pulp and paper mills contains solids, nutrients, and dissolved organic matter that are classified as pollutants. Nutrients such as nitrogen and phosphorus can cause or exacerbate eutrophication of fresh water bodies.

Printing inks and toners are very expensive and use environment-damaging volatile organic compounds, heavy metals and non-renewable oils, although standards for the amount of heavy metals in ink have been set by some regulatory bodies. Deinking recycled paper pulp results in a waste slurry, sometimes weighing 22% of the weight of the recycled wastepaper, which may go to landfills.

The need for paper is eliminated by using online systems, such as replacing index cards and rolodexes with databases, typed letters and faxes with email, and reference books with the internet. Another way to eliminate paper is to automate paper-based processes that rely on forms, applications and surveys to capture and share data. This method is referred to as "electronic forms" or e-forms and is typically accomplished by using existing print-perfect documents in electronic format to allow for pre-filling of existing data, capturing data manually entered online by end-users, providing secure methods to submit form data to processing systems, and digitally signing the electronic documents without printing.

The technologies that may be used with electronic forms automation include -

- Portable Document Format (PDF) - to create, display and interact with electronic documents and forms
- E-form (electronic form) management software - to create, integrate and route forms and form data with processing systems
- Databases - to capture data for prefilling and processing documents
- Workflow platforms - to route information, documents and direct process flow
- E-mail (electronics email) communication which allows sending and receiving information of all kinds and enable attachments
- Digital signature solutions - to digitally sign documents (used by end-users)
- Web servers - to host the process, receive submitted data, store documents and manage document rights

One of the main issues that has kept companies from adopting paperwork automation is difficulty capturing digital signatures in a cost-effective and compliant manner. The E-Sign Act of 2000 in the United States provided that a document cannot be rejected on the basis of an electronic signature and required all companies to accept digital signatures on documents. Today there are sufficient cost-effective options available, including solutions that do not require end-users to purchase hardware or software.

One of the great benefits of this type of software is that you can use OCR (Optical Character Recognition) to search the full text of any file. Additionally, tags can be added to each file to make it easier to locate certain files throughout the entire system.

Some paperless software offers a scanner, hardware and software and works seamlessly in separating and organizing important documents. Paperless software might also allow people to enable online signatures for important documents that can be used in any small business or office. Document management and archiving systems do offer some methods of automating forms. Typically, the point in which document management systems start working with a document is when the document is scanned and/or sent into the system. Many document management systems include the ability to read documents via optical character recognition (OCR) and use that data within the document management system's framework. While this technology is essential to achieving a paperless office it does not address the processes that generate paper in the first place.

DIGITIZING PAPER-BASED DOCUMENTS

Another key aspect of the paperless office philosophy is the conversion of paper documents, photos, engineering plans, microfiche and all the other paper based systems to digital documents. Technologies that may be used for this include scanners, digital mail solutions, book copiers, wide format scanners (for engineering drawings), microfiche scanners, fax to PDF conversion, online post offices, multifunction printers and document management systems. Each of these technologies uses software that converts the raster formats (bitmaps) into other forms depending on need. Generally, they involve some form of image compression technology that produces smaller raster images or use optical character recognition (OCR) to convert a document into text. A combination of OCR and raster is used to enable search ability while maintaining the original form of the document. An important step is the labeling related to paper-to-digital conversion and the cataloging of scanned documents. Some technologies have been developed to do this, but they generally involve either human cataloging or automated indexing on the OCR document. However, scanners and software continue to improve with the development of small, portable scanners that are able to scan doubled-sided A4 documents at around 30-35ppm to a raster format (typically TIFF fax 4 or PDF).

An issue faced by those wishing to take the paperless philosophy to the limit has been copyright laws. These laws may restrict the transfer of documents protected by copyright from one medium to another, such as converting books to electronic format.

Securing and tracing documents

As awareness of identity theft and data breaches became more widespread, new laws and regulations were enacted, requiring companies that manage or store personally identifiable information to take proper care of those documents. Paperless office systems are easier to secure than traditional filing cabinets, and can track individual accesses to each document.

Difficulties in adopting the paperless office

A major difficulty in "going paperless" is that much of a business's communication is with other businesses and individuals, as opposed to just being internal. Electronic communication requires both the sender and the recipient to have easy access to appropriate software and hardware. Costs and temporary productivity losses when converting to a paperless office are also a factor, as are government regulations, industry standards, legal requirements, and business policies which may also slow down the change. Businesses may encounter technological difficulties such as file format compatibility, longevity of digital documents, system stability, and employees and clients not having appropriate technological skills.

For these reasons, while there may be a reduction of paper, some uses of paper will likely remain indefinitely. However, a 2015 questionnaire suggested that nearly half of small/medium-sized businesses believed they were or could go paperless by the end of that year.

Machine-readable document

A machine-readable document is a document whose content can be readily processed by computers. Such documents are distinguished from machine-readable data by virtue of having sufficient structure to provide the necessary context to support the business processes for which they are created.

Definition

Data without context (language use) is meaningless and lacks the four essential characteristics of trustworthy business records specified in ISO 15489 Information and documentation -- Records management:

- Reliability
- Authenticity
- Integrity
- Usability

The vast bulk of information is unstructured data and, from a business perspective, that means it is "immature", i.e., Level 1 (chaotic) of the Capability Maturity Model. Such immaturity fosters inefficiency, diminishes quality, and limits effectiveness. Unstructured information is also ill-suited for records management functions, provides inadequate evidence for legal purposes, drives up the cost of discovery in litigation, and makes access and usage needlessly cumbersome in routine, ongoing business processes.

There are at least four aspects to machine-readability:

- First, words or phrases should be discretely delineated (tagged) so that computer software and/or hardware logic can be applied to them as individual conceptual elements.
- Second, the semantics of each element should be specified so that computers can help human beings achieve a common understanding of their meanings and potential usages.
- Third, if the relationships among the individual elements are also specified, computers can automatically apply inferences to them, thereby further relieving human beings of the burden of trying to understand them, particularly for purposes of inquiry, discovery, and analysis.
- Fourth, if the structures of the documents in which the elements occur are also specified, human understanding is further enhanced and the data becomes more reliable for legal and business-quality purposes.

As early as 1981, the U.S. Government Accountability Office (GAO) began reporting on the problem of inadequate record-keeping practices in the U.S. federal government. Such deficiencies are not unique to government and advances in information technology mean that most information is now "born digital" and thus potentially far more easily managed by automated means. However, in testimony to Congress in 2010, GAO highlighted problems with managing electronic records, and as recently as 2015, GAO has continued to report inadequacies in the performance of Executive Branch agencies in meeting records management requirements. Moreover, more than two decades after a major and formerly highly respected auditing firm, Arthur Andersen, met its demise due to a records destruction scandal, record-keeping practices became a central issue in the 2016 Presidential election.

On January 4, 2011, President Obama signed H.R. 2142, the Government Performance and Results Act (GPRA) Modernization Act of 2010 (GPRAMA), into law as P.L. 111-352. Section 10 of GPRAMA requires U.S. federal agencies to publish their strategic and performance plans and reports in searchable, machine-readable format. Additionally, in 2013, he issued Executive Order 13642, Making Open and Machine Readable the New Default for Government Information in general.

On July 28, 2016, the Office of Management and Budget (OMB) followed up by including in the revised issuance of Circular A-130 direction for agencies to use open, machine-readable formats and to publish "public information online in a manner that promotes analysis and reuse for the widest possible range of purposes", meaning that the information is both publicly accessible and machine-readable. On January 14, 2019, President Trump signed into law H.R. 4174, including Title II, the OPEN Government Data Act (OGDA), which codifies in law the requirement for agencies to make their public data assets available in machine-readable format.

In support of such policy direction, technological advancement is enabling more efficient and effective management and use of machine-readable electronic records. Document-oriented databases have been developed for storing, retrieving, and managing document-oriented information, also known as semi-structured data. Extensible Markup Language (XML) is a World Wide Web Consortium (W3C) Recommendation setting forth rules for encoding documents in a format that is both human-readable and machine-readable. Many XML editor tools have been developed and most, if not all major information technology applications support XML to greater or lesser degrees. The fact that XML itself is an open, standard, machine-readable format makes it relatively easy for application developers to do so.

The W3C's accompanying XML Schema (XSD) Recommendation specifies how to formally describe the elements in an XML document. With respect to the specification of XML schemas, the Organization for the Advancement of Structured Information Standards (OASIS) is a leading standards-developing organization. However, many technical developers prefer to work with JSON, and to define the structure of JSON data for validation, documentation, and interaction control, JSON Schema was developed by the Internet Engineering Task Force (IETF).

The Portable Document Format (PDF) is a file format used to present documents in a manner independent of application software, hardware, and operating systems. Each PDF file encapsulates a complete description of the presentation of the document, including the text, fonts, graphics, and other information needed to display it. PDF/A is an ISO-standardized version of the PDF specialized for use in the archiving and long-term preservation of electronic documents. PDF/A-3 allows embedding of other file formats, including XML, into PDF/A conforming documents, thus potentially providing the best of both human- and machine-readability. The W3C's XSL-FO (XSL Formatting Objects) markup language is commonly used to generate PDF files

Metadata, data about data, can be used to organize electronic resources, provide digital identification, and support the archiving and preservation of resources. In well-structured, machine-readable electronic records, the content can be repurposed as both data and metadata. In the context of electronic record-keeping systems, the terms "management" and "metadata" are virtually synonymous. Given proper metadata, records management functions can be automated, thereby reducing the risk of spoliation of evidence and other fraudulent manipulations of records. Moreover, such records can be used to automate the process of auditing data maintained in databases, thereby reducing the risk of single points of failure associated with the Machiavellian concept of a single source of truth.

Blockchain (database) is a new technology for maintaining continuously-growing lists of records secured from tampering and revision. A key feature is that every node in a decentralized system has a copy of the blockchain so there is no single point of failure subject to manipulation and fraud.

DIRKS, an acronym for Designing and Implementing Recordkeeping Systems, is a comprehensive manual outlining the process for creating records management systems including various business information records and transactions as outlined in the Australian Standard for Records Management - AS ISO 15489. DIRKS was developed by the National Archives of Australia in collaboration with the State Records Authority of New South Wales.

The manual consists of two parts, part one is the user's guide and part two is the set of steps themselves. DIRKS is an eight-step process in which all aspects, or as many as possible, of a business are studied in order to achieve a complete records management practice. In addition to these eight steps DIRKS includes several templates and questionnaires to guide one through the DIRKS methodology.

DIRKS was replaced in 2007 at the Australian Commonwealth level, but continues to be in use at state level in New South Wales as a non-tool to assist the public sector in complying with the State Records Authority of New South Wales State Records Act 1998.

Steps of the DIRKS methodology

Before a preliminary investigation occurs DIRKS suggests a pre-preliminary investigation is performed where it is established if there is a need for a records management program at the organization and is there support for a record keeping system to be put in place. If so the preliminary investigation can take place. There are four components to the DIRKS preliminary investigation.

1. Determine the scope of the preliminary investigation
2. Collect Information
3. Document the research of the investigation
4. Report to Senior Management

Step B: Analysis of business activity;

The purpose of Step B is to create a set of advisory statements from which an analysis of the organization's business activities can be determined. DIRKS suggests a set of systematic approaches to analyze an organization in a systematic way in order to reveal various business activities, how they are completed and who completes them.

Step C: Identification of recordkeeping requirements;

Step C has two main objectives. The first is to determine an organization's requirements in creation and retention of records of its business activities. The second objective is to document the determined requirements in a clear manner that can be used as a reference in the future.

Step D: Assessment of existing systems;

The main objective of Step D is to assess the existing recordkeeping systems and any other related information management systems that have the capacity to capture and maintain records. This assessment is to identify weaknesses and strengths within the existing system.

Step E: Identification of strategies for recordkeeping;

The main objective of Step E is to determine which policies, procedures, standards and various other tools will help the organization achieve its recordkeeping goals. With these strategies established a model for both record management and recordkeeping can be created.

Step F: Design of a recordkeeping system;

The objective in Step F is to use the information gained in steps A through E a plan can be developed that fulfills the requirements set out in Step C. The design should repair any faults found in Step D and include a full plan for integrating the new recordkeeping system

Step G: Implementation of a recordkeeping system;

The objective of Step G is put the recordkeeping system that was designed in Step F in place.

Step H: Post-implementation review.

The objective of Step H is to measure the effectiveness of the installed system and to make sure that in practice in fulfills all requirements as established and documented throughout the DIRKS manual.

Governance, risk management and compliance (GRC) is the umbrella term covering an organization's approach across these three areas: Governance, risk management, and compliance. The first scholarly research on GRC was published in 2007 where GRC was formally defined as "the integrated collection of capabilities that enable an organization to reliably achieve objectives, address uncertainty and act with integrity." The research referred to common "keep the company on track" activities conducted in departments such as internal audit, compliance, risk, legal, finance, IT, HR as well as the lines of business, executive suite and the board itself.

Overview

Governance, risk management, and compliance are three related facets that help assure an organization reliably achieves objectives, addresses uncertainty and acts with integrity. Governance is the combination of processes established and executed by the directors (or the board of directors) that are reflected in the organization's structure and how it is managed and led toward achieving goals. Risk management is predicting and managing risks that could hinder the organization from reliably achieving its objectives under uncertainty. Compliance refers to adhering with the mandated boundaries (laws and regulations) and voluntary boundaries (company's policies, procedures, etc.).

GRC is a discipline that aims to synchronize information and activity across governance, and compliance in order to operate more efficiently, enable effective information sharing, more effectively report activities and avoid wasteful overlaps. Although interpreted differently in various organizations, GRC typically encompasses activities such as corporate governance, enterprise risk management (ERM) and corporate compliance with applicable laws and regulations.

Organizations reach a size where coordinated control over GRC activities is required to operate effectively. Each of these three disciplines creates information of value to the other two, and all three impact the same technologies, people, processes and information. Substantial duplication of tasks evolves when governance, risk management and compliance are managed independently. Overlapping and duplicated GRC activities negatively impact both operational costs and GRC matrices. For example, each internal service might be audited and assessed by multiple groups on an annual basis, creating enormous cost and disconnected results. A disconnected GRC approach will also prevent an organization from providing real-time GRC executive reports. GRC supposes that this approach, like a badly planned transport system, every individual route will operate, but the network will lack the qualities that allow them to work together effectively.

If not integrated, if tackled in a traditional "silo" approach, most organizations must sustain unmanageable numbers of GRC-related requirements due to changes in technology, increasing data storage, market globalization and increased regulation.

Basic concepts

- Governance describes the overall management approach through which senior executives direct and control the entire organization, using a combination of management information and hierarchical management control structures. Governance activities ensure that critical management information reaching the executive team is sufficiently complete, accurate and timely to enable appropriate management decision making, and provide the control mechanisms to ensure that strategies, directions and instructions from management are carried out systematically and effectively.

- Risk management is the set of processes through which management identifies, analyzes, and, where necessary, responds appropriately to risks that might adversely affect realization of the organization's business objectives. The response to risks typically depends on their perceived gravity, and involves controlling, avoiding, accepting or transferring them to a third party. Whereas organizations routinely manage a wide range of risks (e.g. technological risks, commercial/financial risks, information security risks etc.), external legal and regulatory compliance risks are arguably the key issue in GRC.
- Compliance means conforming with stated requirements. At an organizational level, it is achieved through management processes which identify the applicable requirements (defined for example in laws, regulations, contracts, strategies and policies), assess the state of compliance, assess the risks and potential costs of non-compliance against the projected expenses to achieve compliance, and hence prioritize, fund and initiate any corrective actions deemed necessary.

GRC MARKET SEGMENTATION

A GRC program can be instituted to focus on any individual area within the enterprise, or a fully integrated GRC is able to work across all areas of the enterprise, using a single framework. A fully integrated GRC uses a single core set of control material, mapped to all of the primary governance factors being monitored. The use of a single framework also has the benefit of reducing the possibility of duplicated remedial actions.

When reviewed as individual GRC areas, the three most common individual headings are considered to be Financial GRC, IT GRC, and Legal GRC.

- Financial GRC relates to the activities that are intended to ensure the correct operation of all financial processes, as well as compliance with any finance-related mandates.
- IT GRC relates to the activities intended to ensure that the IT (Information Technology) organization supports the current and future needs of the business, and complies with all IT-related mandates.
- Legal GRC focuses on tying together all three components via an organization's legal department and chief compliance officer.

Analysts disagree on how these aspects of GRC are defined as market categories. Gartner has stated that the broad GRC market includes the following areas:

- Finance and audit GRC

- IT GRC management
- Enterprise risk management.

They further divide the IT GRC management market into these key capabilities. Although this list relates to IT GRC, a similar list of capabilities would be suitable for other areas of GRC.

- Controls and policy library
- Policy distribution and response
- IT Controls self-assessment and measurement
- IT Asset repository
- Automated general computer control (GCC) collection
- Remediation and exception management
- Reporting
- Advanced IT risk evaluation and compliance dashboards

GRC PRODUCT VENDORS

The distinctions between the sub-segments of the broad GRC market are often not clear. With a large number of vendors entering this market recently, determining the best product for a given business problem can be challenging. Given that the analysts don't fully agree on the market segmentation, vendor positioning can increase the confusion.

Due to the dynamic nature of this market, any vendor analysis is often out of date relatively soon after its publication.

Broadly, the vendor market can be considered to exist in 3 segments:

- Integrated GRC solutions (multi-governance interest, enterprise wide)
- Domain specific GRC solutions (single governance interest, enterprise wide)
- Point solutions to GRC (relate to enterprise wide governance or enterprise wide risk or enterprise wide compliance but not in combination.)

Integrated GRC solutions attempt to unify the management of these areas, rather than treat them as separate entities. An integrated solution is able to administer one central library of compliance controls, but manage, monitor and present them against every governance factor. For example, in a domain specific approach, three or more findings could be generated against a single broken activity. The integrated solution recognizes this as one break relating to the mapped governance factors.

Domain specific GRC vendors understand the cyclical connection between governance, risk and compliance within a particular area of governance. For example, within financial processing - that a risk will either relate to the absence of a control (need to update governance) and/or the lack of adherence to (or poor quality of) an existing control. An initial goal of splitting out GRC into a separate market has left some vendors confused about the lack of movement. It is thought that a lack of deep education within a domain on the audit side, coupled with a mistrust of audit in general causes a rift in a corporate environment. However, there are vendors in the marketplace that, while remaining domain-specific, have begun marketing their product to end users and departments that, while either tangential or overlapping, have expanded to include the internal corporate internal audit (CIA) and external audit teams (tier 1 big four AND tier two and below), information security and operations/production as the target audience. This approach provides a more 'open book' approach into the process. If the production team will be audited by CIA using an application that production also has access to, is thought to reduce risk more quickly as the end goal is not to be 'compliant' but to be 'secure,' or as secure as possible.

Point solutions to GRC are marked by their focus on addressing only one of its areas. In some cases of limited requirements, these solutions can serve a viable purpose. However, because they tend to have been designed to solve domain specific problems in great depth, they generally do not take a unified approach and are not tolerant of integrated governance requirements. Information systems will address these matters better if the requirements for GRC management are incorporated at the design stage, as part of a coherent framework.

GRC data warehousing and business intelligence

GRC vendors with an integrated data framework are now able to offer custom built GRC data warehouse and business intelligence solutions. This allows high value data from any number of existing GRC applications to be collated and analysed.

The aggregation of GRC data using this approach adds significant benefit in the early identification of risk and business process (and business control) improvement.

Further benefits to this approach include (i) it allows existing, specialist and high value applications to continue without impact (ii) organizations can manage an easier transition into an integrated GRC approach because the initial change is only adding to the reporting layer and (iii) it provides a real-time ability to compare and contrast data value across systems that previously had no common data scheme.'

GRC research

A publication review carried out in 2009 found that there was hardly any scientific research on GRC. The authors went on to derive the first GRC short-definition from an extensive literature review. Subsequently, the definition was validated in a survey among GRC professionals. "GRC is an integrated, holistic approach to organisation-wide GRC ensuring that an organisation acts ethically correct and in accordance with its risk appetite, internal policies and external regulations through the alignment of strategy, processes, technology and people, thereby improving efficiency and effectiveness." The authors then translated the definition into a frame of reference for GRC research.

Each of the core disciplines - Governance, Risk Management and Compliance - consists of the four basic components: strategy, processes, technology and people. The organisation's risk appetite, its internal policies and external regulations constitute the rules of GRC. The disciplines, their components and rules are now to be merged in an integrated, holistic and organisation-wide (the three main characteristics of GRC) manner - aligned with the (business) operations that are managed and supported through GRC. In applying this approach, organisations long to achieve the objectives: ethically correct behaviour, and improved efficiency and effectiveness of any of the elements involved.

A hot topic is Records Classification. Discussions surrounding records classification do not seem to cease, as this continues to be the centre of records management issues experienced by many. In my view as a records manager, the importance of classification often tends to be misunderstood or dismissed by end-users and even IT professionals. On the other hand, I realize that records managers should put more effort into developing strategies that address the concerns expressed by others.

For those new to the concept, classification is the "systematic identification and arrangement of business activities and/or records into categories according to logically structured conventions, methods, and procedural rules represented in a classification system" (ISO 15489-1). The term is also referred to as classification system, classification scheme, file plan, and records retention and disposition schedule (makes up a part of a classification system). Readers may also point out that classification and classification system are considered two different terms. In this blog, I treat both the same, but either approach is fine; basically, classification is represented in a system (classification system).

1. Classification provides context of records

Many people, particularly IT professionals, question the need for classifying documents when enterprise systems can fully index content. Indexing of content or metadata is not sufficient for establishing the context of records. This is important because we can segregate records of value from records of little or no value. While the value of certain information can be a subjective matter and differs depending on the goals for seeking the particular information, records classification helps narrow down places where reliable information may reside.

Subsequently, it aids searchability. When there is a particular topic of records to search but hardly any information other than a few keywords are provided, users initiate the research by identifying classifications that may apply to that particular topic. When records are filed properly and/or they are audited systematically by records managers, the success rate for this methodology is often high.

2. Classification specifies retention and disposition of records

"Storage is cheap, so why bother deleting data" is another popular remark I often hear others say. Indeed portable storage units are getting cheaper. But to acquire sturdy, reliable and corporate-capable storage can be expensive. In fact, why keep records when you don't need them or are not required to keep them and become subject to unnecessary litigation Records that are destroyed according to law and organizational policy along with the retention/disposition schedule are far less likely, or not at all likely, to be subject to litigation or accused of spoliation. This is a financially sound risk management strategy.

4 Tips To Improve Filing Accuracy

Many would agree with me that an Electronic Document Records Management System (EDRMS) is only as good as its implementation success rate. An organization may have purchased the most up-to-date records management application with all the bells and whistles, but if end-users do not favour using it, the application hardly has any value or use to the organization. In other words, if records are not filied to the correct classification, they cannot be found easily, and the retention and disposition applied to them may be incorrect. On the other hand, end-users often find identifying the correct classification to file documents a time-consuming task while others fear filing them incorrectly. Here are 4 tips to improve your organization's filing accuracy while allowing users to classify records more easily:

1. Simplify your file plan scheme

Do you have too many classification code subsets or subsets of subsets While end-users often favour a desktop folder-like structure, it can also be a cumbersome task to continuously drill down to aggregates of aggregates to find the right classification. Analyze which aggregates can be grouped together and which should be broken down. Break down groups only if functional activities seem too broad, the volume of records they fall under are so high that it is hard to navigate through them or manage them, or when the retention schedules are significantly different.

2. Use easily recognized codes

File codes should be easy to recognize. Utilize numeric or alphabetic codes that are easy to identify or frequently used by end-users as part of their business activities.

- Acronyms and abbreviations can be easier to recognize, if they are adopted organization-wide. Incorporate them as part of the classification code. Which classification code is easier to understand and identify For Circulation - Times Magazine, "055-33" or "055-TIMES"

- Incorporate unique identifiers or device numbers that the organization (office of the primary responsibility) uses to specify any procedural or contract documents. The fewer numbers or codes users need to become familiar with, the easier it is to adopt.

3. Create Cheat-sheets For Users

Perform a quick analysis of the end-user's (or his/her colleague's) types of documents they often generate or receive. Find those codes and create a commonly-used-classification list for the user to use as a reference. Or create a list for a group of users who share a similar job responsibility.

4. Consider an Intuitive Solution

What if we can still classify documents correctly while freeing users from having to perform that task Can we really have the cake and eat it, too Collabware CLM for SharePoint offers a way to classify documents automatically by utilizing a type of metadata value that end users input or select as part of their regular activities. For example, when a user creates a Contract document and inputs a contract number into the document, CLM will recognize that contract number value and classify the document accordingly. Furthermore, it can also complete (populate) other necessary values that are associated to the classification to metadata fields in the document's profile. Sounds too good to be true

Purpose

The Records Management policy establishes a framework for the implementation of the University's records management programme and ensures that full and accurate records of the University's activities are created, captured, maintained, made accessible, stored and legally disposed of in accordance with legislative requirements. The Records Management policy also outlines the responsibilities of staff in support of these requirements.

Organisational Scope

This policy applies to all University of Otago staff and all staff in controlled entities of the University of Otago, including persons contracted to the University either directly or in partnership with it. This policy applies to all records owned by the University which fall under the coverage of the Public Records Act (PRA) 2005, regardless of format and media.

Definitions

- Disposal is the final decision concerning the fate of records, i.e. their destruction or transfer to archives.
- Document Management is the process of storing, locating, updating and sharing documents in a work-group environment.

- Electronic Document and Records Management System (EDRMS) is a type of content management system that combines document management and records management in an integrated system.
- Electronic Records are records that require the use of a computer for creation, access and use. This can include emails, databases, websites, audiovisual files, images and records migrated or transformed into digital formats.
- GDA refers to the New Zealand Universities General Disposal Authority. This document sets out the retention periods and disposal actions for those records that are common to all New Zealand universities. This document is the University of Otago's legal authority to retain, dispose of, or transfer its records.
- OURDrive is the University of Otago's custom Electronic Document and Records Management System.
- Public Records are defined as records that are created or received by a public office in the conduct of its affairs. (N.B. this does not mean records that are available for public inspection, but rather records created in the course of a public office's normal business practice.) The following types of records are not considered to be public records:

(a) Teaching materials of staff used to deliver a lecture or other presentation;

(b) Research materials generated by staff and students including, but not exclusively, raw data, analysed data, working notes and publications;

(c) Material generated by subsidiary companies where the University holds or controls 50 percent or less of the company.

- Records are all those documents which facilitate the activities carried out by the University and which are thereafter retained (for a set period) to provide evidence of its transactions and activities. These records may be created, received or maintained in hard copy, electronically or a hybrid of the two. They include, but are not limited to, emails, documents, spreadsheets, letters, photographs, images, sound, plans and signatures.
- Records Management is the field of management which utilises an administrative system to direct and control the creation, distribution, filing, retention, storage and disposal of records.
- Recordkeeping Systems are business information systems which include amongst their functions the capability to capture, maintain and provide access to records.

Policy Content

1. *Records Management Programme*

(a) The University is required to establish a records management programme that complies with the requirements of the Public Records Act 2005 and the mandatory standard(s) issued under it.

(b) The Records Management Programme is the management framework, which includes the people, and the recordkeeping and/or information systems required to manage and maintain full, authentic, accurate and accessible records over time. The University of Otago will ensure that all staff comply with the University's approved recordkeeping framework and will provide training and guidance in support of this.

(c) The Records Management Programme delivers the following key benefits to the organisation:

(i) Cost savings and efficiency in terms of significantly reducing duplication of effort and the time staff spend looking for information.

(ii) Effective management in ensuring awareness of and access to the University's records.

(iii) Accountability by ensuring that records which document important activity are safely retained for an appropriate length of time.

(iv) Preserving the institution's corporate memory by enabling records of enduring cultural and historical value to be identified, captured, and transferred to the possession of an approved repository at the end of their life cycle.

2. *Recordkeeping Systems*

(a) The University shall employ a variety of appropriate recordkeeping systems to meet legislative requirements and the responsibilities detailed in clauses 3 and 4 of this Policy below.

(b) OURDrive, the University's EDRMS, shall be the University's primary system for managing most public records (that is those that are not managed in a line-of-business system, and that are not low level administrative or housekeeping records).

3. *University Responsibilities*

(a) The University of Otago will create full and accurate records of its affairs, in accordance with normal prudent business practice. This shall include records of any matters contracted out to independent parties, from whom the University will require any relevant documentation so as to ensure proper record keeping.

(b) The University of Otago will maintain, in an accessible form, so as to be able to be used for subsequent reference, all records that are in its control, until their disposal is authorised by or under the Public Records Act or required by or under another Act.

(c) The University of Otago will not dispose of, or authorise the disposal of, records or protected records except with the authority of the Chief Archivist, given in accordance with the provisions of the Public Records Act. The General Disposal Authority for all New Zealand Universities is the University of Otago's written authority to legally dispose of its records.

(d) The University of Otago will transfer from its possession and control any records that have been in existence for 25 years and that are no longer in current use to the possession of the Hocken Library and the control of the Chief Archivist.

(e) The University of Otago will store its records in conditions which will ensure that they are preserved for as long as they are required, and are protected so as to prevent damage, loss, theft, vandalism, misuse or inadvertent release through the use of appropriate packaging, shelving, equipment and a secure environment.

4. *Staff Responsibilities*

(a) The Vice-Chancellor, as the person responsible for the performance of the University of Otago, has ultimate responsibility for ensuring that the University complies with the legislative requirements for recordkeeping.

(b) Academic and Service Division Directors, Deans and Departmental Heads are responsible for supporting and monitoring their staff in terms of compliance and ensuring where appropriate that:

(i) Resources (time and people) are provided in support of this.

(ii) Appropriate storage provisions are made in support of this.

(iii) Records management expectations are included in job descriptions and performance reviews.

(iv) Staff who report to them are creating and maintaining records in a manner consistent with relevant standards, policies and procedures.

(c) Each Faculty, Department, School, Centre or Service Division is expected to:

(i) Manage its records in accordance with University requirements.

(ii) Nominate a records officer or records officers as appropriate for their area who will undergo regular training and be the primary contact for the Corporate Records Service.

(iii) Ensure the following recordkeeping principles are applied:

LEGAL COMPLIANCE

The following legislation (accessible at www.legislation.govt.nz) is relevant to the Records Management Policy and to record keeping activities at the University of Otago.

Financial Legislation

Financial Reporting Act 1993 defines the standards to be used in preparing financial reports and obligations in respect of the preparation and audit of financial statements. See also Public Finance Act 1989 for relevant sections.

Goods and Services Tax Act 1985 includes requirements for the keeping of records to support the administration of the Goods and Services Tax system (s 75) and their retention for a period of at least seven years after the end of the taxable period to which they relate. Income Tax Act 1994 includes requirements to furnish records to support specific rebates or deductions, such as those for demonstrating the business use of motor vehicles (sDH2 - 3).

Tax Administration Act 1994 requires taxpayers and employers to keep records in relation to business matters for tax purposes. Such records are to be retained for at least seven years after the end of the income year to which they relate (s22 (2)). Other recordkeeping provisions include the Inland Revenue Commissioner's powers to obtain information, the furnishing of tax returns, and the secrecy of information provided in relation to tax matters.

PRIVACY LEGISLATION

Privacy Act 1993 establishes a set of privacy principles to ensure the protection of personal privacy in respect of both public and private sector organisations. The Act is of prime importance and should be clearly understood by all information management professionals.

Employment Legislation

Employment Contracts Act 1991 contains recordkeeping requirements for redundancy of employment records (s47). Wages and time records for any period in the preceding six years must be available for the employee. There is also a requirement to retain records of any strikes and lockouts (s142)

Health and Safety in Employment Act 1992 requires employers to maintain a register of accidents and serious harm.

Commercial Legislation

Companies Act 1993 includes provisions requiring the maintenance of a share register (s87-94), company records (s189-191), accounting records (s194), and audit and reporting obligations. It allows the inspection of company records (s178-179 and s215-218). Other provisions include the registration of companies with the Registrar of Companies.

Public Sector Legislation

Public Records Act 2005 provides for the selection of public records and archives for creation, maintenance and retention; directs that public records and archives may only be destroyed or disposed of with the authority of the Chief Archivist. Provides for the deposit of public archives with the Archives of New Zealand and describes conditions for the management of material so deposited; and sets out the powers of the Chief Archivist in respect of current public records.

Official Information Act 1982 provides for access to official information, except where specific reasons for withholding it exist, such as national security or the protection of personal privacy. Ombudsmen Act 1975 contains requirements for documenting complaints and the supply of written evidence to support complaints; specifies access restrictions on a complaint or supplied evidence, and on publication of any summary report resulting from a complaint; and allows the Ombudsman to review complaints, records and decision-making processes and procedures. Public Finance Act 1989 covers the reporting requirements of the Crown, Government Departments and Crown Entities, including requirements for Audit Office issuing of Audit Opinions.

Intellectual Property Legislation

Copyright Act 1994 contains references to the requirements for documenting copyright in original works, transferring copyright and licensing for use/copying. It also includes documentation requirements for hearings of the Copyright Tribunal. Copyright Regulations also apply.

Designs Act 1953 contains recordkeeping requirements for all documents associated with the creation and registration of a design with the Patents Office. It also includes specific requirements regarding the creation and accessibility of the Register of Designs. Designs Regulations also apply.

Patents Act 1953 contains recordkeeping requirements for all documents associated with the application for and certification of New Zealand patents. It also includes specific requirements regarding the creation and accessibility of the Register of Patents. Patents Regulations also apply.

Trade Marks Act 1953 covers recordkeeping requirements for all documents relating to the application for and certification of New Zealand registered trademarks. It also includes specific requirements regarding the creation and accessibility of the Register of Trademarks. Trade Marks Regulations also apply.

Education Sector Legislation

Education Act 1989 and amendments covers recordkeeping requirements for all documents relating to the creation of annual reports, minutes and other statutory council and board records.

Health-related Legislation

Health Act 1956 and amendments addresses the legal implications and requirements for the use and transfer of patient records.

Health (Retention of Health Information) Regulations 1996 addresses outlines the legal requirements for the retention of patient records by PHOs, private hospitals and doctors in private practice.

Health Information Privacy Code 1994 outlines the requirements for storage of patient records and also provides for the non-release of information to patients in certain circumstances.

Code of Health and Disability Services Consumers' Rights addresses the requirements for recordkeeping relating to the rights of patients cared for under the provisions of the Health and Disability acts.

General Disposal Authority for District Health Boards provides best practice for the retention and disposal of patient records.

Other Legislation

Electronic Transactions Act 2002 addresses the legal implication and requirements for the use of electronic information and media. Evidence Act 1908, Evidence Amendment Act 1948 and Evidence Amendment Act 1980 and amendments govern the admissibility of documents and records in Courts.

National Library of New Zealand Act 2003 provides for the deposit of published documents by Crown Entities and other State owned or funded enterprises. The act requires that identical copies of the published document be provided.

Principles and Objectives of Records Management

The records management should be effective and successful. For which, the records management should be based on certain fundamental principles. They are listed below.

Principles of Records Management

1. Justification: The purpose for which records are maintained should be justifiable. There is no need of keeping all information on the ground that they may be useful in future. If the records are maintained in the light of the principle of purpose,

there may be many records which have no purpose and should not be preserved at all.

2. Verification: A record should be capable of verification. A record has no value if the concerned record cannot be verifiable.
3. Classification: Records should be properly classified according to its requirements in future. If the facts of a business are recorded chronologically, it is very difficult to analyze the facts of a business. In certain cases, classification itself is a form of analysis of the recorded facts.
4. Simplicity: Records should be maintained in a simple manner and according to the requirements of the business office.
5. Availability of Information: The desired information should be available when required. All the records are not necessary at one time. Hence, there is no need of instant availability of all the records. But, the required records should be available in the shortest possible period of time.
6. Accuracy: Records should be maintained accurately so as to minimize the chances of errors and fraud.
7. Reasonable Cost: The expenses of records management should not be ignored. All types of records have no equal importance. More safety arrangement is necessary to keep valuable and important documents. Some records are more important than others. Hence, safety lockers may be used to keep such records. Under strict control of the office manager, less important and less valuable records are also maintained.
8. Flexibility: The systems of records maintenance should be elastic. The system may be changed as and when on account of changing requirements of the business organization with out difficulty.

Objectives of Records Management

1. To keep the accounts of progress in an order.
2. To facilitate the preparation of financial statements.
3. To know the true condition of the business organization
4. To facilitate in business plans and decision making particularly in the context of changing environment.
5. To facilitate comparisons between one period of time with another.
6. To facilitate comparisons between different product lines.

7. To facilitate comparisons between two similar business firms.
8. To detect errors, prevent frauds and avoid wastage.
9. To facilitate the performance of the business functions.
10. To keep the various records under various laws and fulfill the legal requirements.
11. To use the records as written proof of the every business transaction.
12. To bring and keep the efficiency in office operations.

Organizational memory (OM) (sometimes called institutional or corporate memory) is the accumulated body of data, information, and knowledge created in the course of an individual organization's existence. Falling under the wider disciplinary umbrella of knowledge management, it has two repositories: an organization's archives, including its electronic data bases; and individuals' memories.

Kenneth Megill says corporate memory is information of value for re-use. He views corporate memory from the perspective of information services such as libraries, records management and archival management.

Organizational memory can only be applied if it can be accessed. To make use of it, organizations must have effective retrieval systems for their archives and good memory recall among the individuals that make up the organization. Its importance to an organization depends upon how well individuals can apply it, a discipline known as experiential learning or evidence-based practice. In the case of individuals' memories, organizational memory's veracity is invariably compromised by the inherent limitations of human memory. Individuals' reluctance to admit to mistakes and difficulties compounds the problem. The actively encouraged flexible labor market has imposed an Alzheimer's-like corporate amnesia on organizations that creates an inability to benefit from hindsight.

Nature

Organizational memory is composed of:

- Prior data and information
- All internally generated documentation related to the organization's activities
- Intellectual property (patents, copyrights, trademarks, brands, registered design, trade secrets and processes whose ownership is granted to the company by law, licensing and partnering agreements)
- Details of events, products and individuals (including relationships with people in outside organizations and professional bodies),
- Relevant published reference material
- Institution-created knowledge

Of these, institution-created knowledge is the most important. The three main facets of organizational memory are data, information, and knowledge. It is important to understand the differences between each of these. Data is a fact depicted as a figure or a statistic, while data in context-such as in a historical time frame-is information.

By contrast, knowledge is interpretative and predictive. Its deductive character allows a person with knowledge to understand the implications of information, and act accordingly. The term has been defined variously by different experts: Alvin Goldman described it as justified true belief; Bruce Aune saw it as information in context; Verna Alee defined it as experience or information that can be communicated or shared; and Karl Wiig said it was a body of understanding and insights for interpreting and managing the world around us.

The word knowledge comes from the Saxon word cnaw-lec. The suffix lec has become, in modern English, -like. So, knowledge means "cnaw-like", with cnaw meaning "emerge". Its best interpretation, then, is that it is an emergent phenomenon, an extension of existing erudition.

Once knowledge is documented, it reverts to being information. New knowledge-what some academics call knowledge in action-is that which is either created incrementally, accidentally, or through innovation. Incremental knowledge is the product of prior experience that is already established and recognized-so-called "organic learning" that builds one experience on another (also known as existent or historical knowledge). It is the most common form of learning. By way of a simple illustration, existent knowledge is the established awareness that, because it is hot, it is necessary to avoid sunburn and dehydration.

Existent knowledge becomes new knowledge when (for example) a European on a summer vacation in Mexico, being used to wearing a cap on sunny days at home, decides to wear a sombrero.

The second type of knowledge, accidental knowledge, happens unexpectedly-such as what happened in 1928 when a mold spore drifted onto a culture dish in the laboratory of Scottish research scientist Alexander Fleming while he was on a two-week holiday. It seeded a blue mold-penicillin-that killed off a harmful bacterium.

The third type of knowledge, innovative knowledge, is the labor of genius, such as the work of Leonardo da Vinci-who, in the late 15th century, conceptualized cutting-edge ideas like the aeroplane, the parachute, cranes, submarines, tanks, water pumps, canals, and drills. Innovative knowledge encompasses the type of learning that leapfrogs the other types, and-in da Vinci's case-was so advanced that it had to wait hundreds of years for incremental learning to catch up.

The difference between explicit and tacit knowledge

In its modern understanding, knowledge is made up of explicit knowledge, sometimes called skilled knowledge; and tacit or cognitive knowledge (sometimes known as "coping skills"), a category first identified by Michael Polanyi in 1958.

Explicit knowledge is the "what" of know-how: knowledge such as the professional or vocational skills that are recorded in manuals, textbooks, and training courses. Tacit knowledge, on the other hand, is the non-technical "how" of getting things done-what Edward de Bono, the inventor of lateral thinking, calls operacy, or the skill of action, and what Peter Drucker identifies in the use of the word techne, the Greek for "skill". Much of it is implicit and ambiguous, acquired largely by functional, context-specific experience. Typically existing only in the minds of individuals, tacit knowledge is normally very difficult to capture, with most organizations depending almost entirely on the explicit knowledge. This makes experiential learning, productivity gains, and competitiveness slow and expensive to acquire. In business terms, tacit knowledge is a passive misnomer for active sharing of knowledge to make an organization more effective. Training programs, for instance, cannot be limited to a source-recipient model, and should leverage mutual exchanges across generations.

The reality is that even though most organizational work processes are largely designed around documentation, much remains unrecorded, especially that to do with decision-making. The record often reflects the desire to gloss over disagreements and serious questions, or the desire to sell or excuse.

Given the high levels of corporate amnesia in commerce and industry, some organizations are turning to new techniques to preserving their organizational memory and, in particular, their tacit knowledge. The latest capture tools to get attention are the traditional corporate history, usually produced once or twice every 100 years as a public relations medium; and oral debriefing, an augmentation of the old-fashioned prescriptive and formulaic exit interview. Instead of hagiography, organizational memory is being produced as an induction and educational tool that transmits long-term information. Oral debriefing, which concentrates on short- and medium-term memory, targets exiting and key occupant employees, recurring corporate events, and important projects in detailed testimony of participants. Both are designed to extract tacit knowledge in an easily accessible format that also generates the "lessons of history". Its permanent character also means that it does not have to be continually reproduced, just updated, and that its necessary re-interpretation alongside changing circumstances is predicated on a more reliable evidential base.

How experiential learning works

When it comes to experiential learning, an awareness of both the explicit and tacit components of organizational memory on their own is not generally enough to create new knowledge efficiently. As a general rule, it needs to be accompanied by a focused learning phase.

Most models of experiential learning are cyclical and have three basic phases:

1. Awareness of an experience or problem situation;
2. A reflective phase within which the learner examines the OM around the experience and draws erudition from that reflection; and
3. A testing phase within which the new insights or learnings, having been integrated with the learner's own conceptual framework, are applied to a new problem situation or experience.

The concept's starting point is that individuals or organizations seldom learn from experience, unless the experience is assessed and then assigned its own meaning in terms of individual and/or the organization's own goals, aims, ambitions, and expectations. From these processes come insights and added meaning, which is then applied to new circumstances. The end product is better decision-making.

Exploring

Key decisions organizations make when exploring organizational memory include:

- What knowledge representation to use (stories, patterns, cases, rules, predicate logic, etc.)
- Who will be the users - what are their information and learning needs
- How to ensure security and who will be granted access
- How to best integrate with existing sources, stores and systems
- What to do to ensure the current content is correct, applicable, timely and weeded
- How to motivate experts to contribute
- What to do about ephemeral insights, how to capture informal scripts (e.g. e-mail and instant-messenger posts).

Most commercial knowledge management efforts have included building some form of organizational memory to capture expertise, speed learning, help the organization remember, record decision rationale, document achievements, or learn from past failures.

Enterprise content management (ECM) extends the concept of content management by adding a time line for each content item and possibly enforcing processes for the creation, approval and distribution of them. Systems that implement ECM generally provide a secure repository for managed items, be they analog or digital, that indexes them. They also include one or more methods for importing content to bring new items under management and several presentation methods to make items available for use.

While it is possible that content in an ECM is protected by DRM it is not required.

The key feature of ECM that distinguishes it from "simple" content management is that an ECM is at least cognizant of the processes and procedures of the enterprise it is created for, and as such is particular to it. Enterprise content management is the technology used to capture, manage, store, preserve, and deliver content and documents related to organizational processes.

Early 2006

Enterprise content management is the technology used to capture, manage, store, preserve, and deliver content and documents related to organizational processes. ECM tools and strategies allow the management of an organization's unstructured information, wherever that information exists.

Early 2008

Enterprise Content Management (ECM) is the strategies, methods, and tools used to capture, manage, store, preserve, and deliver content and documents related to organizational processes. ECM tools and strategies allow the management of an organization's unstructured information, wherever that information exists.

Early 2010

Enterprise Content Management (ECM) is the strategies, methods, and tools used to capture, manage, store, preserve, and deliver content and documents related to organizational processes. ECM covers the management of information within the entire scope of an enterprise whether that information is in the form of a paper document, an electronic file, a database print stream, or even an email.

March 2017

AIIM retired the term ECM in favor of a more encompassing term, Intelligent Information Management (IIM). IIM is defined as the strategies, methods, and tools used to create, capture, automate, deliver, secure, and analyze content and documents related to organizational processes. IIM refers to the management of content AND data, not just content itself.

The latest definition encompasses areas that have traditionally been addressed by records management and by document management systems. It also implies the conversion of data between various digital and traditional forms, including paper and microfilm.

ECM as an umbrella term covers document management, Web content management, search, collaboration, records management, digital asset management (DAM), workflow management, capture and scanning. ECM is primarily aimed at managing the life-cycle of information from initial publication or creation all the way through archival and eventual disposal. ECM applications are delivered in four ways:

- on-premises software (installed on an organization's own network)
- software as a service (SaaS) (Web access to information that is stored on a software manufacturer's system)
- a hybrid composed of both on-premises and SaaS components
- Infrastructure as a Service (IaaS) (which refers to online services that abstract the user from the details of infrastructure like physical computing resources, location, data partitioning, scaling, security, backup etc.)

ECM aims to make the management of corporate information easier through simplifying storage, security, version control, process routing, and retention. The benefits to an organization include improved efficiency, better control, and reduced costs. For example, many banks have converted to storing copies of old cheques within ECM systems (ECMSs) as opposed to the older method of keeping physical cheques in massive paper warehouses. Under the old system, a customer request for a copy of a cheque might take weeks, as the bank employees had to contact the warehouse where the right box, file, and cheque, would need to be located. The cheque would then need to be pulled, a copy made and mailed to the bank where it would finally be mailed to the customer. With a suitable ECM system in place, the bank employee might simply query the system for the customer's account number and the number of the requested cheque. When the image of the cheque appears on-screen, the bank can mail a copy immediately to the customer, usually while the customer is still on the phone.

SCOPE

Enterprise content management, as a form of content management, combines the capture, search and networking of documents with digital archiving, document management and workflow. It specifically includes the special challenges involved in using and preserving a company's internal, often unstructured information, in all of its forms. Therefore, most ECM solutions focus on business-to-employee (B2E) systems.

As ECM solutions have evolved, new components have emerged. For example, as content is checked in and out, each use generates new metadata about the content, to some extent automatically; information about how and when people use the content can allow the system to gradually acquire new filtering, routing and search pathways, corporate taxonomies and semantic networks, and retention-rule decisions. Email and instant messaging feature increasingly in decision-making processes; ECM can provide access to data about these communications, which can be used in business decisions.

Solutions can provide intranet services to employees (B2E), and can also include enterprise portals for business-to-business (B2B), business-to-government (B2G), government-to-business (G2B), or other business relationships. This category includes most former document-management groupware and workflow solutions that have not yet fully converted their architecture to ECM, but provide a Web interface. Digital asset management is a form of ECM concerned with content stored using digital technology.

History

The technologies that comprise ECM as of 2016 descend from the electronic document management systems (EDMS) of the late 1980s and early 1990s. The original EDMS products were stand-alone products, providing functionality in one of four areas: imaging, workflow, document management, or ERM (see components below).

The typical early EDMS adopter deployed a small-scale imaging and workflow system, possibly to just a single department, in order to improve a paper-intensive process and to migrate towards the mythical paperless office. The first stand-alone EDMS technologies aimed to save time or to improve information access by reducing paper handling and paper storage, thereby reducing document loss and providing faster access to information. EDMS could provide online access to information formerly available only on paper, microfilm, or microfiche. By improving control over documents and document-oriented processes, EDMS streamlined time-consuming business practices. The audit trail generated by EDMS enhanced document security and provided metrics to help measure productivity and identify efficiencies.

Through the late 1990s, the EDMS industry continued to grow steadily.

As more organizations achieved "pockets" of productivity with these technologies, it became clear that the various EDMS product categories were complementary. Organizations increasingly wanted to leverage multiple EDMS products. Consider, for example, a customer-service department-where imaging, document management, and workflow could combine to allow agents to better resolve customer inquiries. Likewise, an accounting department might access supplier invoices from an ERM system, purchase orders from an imaging system, and contracts from a document management system as part of an approval workflow. As organizations established an Internet presence, they wanted to present information via the Web, which required managing Web content. Organizations that had automated individual departments now began to envision wider benefits from broader deployment. Many documents across multiple departments and affect multiple processes.

The movement toward integrated EDM systems merely reflected a common trend in the software industry: the ongoing integration of point systems into more comprehensive systems. For example, until the early 1990s, word processing, spreadsheet, and presentation software products were standalone products. Thereafter, the market shifted toward integration.

Early leaders already offered multiple stand-alone EDMS technologies. The first phase was to offer multiple systems as a single, packaged "suite", with little or no functional integration. Throughout the 1990s, integration increased. Beginning in approximately 2001, the industry began to use the term enterprise content management to refer to these integrated systems. In 2006, Microsoft (with its SharePoint product family) and Oracle Corporation (with Oracle Content Management) joined also entered the entry-level "value" market segment of ECM.

Open source ECM products are also available.

Government standards, including HIPAA, SAS 70, BS 7799 and ISO/IEC 27001, influence the development and deployment of ECM. Standards compliance may make outsourcing to certified service providers a viable alternative to an internal ECM deployment.

As of 2016 organizations can deploy a single, flexible ECM system to manage information in all functional departments, including customer service, accounting, human resources, etc.

ADOPTION DRIVERS

There are numerous factors driving businesses to adopt an ECM solution, such as the need to increase efficiency, improving control of information, and reducing the overall cost of information management for the enterprise. ECM applications streamline access to records through keyword and full-text search allowing employees to get to the information they need directly from their desktops in seconds rather than searching multiple applications or digging through paper records.

These management systems can enhance record control to help businesses to comply with government and industry regulations such as HIPAA, Sarbanes-Oxley, PCI DSS, and the Federal Rules of Civil Procedure. Security functions including user-level, function-level, and even record-specific security options protect your most sensitive data. In fact, even information contained on a specific document can be masked using redaction features, so the rest of the document can be shared without compromising individual identity or key data. Every action taken within the system is tracked and reportable for auditing purposes for a wide variety of regulations.

ECM systems can reduce storage, paper and mailing needs, make employees more efficient, and result in better, more informed decisions across the enterprise-all of which reduce the overhead costs of managing information. SaaS ECM services can convert expensive capital outlay for servers and network equipment into a monthly operating expense, while also reducing the IT resources required to manage enterprise records.

Characteristics

Content management includes ECM, Web content management (WCM), content syndication, and media asset management. Enterprise content management is not a closed-system solution or a distinct product category. Therefore, along with Document Related Technologies or Document Lifecycle Management, ECM is just one possible catch-all term for a wide range of technologies and vendors.

The content and structure of today's outward-directed Web portal will be the platform for tomorrow's internal information system. In his article in Computerwoche, Ulrich Kampffmeyer distilled ECM to three key ideas that distinguish such solutions from Web content management:

Enterprise content management as integrative middleware

ECM is used to overcome the restrictions of former vertical applications and island architectures. The user is basically unaware of using an ECM solution. ECM offers the requisite infrastructure for the new world of Web-based IT, which is establishing itself as a kind of third platform alongside conventional host and client/server systems. Therefore, EAI (enterprise application integration) and SOA (service-oriented architecture) will play an important role in the implementation and use of ECM.

Enterprise content management components as independent services

ECM is used to manage information without regard to the source or the required use. The functionality is provided as a service that can be used from all kinds of applications. The advantage of a service concept is that for any given functionality only one general service is available, thus avoiding redundant, expensive and difficult to maintain parallel functions. Therefore, standards for interfaces connecting different services will play an important role in the implementation of ECM.

ECM is used as a content warehouse (both data warehouse and document warehouse) that combines company information in a repository with a uniform structure. Expensive redundancies and associated problems with information consistency are eliminated. All applications deliver their content to a single repository, which in turn provides needed information to all applications. Therefore, content integration and ILM (Information Lifecycle Management) will play an important role in the implementation and use of ECM.

Enterprise content management is working properly when it is effectively "invisible" to users. ECM technologies are infrastructures that support specialized applications as subordinate services.

ECM thus is a collection of infrastructure components that fit into a multi-layer model and include all document related technologies (DRT) for handling, delivering, and managing structured data and unstructured information jointly. As such, enterprise content management is one of the necessary basic components of the overarching e-business application area. ECM also sets out to manage all the information of a WCM and covers archiving needs as a universal repository.

Components

ECM combines components that can also be used as stand-alone systems without being incorporated into an enterprise-wide system. The five ECM components and technologies were first defined by AIIM as capture, manage, store, preserve, and deliver.

Capture

Capture involves converting information from paper documents into an electronic format through scanning. Capture is also used to collect electronic files and information into a consistent structure for management. Capture technologies also encompass the creation of metadata (index values) that describe characteristics of a document for easy location through search technology. For example, a medical chart might include the patient ID, patient name, date of visit, and procedure as index values to make it easy for medical personnel to locate the chart.

Earlier document automation systems photographed documents for storage on microfilm or microfiche. Optical scanners now make digital copies of paper documents. Documents already in digital form can be copied or linked to, if they are already available online. Automatic or semi-automatic capture can use EDI or XML documents, business and ERP applications or existing specialist application systems as sources.

Forms processing

In forms capture, there are two groups of technologies, although the information content and character of the documents may be identical. Forms processing is the capture of printed forms via scanning; recognition technologies are often used here since well-designed forms enable largely automatic processing. Automatic processing can be used to capture electronic forms, such as those submitted via Web pages, as long as the layout, structure, logic, and contents are known to the capture system.

COLD

Computer Output to Laser Disc (COLD) records reports and other documents on optical disks, or any form of digital storage for ongoing management by ECM systems. Another term for this is enterprise report management (ERM). Originally, the technology only worked with laserdiscs; the name was not changed after other technologies supplanted the laserdisc.

Aggregation

Aggregation combines documents from different applications. The goal is to unify data from different sources, forwarding them to storage and processing systems in a uniform structure and format.

Indexing components

Indexing improves searches, and provides alternative ways to organize the information. Manual indexing assigns index database attributes to content by hand, typically used by the database of a "manage" component for administration and access. Manual indexing may make use of input designs to limit the information that can be entered; for example, entry masks may use program logic to restrict inputs based on other information known about the document.

Both automatic and manual attribute indexing can be made easier and better with preset input-design profiles; these can describe document classes that limit the number of possible index values, or automatically assign certain criteria.

Automatic classification programs can extract index, category, and transfer data autonomously. Automatic classification or categorizing, based on the information contained in electronic information objects, can evaluate information based on predefined criteria or in a self-learning process. This technique can be used with OCR-converted faxes, office files, or output files.

Manage

The Manage category includes five traditional application areas:

- Document management (DM)
- Collaboration (or collaborative software, a.k.a. groupware)
- Web content management (including Web portals)
- Records management
- Workflow and business process management (BPM)

The Manage category connects the other components, which can be used in combination or separately. Document management, Web content management, collaboration, workflow and business process management address the dynamic part of the information's lifecycle. Records management focuses on managing finalized documents in accordance with the organization's document retention policy, which in turn must comply with government mandates and industry practices. All Manage components incorporate databases and access authorization systems. Manage components are offered individually or integrated as suites. In many cases they already include the "store" components.

Document management

Document management, in this context, refers to document management systems in the narrow sense of controlling documents from creation to archiving. Document management includes functions like:

Version management

To keep track of different versions of the same information with revisions and renditions (same information in a different format)

Search and navigation

However, document management increasingly overlaps with other "Manage" components, office applications like Microsoft Outlook and Exchange, or Lotus Notes and Domino, as well as "library services" for administering information storage.

Collaboration

Collaboration components in an ECM system help users work with each other to develop and process content. Many of these components were developed from collaborative software, or groupware, packages; ECM collaborative systems go much further, and include elements of knowledge management. ECM systems facilitate collaboration by using information databases and processing methods that are designed to be used simultaneously by multiple users, even when those users are working on the same content item. They make use of knowledge based on skills, resources and background data for joint information processing. Administration components, such as virtual whiteboards for brainstorming, appointment scheduling, and project management systems, communications application such as video conferencing, etc., may be included. Collaborative ECM may also integrate information from other applications, permitting joint information processing.

Web content management

The scope of Enterprise content management integrates Web content management systems. WCM as ECM component is used to present information already existing and managed in the ECM repository. However, information presented via Web technologies-on the Internet, an extranet, or on a portal-uses the workflow, access control, versioning, delivery and authorization modules of the WCM instead of integrated ECM functionality. There are only few examples of successful implementations whereby a shared repository for documents and Web content are managed together.

Records management (file and archive management)

Unlike traditional electronic archival systems, records management refers to the pure administration of records, important information, and data that companies are required to archive. Records management is independent of storage media; managed information does not necessarily need to be stored electronically, but can be on traditional physical media as well. Some of the functions of records management are:

- Visualisation of file plans and other structured indexes for the orderly storage of information
- Unambiguous indexing of information, supported by thesauri or controlled wordlists
- Management of record retention schedules and deletion schedules
- Protection of information in accordance with its characteristics, sometimes down to individual content components in documents
- Use of international, industry-specific or company-wide standardized metadata for the unambiguous identification and description of stored information

Workflow/business process management

There are different types of workflow: production workflow uses predefined sequences to guide and control processes, whereas in an ad-hoc workflow, the user determines the process sequence on the fly.

Workflow can be implemented as workflow solutions with which users interact, or as workflow engines, which act as a background service controlling the information and data flow.

Workflow management includes the following functions:

- Visualization of process and organization structures
- Capture, administration, visualization, and delivery of grouped information with its associated documents or data
- Incorporation of data processing tools (such as specific applications) and documents (such as office products)
- Parallel and sequential processing of procedures including simultaneous saving
- Reminders, deadlines, delegation and other administration functionalities
- Monitoring and documentation of process status, routing, and outcomes
- Tools for designing and displaying process

The objective is to automate processes as much as possible by incorporating all necessary resources.

2

ACCESS TO DATABASE

A database is an organized collection of data. It is the collection of schemas, tables, queries, reports, views, and other objects. The data are typically organized to model aspects of reality in a way that supports processes requiring information, such as modelling the availability of rooms in hotels in a way that supports finding a hotel with vacancies. A database management system (DBMS) is a computer software application that interacts with the user, other applications, and the database itself to capture and analyze data. A general-purpose DBMS is designed to allow the definition, creation, querying, update, and administration of databases. Well-known DBMSs include MySQL, PostgreSQL, MongoDB, MariaDB, Microsoft SQL Server, Oracle, Sybase, SAP HANA, MemSQL and IBM DB2. A database is not generally portable across different DBMSs, but different DBMS can interoperate by using standards such as SQL and ODBC or JDBC to allow a single application to work with more than one DBMS. Database management systems are often classified according to the database model that they support; the most popular database systems since the 1980s have all supported the relational model as represented by the SQL language. Sometimes a DBMS is loosely referred to as a 'database'.

TERMINOLOGY AND OVERVIEW

Formally, a "database" refers to a set of related data and the way it is organized. Access to this data is usually provided by a "database management system" (DBMS) consisting of an integrated set of computer software that allows users to interact with one or more databases and provides access to all of the data contained in the database (although restrictions may exist that limit access to particular data). The DBMS provides various functions that allow entry, storage and retrieval of large quantities of information and provides ways to manage how that information is organized.

Because of the close relationship between them, the term "database" is often used casually to refer to both a database and the DBMS used to manipulate it. Outside the world of professional information technology, the term database is often used to refer to any collection of related data (such as a spreadsheet or a card index). This article is concerned only with databases where the size and usage requirements necessitate use of a database management system.

Existing DBMSs provide various functions that allow management of a database and its data which can be classified into four main functional groups:

- Data definition – Creation, modification and removal of definitions that define the organization of the data.
- Update – Insertion, modification, and deletion of the actual data.
- Retrieval – Providing information in a form directly usable or for further processing by other applications. The retrieved data may be made available in a form basically the same as it is stored in the database or in a new form obtained by altering or combining existing data from the database.
- Administration – Registering and monitoring users, enforcing data security, monitoring performance, maintaining data integrity, dealing with concurrency control, and recovering information that has been corrupted by some event such as an unexpected system failure.

Both a database and its DBMS conform to the principles of a particular database model."Database system" refers collectively to the database model, database management system, and database. Physically, database servers are dedicated computers that hold the actual databases and run only the DBMS and related software. Database servers are usually multiprocessor computers, with generous memory and RAID disk arrays used for stable storage. RAID is used for recovery of data if any of the disks fail. Hardware database accelerators, connected to one or more servers via a high-speed channel, are also used in large volume transaction processing environments. DBMSs are found at the heart of most database applications. DBMSs may be built around a custom multitasking kernel with built-in networking support, but modern DBMSs typically rely on a standard operating system to provide these functions from databases before the inception of Structured Query Language (SQL). The data recovered was disparate, redundant and disorderly, since there was no proper method to fetch it and arrange it in a concrete structure.

Since DBMSs comprise a significant economical market, computer and storage vendors often take into account DBMS requirements in their own development plans.

Databases and DBMSs can be categorized according to the database model(s) that they support (such as relational or XML), the type(s) of computer they run on (from a server cluster to a mobile phone), the query language(s) used to access the database (such as SQL or XQuery), and their internal engineering, which affects performance, scalability, resilience, and security.

Applications

Databases are used to support internal operations of organizations and to underpin online interactions with customers and suppliers.

Databases are used to hold administrative information and more specialized data, such as engineering data or economic models. Examples of database applications include computerized library systems, flight reservation systems, computerized parts inventory systems, and many content management systems that store websites as collections of webpages in a database.

General-purpose and special-purpose DBMSs

A DBMS has evolved into a complex software system and its development typically requires thousands of human years of development effort. Some general-purpose DBMSs such as Adabas, Oracle and DB2 have been undergoing upgrades since the 1970s. General-purpose DBMSs aim to meet the needs of as many applications as possible, which adds to the complexity. However, the fact that their development cost can be spread over a large number of users means that they are often the most cost-effective approach. However, a general-purpose DBMS is not always the optimal solution: in some cases a general-purpose DBMS may introduce unnecessary overhead. Therefore, there are many examples of systems that use special-purpose databases. A common example is an email system that performs many of the functions of a general-purpose DBMS such as the insertion and deletion of messages composed of various items of data or associating messages with a particular email address; but these functions are limited to what is required to handle email and don't provide the user with all of the functionality that would be available using a general-purpose DBMS.

Many other databases have application software that accesses the database on behalf of end-users, without exposing the DBMS interface directly. Application programmers may use a wire protocol directly, or more likely through an application programming interface. Database designers and database administrators interact with the DBMS through dedicated interfaces to build and maintain the applications' databases, and thus need some more knowledge and understanding about how DBMSs operate and the DBMSs' external interfaces and tuning parameters.

History

Following the technology progress in the areas of processors, computer memory, computer storage, and computer networks, the sizes, capabilities, and performance of databases and their respective DBMSs have grown in orders of magnitude. The development of database technology can be divided into three eras based on data model or structure: navigational, SQL/relational, and post-relational.

The two main early navigational data models were the hierarchical model, epitomized by IBM's IMS system, and the CODASYL model (network model), implemented in a number of products such as IDMS.

The relational model, first proposed in 1970 by Edgar F. Codd, departed from this tradition by insisting that applications should search for data by content, rather than by following links. The relational model employs sets of ledger-style tables, each used for a different type of entity. Only in the mid-1980s did computing hardware become powerful enough to allow the wide deployment of relational systems (DBMSs plus applications). By the early 1990s, however, relational systems dominated in all large-scale data processing applications, and as of 2015 they remain dominant : IBM DB2, Oracle, MySQL, and Microsoft SQL Server are the top DBMS. The dominant database language, standardised SQL for the relational model, has influenced database languages for other data models.

Object databases were developed in the 1980s to overcome the inconvenience of object-relational impedance mismatch, which led to the coining of the term "post-relational" and also the development of hybrid object-relational databases.

The next generation of post-relational databases in the late 2000s became known as NoSQL databases, introducing fast key-value stores and document-oriented databases. A competing "next generation" known as NewSQL databases attempted new implementations that retained the relational/SQL model while aiming to match the high performance of NoSQL compared to commercially available relational DBMSs.

1960s, navigational DBMS

The introduction of the term database coincided with the availability of direct-access storage (disks and drums) from the mid-1960s onwards. The term represented a contrast with the tape-based systems of the past, allowing shared interactive use rather than daily batch processing. The Oxford English Dictionary cites a 1962 report by the System Development Corporation of California as the first to use the term "data-base" in a specific technical sense.

As computers grew in speed and capability, a number of general-purpose database systems emerged; by the mid-1960s a number of such systems had come into commercial use. Interest in a standard began to grow, and Charles Bachman, author of one such product, the Integrated Data Store (IDS), founded the "Database Task Group" within CODASYL, the group responsible for the creation and standardization of COBOL. In 1971, the Database Task Group delivered their standard, which generally became known as the "CODASYL approach", and soon a number of commercial products based on this approach entered the market.

The CODASYL approach relied on the "manual" navigation of a linked data set which was formed into a large network. Applications could find records by one of three methods:

1. Use of a primary key (known as a CALC key, typically implemented by hashing)
2. Navigating relationships (called sets) from one record to another
3. Scanning all the records in a sequential order

Later systems added B-trees to provide alternate access paths. Many CODASYL databases also added a very straightforward query language. However, in the final tally, CODASYL was very complex and required significant training and effort to produce useful applications.

IBM also had their own DBMS in 1966, known as Information Management System (IMS). IMS was a development of software written for the Apollo program on the System/360. IMS was generally similar in concept to CODASYL, but used a strict hierarchy for its model of data navigation instead of CODASYL's network model. Both concepts later became known as navigational databases due to the way data was accessed, and Bachman's 1973 Turing Award presentation was The Programmer as Navigator. IMS is classified as a hierarchical database. IDMS and Cincom Systems' TOTAL database are classified as network databases. IMS remains in use as of 2014.

1970s, relational DBMS

Edgar Codd worked at IBM in San Jose, California, in one of their offshoot offices that was primarily involved in the development of hard disk systems. He was unhappy with the navigational model of the CODASYL approach, notably the lack of a "search" facility. In 1970, he wrote a number of papers that outlined a new approach to database construction that eventually culminated in the groundbreaking A Relational Model of Data for Large Shared Data Banks.

In this paper, he described a new system for storing and working with large databases. Instead of records being stored in some sort of linked list of free-form records as in CODASYL, Codd's idea was to use a "table" of fixed-length records, with each table used for a different type of entity. A linked-list system would be very inefficient when storing "sparse" databases where some of the data for any one record could be left empty. The relational model solved this by splitting the data into a series of normalized tables (or relations), with optional elements being moved out of the main table to where they would take up room only if needed. Data may be freely inserted, deleted and edited in these tables, with the DBMS doing whatever maintenance needed to present a table view to the application/user.

The relational model also allowed the content of the database to evolve without constant rewriting of links and pointers. The relational part comes from entities referencing other entities in what is known as one-to-many relationship, like a traditional hierarchical model, and many-to-many relationship, like a navigational (network) model. Thus, a relational model can express both hierarchical and navigational models, as well as its native tabular model, allowing for pure or combined modeling in terms of these three models, as the application requires.

For instance, a common use of a database system is to track information about users, their name, login information, various addresses and phone numbers. In the navigational approach, all of this data would be placed in a single record, and unused items would simply not be placed in the database. In the relational approach, the data would be normalized into a user table, an address table and a phone number table (for instance). Records would be created in these optional tables only if the address or phone numbers were actually provided.

Linking the information back together is the key to this system. In the relational model, some bit of information was used as a "key", uniquely defining a particular record. When information was being collected about a user, information stored in the optional tables would be found by searching for this key. For instance, if the login name of a user is unique, addresses and phone numbers for that user would be recorded with the login name as its key. This simple "re-linking" of related data back into a single collection is something that traditional computer languages are not designed for.

Just as the navigational approach would require programs to loop in order to collect records, the relational approach would require loops to collect information about any one record. Codd's solution to the necessary looping was a set-oriented language, a suggestion that would later spawn the ubiquitous SQL. Using a branch of mathematics known as tuple calculus, he demonstrated that such a system could support all the operations of normal databases (inserting, updating etc.) as well as providing a simple system for finding and returning sets of data in a single operation.

Codd's paper was picked up by two people at Berkeley, Eugene Wong and Michael Stonebraker. They started a project known as INGRES using funding that had already been allocated for a geographical database project and student programmers to produce code. Beginning in 1973, INGRES delivered its first test products which were generally ready for widespread use in 1979. INGRES was similar to System R in a number of ways, including the use of a "language" for data access, known as QUEL. Over time, INGRES moved to the emerging SQL standard.

IBM itself did one test implementation of the relational model, PRTV, and a production one, Business System 12, both now discontinued. Honeywell wrote MRDS for Multics, and now there are two new implementations: Alphora Dataphor and Rel. Most other DBMS implementations usually called relational are actually SQL DBMSs.

In 1970, the University of Michigan began development of the MICRO Information Management System based on D. L. Childs' Set-Theoretic Data model. MICRO was used to manage very large data sets by the US Department of Labor, the U. S. Environmental Protection Agency, and researchers from the University of Alberta, the University of Michigan, and Wayne State University. It ran on IBM mainframe computers using the Michigan Terminal System. The system remained in production until 1998.

Integrated approach

In the 1970s and 1980s, attempts were made to build database systems with integrated hardware and software. The underlying philosophy was that such integration would provide higher performance at lower cost. Examples were IBM System/38, the early offering of Teradata, and the Britton Lee, Inc. database machine.

Another approach to hardware support for database management was ICL's CAFS accelerator, a hardware disk controller with programmable search capabilities. In the long term, these efforts were generally unsuccessful because specialized database machines could not keep pace with the rapid development and progress of general-purpose computers. Thus most database systems nowadays are software systems running on general-purpose hardware, using general-purpose computer data storage. However this idea is still pursued for certain applications by some companies like Netezza and Oracle (Exadata).

Late 1970s, SQL DBMS

IBM started working on a prototype system loosely based on Codd's concepts as System R in the early 1970s. The first version was ready in 1974/5, and work then started on multi-table systems in which the data could be split so that all of the data for a record (some of which is optional) did not have to be stored in a single large "chunk". Subsequent multi-user versions were tested by customers in 1978 and 1979, by which time a standardized query language – SQL – had been added. Codd's ideas were establishing themselves as both workable and superior to CODASYL, pushing IBM to develop a true production version of System R, known as SQL/DS, and, later, Database 2 (DB2). Larry Ellison's Oracle started from a different chain, based on IBM's papers on System R, and beat IBM to market when the first version was released in 1978.

Stonebraker went on to apply the lessons from INGRES to develop a new database, Postgres, which is now known as PostgreSQL. PostgreSQL is often used for global mission critical applications (the. org and. info domain name registries use it as their primary data store, as do many large companies and financial institutions). In Sweden, Codd's paper was also read and Mimer SQL was developed from the mid-1970s at Uppsala University. In 1984, this project was consolidated into an independent enterprise. In the early 1980s, Mimer introduced transaction handling for high robustness in applications, an idea that was subsequently implemented on most other DBMSs.

Another data model, the entity–relationship model, emerged in 1976 and gained popularity for database design as it emphasized a more familiar description than the earlier relational model. Later on, entity–relationship constructs were retrofitted as a data modeling construct for the relational model, and the difference between the two have become irrelevant.

1980s, on the desktop

The 1980s ushered in the age of desktop computing. The new computers empowered their users with spreadsheets like Lotus 1-2-3 and database software like dBASE. The dBASE product was lightweight and easy for any computer user to understand out of the box. C. Wayne Ratliff the creator of dBASE stated: "dBASE was different from programs like BASIC, C, FORTRAN, and COBOL in that a lot of the dirty work had already been done. The data manipulation is done by dBASE instead of by the user, so the user can concentrate on what he is doing, rather than having to mess with the dirty details of opening, reading, and closing files, and managing space allocation." dBASE was one of the top selling software titles in the 1980s and early 1990s.

1990s, object-oriented

The 1990s, along with a rise in object-oriented programming, saw a growth in how data in various databases were handled. Programmers and designers began to treat the data in their databases as objects. That is to say that if a person's data were in a database, that person's attributes, such as their address, phone number, and age, were now considered to belong to that person instead of being extraneous data. This allows for relations between data to be relations to objects and their attributes and not to individual fields. The term "object-relational impedance mismatch" described the inconvenience of translating between programmed objects and database tables. Object databases and object-relational databases attempt to solve this problem by providing an object-oriented language (sometimes as extensions to SQL) that programmers can use as alternative to purely relational SQL. On the programming side, libraries known as object-relational mappings (ORMs) attempt to solve the same problem.

2000s, NoSQL and NewSQL

XML databases are a type of structured document-oriented database that allows querying based on XML document attributes. XML databases are mostly used in enterprise database management, where XML is being used as the machine-to-machine data interoperability standard. XML database management systems include commercial softwareMarkLogic and Oracle Berkeley DB XML, and a free use software Clusterpoint Distributed XML/JSON Database. All are enterprise software database platforms and support industry standard ACID-compliant transaction processing with strong database consistency characteristics and high level of database security.

NoSQL databases are often very fast, do not require fixed table schemas, avoid join operations by storing denormalized data, and are designed to scale horizontally. The most popular NoSQL systems include MongoDB, Couchbase, Riak, Memcached, Redis, CouchDB, Hazelcast, Apache Cassandra, and HBase, which are all open-source software products.

In recent years, there was a high demand for massively distributed databases with high partition tolerance but according to the CAP theorem it is impossible for a distributed system to simultaneously provide consistency, availability, and partition tolerance guarantees. A distributed system can satisfy any two of these guarantees at the same time, but not all three. For that reason, many NoSQL databases are using what is called eventual consistency to provide both availability and partition tolerance guarantees with a reduced level of data consistency.

NewSQL is a class of modern relational databases that aims to provide the same scalable performance of NoSQL systems for online transaction processing (read-write) workloads while still using SQL and maintaining the ACID guarantees of a traditional database system. Such databases include ScaleBase, Clustrix, EnterpriseDB, MemSQL, NuoDB, and VoltDB.

Research

Database technology has been an active research topic since the 1960s, both in academia and in the research and development groups of companies (for example IBM Research). Research activity includes theory and development of prototypes. Notable research topics have included models, the atomic transaction concept, and related concurrency control techniques, query languages and query optimization methods, RAID, and more.

The database research area has several dedicated academic journals (for example, ACM Transactions on Database Systems-TODS, Data and Knowledge Engineering-DKE) and annual conferences (e. g., ACM SIGMOD, ACM PODS, VLDB, IEEE ICDE).

Examples

One way to classify databases involves the type of their contents, for example: bibliographic, document-text, statistical, or multimedia objects. Another way is by their application area, for example: accounting, music compositions, movies, banking, manufacturing, or insurance. A third way is by some technical aspect, such as the database structure or interface type. This section lists a few of the adjectives used to characterize different kinds of databases.

- An in-memory database is a database that primarily resides in main memory, but is typically backed-up by non-volatile computer data storage. Main memory databases are faster than disk databases, and so are often used where response time is critical, such as in telecommunications network equipment. SAP HANA platform is a very hot topic for in-memory database. By May 2012, HANA was able to run on servers with 100TB main memory powered by IBM. The co founder of the company claimed that the system was big enough to run the 8 largest SAP customers.
- An active database includes an event-driven architecture which can respond to conditions both inside and outside the database. Possible uses include security monitoring, alerting, statistics gathering and authorization. Many databases provide active database features in the form of database triggers.
- A cloud database relies on cloud technology. Both the database and most of its DBMS reside remotely, "in the cloud", while its applications are both developed by programmers and later maintained and utilized by (application's) end-users through a web browser and Open APIs.
- Data warehouses archive data from operational databases and often from external sources such as market research firms. The warehouse becomes the central source of data for use by managers and other end-users who may not have access to operational data. For example, sales data might be aggregated to weekly totals and converted from internal product codes to use UPCs so that they can be compared with ACNielsen data. Some basic and essential components of data warehousing include extracting, analyzing, and mining data, transforming, loading, and managing data so as to make them available for further use.
- A deductive database combines logic programming with a relational database, for example by using the Datalog language.
- A distributed database is one in which both the data and the DBMS span multiple computers.
- A document-oriented database is designed for storing, retrieving, and managing document-oriented, or semi structured data, information. Document-oriented databases are one of the main categories of NoSQL databases.
- An embedded database system is a DBMS which is tightly integrated with an application software that requires access to stored data in such a way that the DBMS is hidden from the application's end-users and requires little or no ongoing maintenance.

- End-user databases consist of data developed by individual end-users. Examples of these are collections of documents, spreadsheets, presentations, multimedia, and other files. Several products exist to support such databases. Some of them are much simpler than full-fledged DBMSs, with more elementary DBMS functionality.
- A federated database system comprises several distinct databases, each with its own DBMS. It is handled as a single database by a federated database management system (FDBMS), which transparently integrates multiple autonomous DBMSs, possibly of different types (in which case it would also be a heterogeneous database system), and provides them with an integrated conceptual view.
- Sometimes the term multi-database is used as a synonym to federated database, though it may refer to a less integrated (e. g., without an FDBMS and a managed integrated schema) group of databases that cooperate in a single application. In this case, typically middleware is used for distribution, which typically includes an atomic commit protocol (ACP), e. g., the two-phase commit protocol, to allow distributed (global) transactions across the participating databases.
- A graph database is a kind of NoSQL database that uses graph structures with nodes, edges, and properties to represent and store information. General graph databases that can store any graph are distinct from specialized graph databases such as triplestores and network databases.
- An array DBMS is a kind of NoSQL DBMS that allows to model, store, and retrieve (usually large) multi-dimensional arrays such as satellite images and climate simulation output.
- In a hypertext or hypermedia database, any word or a piece of text representing an object, e. g., another piece of text, an article, a picture, or a film, can be hyperlinked to that object. Hypertext databases are particularly useful for organizing large amounts of disparate information. For example, they are useful for organizing online encyclopedias, where users can conveniently jump around the text. The World Wide Web is thus a large distributed hypertext database.
- A knowledge base (abbreviated KB, kb or Ä) is a special kind of database for knowledge management, providing the means for the computerized collection, organization, and retrieval of knowledge. Also a collection of data representing problems with their solutions and related experiences.
- A mobile database can be carried on or synchronized from a mobile computing device.

- Operational databases store detailed data about the operations of an organization. They typically process relatively high volumes of updates using transactions. Examples include customer databases that record contact, credit, and demographic information about a business' customers, personnel databases that hold information such as salary, benefits, skills data about employees, enterprise resource planning systems that record details about product components, parts inventory, and financial databases that keep track of the organization's money, accounting and financial dealings.
- A parallel database seeks to improve performance through parallelization for tasks such as loading data, building indexes and evaluating queries.
- The major parallel DBMS architectures which are induced by the underlying hardware architecture are:
- Shared memory architecture, where multiple processors share the main memory space, as well as other data storage.
- Shared disk architecture, where each processing unit (typically consisting of multiple processors) has its own main memory, but all units share the other storage.
- Shared nothing architecture, where each processing unit has its own main memory and other storage.
- Probabilistic databases employ fuzzy logic to draw inferences from imprecise data.
- Real-time databases process transactions fast enough for the result to come back and be acted on right away.
- A spatial database can store the data with multidimensional features. The queries on such data include location-based queries, like "Where is the closest hotel in my area?".
- A temporal database has built-in time aspects, for example a temporal data model and a temporal version of SQL. More specifically the temporal aspects usually include valid-time and transaction-time.
- A terminology-oriented database builds upon an object-oriented database, often customized for a specific field.
- An unstructured data database is intended to store in a manageable and protected way diverse objects that do not fit naturally and conveniently in common databases. It may include email messages, documents, journals, multimedia objects, etc. The name may be misleading since some objects can be highly structured. However, the entire possible object collection does not fit into a predefined structured

framework. Most established DBMSs now support unstructured data in various ways, and new dedicated DBMSs are emerging.

DESIGN AND MODELING

The first task of a database designer is to produce a conceptual data model that reflects the structure of the information to be held in the database. A common approach to this is to develop an entity-relationship model, often with the aid of drawing tools. Another popular approach is the Unified Modeling Language. A successful data model will accurately reflect the possible state of the external world being modeled: for example, if people can have more than one phone number, it will allow this information to be captured. Designing a good conceptual data model requires a good understanding of the application domain; it typically involves asking deep questions about the things of interest to an organisation, like "can a customer also be a supplier?", or "if a product is sold with two different forms of packaging, are those the same product or different products?", or "if a plane flies from New York to Dubai via Frankfurt, is that one flight or two (or maybe even three)?". The answers to these questions establish definitions of the terminology used for entities (customers, products, flights, flight segments) and their relationships and attributes.

Producing the conceptual data model sometimes involves input from business processes, or the analysis of workflow in the organization. This can help to establish what information is needed in the database, and what can be left out. For example, it can help when deciding whether the database needs to hold historic data as well as current data.

Having produced a conceptual data model that users are happy with, the next stage is to translate this into a schema that implements the relevant data structures within the database. This process is often called logical database design, and the output is a logical data model expressed in the form of a schema. Whereas the conceptual data model is (in theory at least) independent of the choice of database technology, the logical data model will be expressed in terms of a particular database model supported by the chosen DBMS. (The terms data model and database model are often used interchangeably, but in this article we use data model for the design of a specific database, and database model for the modelling notation used to express that design.)

The most popular database model for general-purpose databases is the relational model, or more precisely, the relational model as represented by the SQL language. The process of creating a logical database design using this model uses a methodical approach known as normalization. The goal of normalization is to ensure that each elementary "fact" is only recorded in one place, so that insertions, updates, and deletions automatically maintain consistency.

The final stage of database design is to make the decisions that affect performance, scalability, recovery, security, and the like. This is often called physical database design. A key goal during this stage is data independence, meaning that the decisions made for performance optimization purposes should be invisible to end-users and applications. There are two types of data independence: Physical data independence and logical data independence. Physical design is driven mainly by performance requirements, and requires a good knowledge of the expected workload and access patterns, and a deep understanding of the features offered by the chosen DBMS.

Another aspect of physical database design is security. It involves both defining access control to database objects as well as defining security levels and methods for the data itself.

Models

A database model is a type of data model that determines the logical structure of a database and fundamentally determines in which manner data can be stored, organized, and manipulated. The most popular example of a database model is the relational model (or the SQL approximation of relational), which uses a table-based format.

Common logical data models for databases include:

- Navigational databases
- Hierarchical database model
- Network model
- Graph database
- Relational model
- Entity–relationship model
- Enhanced entity–relationship model
- Object model
- Document model
- Entity–attribute–value model
- Star schema

An object-relational database combines the two related structures.

Physical data models include:

- Inverted index
- Flat file

Other models include:

- Associative model
- Multidimensional model
- Array model
- Multivalue model

Specialized models are optimized for particular types of data:

- XML database
- Semantic model
- Content store
- Event store
- Time series model

External, conceptual, and internal views

A database management system provides three views of the database data:

- The external level defines how each group of end-users sees the organization of data in the database. A single database can have any number of views at the external level.
- The conceptual level unifies the various external views into a compatible global view. It provides the synthesis of all the external views. It is out of the scope of the various database end-users, and is rather of interest to database application developers and database administrators.
- The internal level (or physical level) is the internal organization of data inside a DBMS. It is concerned with cost, performance, scalability and other operational matters. It deals with storage layout of the data, using storage structures such as indexes to enhance performance. Occasionally it stores data of individual views (materialized views), computed from generic data, if performance justification exists for such redundancy. It balances all the external views' performance requirements, possibly conflicting, in an attempt to optimize overall performance across all activities.

While there is typically only one conceptual (or logical) and physical (or internal) view of the data, there can be any number of different external views. This allows users to see database information in a more business-related way rather than from a technical, processing viewpoint. For example, a financial department of a company needs the payment details of all employees as part of the company's expenses, but does not need details about employees that are the interest of the human resources department. Thus different departments need different views of the company's database.

The three-level database architecture relates to the concept of data independence which was one of the major initial driving forces of the relational model. The idea is that changes made at a certain level do not affect the view at a higher level. For example, changes in the internal level do not affect application programs written using conceptual level interfaces, which reduces the impact of making physical changes to improve performance.

The conceptual view provides a level of indirection between internal and external. On one hand it provides a common view of the database, independent of different external view structures, and on the other hand it abstracts away details of how the data are stored or managed (internal level). In principle every level, and even every external view, can be presented by a different data model. In practice usually a given DBMS uses the same data model for both the external and the conceptual levels (e. g., relational model). The internal level, which is hidden inside the DBMS and depends on its implementation, requires a different level of detail and uses its own types of data structure types.

Separating the external, conceptual and internal levels was a major feature of the relational database model implementations that dominate 21st century databases.

Languages

Database languages are special-purpose languages, which do one or more of the following:

- Data definition language – defines data types such as creating, altering, or dropping and the relationships among them
- Data manipulation language – performs tasks such as inserting, updating, or deleting data occurrences
- Query language – allows searching for information and computing derived information

Database languages are specific to a particular data model. Notable examples include:

- SQL combines the roles of data definition, data manipulation, and query in a single language. It was one of the first commercial languages for the relational model, although it departs in some respects from the relational model as described by Codd (for example, the rows and columns of a table can be ordered). SQL became a standard of the American National Standards Institute (ANSI) in 1986, and of the International Organization for Standardization (ISO) in 1987. The standards have been regularly enhanced since and is supported (with varying degrees of conformance) by all mainstream commercial relational DBMSs.

- OQL is an object model language standard (from the Object Data Management Group). It has influenced the design of some of the newer query languages like JDOQL and EJB QL.
- XQuery is a standard XML query language implemented by XML database systems such as MarkLogic and eXist, by relational databases with XML capability such as Oracle and DB2, and also by in-memory XML processors such as Saxon.
- SQL/XML combines XQuery with SQL.

A database language may also incorporate features like:

- DBMS-specific Configuration and storage engine management
- Computations to modify query results, like counting, summing, averaging, sorting, grouping, and cross-referencing
- Constraint enforcement (e. g. in an automotive database, only allowing one engine type per car)
- Application programming interface version of the query language, for programmer convenience

Performance, security, and availability

Because of the critical importance of database technology to the smooth running of an enterprise, database systems include complex mechanisms to deliver the required performance, security, and availability, and allow database administrators to control the use of these features.

Storage

Database storage is the container of the physical materialization of a database. It comprises the internal (physical) level in the database architecture. It also contains all the information needed (e. g., metadata, "data about the data", and internal data structures) to reconstruct the conceptual level and external level from the internal level when needed. Putting data into permanent storage is generally the responsibility of the database engine a. k. a. "storage engine". Though typically accessed by a DBMS through the underlying operating system (and often utilizing the operating systems' file systems as intermediates for storage layout), storage properties and configuration setting are extremely important for the efficient operation of the DBMS, and thus are closely maintained by database administrators. A DBMS, while in operation, always has its database residing in several types of storage (e. g., memory and external storage). The database data and the additional needed information, possibly in very large amounts, are coded into bits. Data typically reside in the storage in structures that look completely different from the way the data look in the conceptual and external levels, but in ways that attempt to optimize (the best possible) these levels' reconstruction when needed by users and programs, as well as for computing additional types of needed information from the data (e. g., when querying the database).

Some DBMSs support specifying which character encoding was used to store data, so multiple encodings can be used in the same database.

Various low-level database storage structures are used by the storage engine to serialize the data model so it can be written to the medium of choice. Techniques such as indexing may be used to improve performance. Conventional storage is row-oriented, but there are also column-oriented and correlation databases.

Materialized views

Often storage redundancy is employed to increase performance. A common example is storing materialized views, which consist of frequently needed external views or query results. Storing such views saves the expensive computing of them each time they are needed. The downsides of materialized views are the overhead incurred when updating them to keep them synchronized with their original updated database data, and the cost of storage redundancy.

Replication

Occasionally a database employs storage redundancy by database objects replication (with one or more copies) to increase data availability (both to improve performance of simultaneous multiple end-user accesses to a same database object, and to provide resiliency in a case of partial failure of a distributed database). Updates of a replicated object need to be synchronized across the object copies. In many cases, the entire database is replicated.

Security

Database security deals with all various aspects of protecting the database content, its owners, and its users. It ranges from protection from intentional unauthorized database uses to unintentional database accesses by unauthorized entities (e. g., a person or a computer program).

Database access control deals with controlling who (a person or a certain computer program) is allowed to access what information in the database. The information may comprise specific database objects (e. g., record types, specific records, data structures), certain computations over certain objects (e. g., query types, or specific queries), or utilizing specific access paths to the former (e. g., using specific indexes or other data structures to access information). Database access controls are set by special authorized (by the database owner) personnel that uses dedicated protected security DBMS interfaces.

This may be managed directly on an individual basis, or by the assignment of individuals and privileges to groups, or (in the most elaborate models) through the assignment of individuals and groups to roles which are then granted entitlements. Data security prevents unauthorized users from viewing or updating the database. Using passwords, users are allowed access to the entire database or subsets of it called "subschemas". For example, an employee database can contain all the data about an individual employee, but one group of users may be authorized to view only payroll data, while others are allowed access to only work history and medical data. If the DBMS provides a way to interactively enter and update the database, as well as interrogate it, this capability allows for managing personal databases.

Data security in general deals with protecting specific chunks of data, both physically (i. e., from corruption, or destruction, or removal; e. g., see physical security), or the interpretation of them, or parts of them to meaningful information (e. g., by looking at the strings of bits that they comprise, concluding specific valid credit-card numbers; e. g., see data encryption).

Change and access logging records who accessed which attributes, what was changed, and when it was changed. Logging services allow for a forensic database audit later by keeping a record of access occurrences and changes. Sometimes application-level code is used to record changes rather than leaving this to the database. Monitoring can be set up to attempt to detect security breaches.

3

INFORMATION ABOUT ARCHIVE

An archive is an accumulation of historical records or the physical place they are located. Archives contain primary source documents that have accumulated over the course of an individual or organization's lifetime, and are kept to show the function of that person or organization. Professional archivists and historians generally understand archives to be records that have been naturally and necessarily generated as a product of regular legal, commercial, administrative, or social activities. They have been metaphorically defined as "the secretions of an organism", and are distinguished from documents that have been consciously written or created to communicate a particular message to posterity.

In general, archives consist of records that have been selected for permanent or long-term preservation on grounds of their enduring cultural, historical, or evidentiary value. Archival records are normally unpublished and almost always unique, unlike books or magazines for which many identical copies exist. This means that archives are quite distinct from libraries with regard to their functions and organization, although archival collections can often be found within library buildings.

A person who works in archives is called an archivist. The study and practice of organizing, preserving, and providing access to information and materials in archives is called archival science. The physical place of storage can be referred to as an archive (more usual in the United Kingdom), an archives (more usual in the United States), or a repository.

When referring to historical records or the places they are kept, the plural form archives is chiefly used. The computing use of the term 'archive' should not be confused with the record-keeping meaning of the term.

Historical documents are original documents that contain important historical information about a person, place, or event and can thus serve as primary sources as important ingredients of the historical methodology. Significant historical documents can be deeds, laws, accounts of battles (often given by the victors or persons sharing their viewpoint), or the exploits of the powerful. Though these documents are of historical interest, they do not detail the daily lives of ordinary people, or the way society functioned. Anthropologists, historians and archeologists generally are more interested in documents that describe the day-to-day lives of ordinary people, indicating what they ate, their interaction with other members of their households and social groups, and their states of mind. It is this information that allows them to try to understand and describe the way society was functioning at any particular time in history. Greek ostraka provide good examples of historical documents from "among the common people".

Many documents that are produced today, such as personal letters, pictures, contracts, newspapers, and medical records, would be considered valuable historical documents in the future. However most of these will be lost in the future since they are either printed on ordinary paper which has a limited lifespan, or even stored in digital formats, then lost track over time.

Some companies and government entities are attempting to increase the number of documents that will survive the passage of time, by taking into account the preservation issues, and either printing documents in a manner that would increase the likelihood of them surviving indefinitely, or placing selected documents in time capsules or other special storage environments.

ETYMOLOGY

First attested in English in early 17th century, the word archive /rkav/ is derived from the French archives (plural), in turn from Latin archum or archvum, which is the romanized form of the Greek (archeion), "public records, town-hall, residence, or office of chief magistrates", itself from (arkh), amongst others "magistracy, office, government" (compare an-archy, mon-archy), which comes from the verb (arkh), "to begin, rule, govern".

The word originally developed from the Greek (arkheion), which refers to the home or dwelling of the Archon, in which important official state documents were filed and interpreted under the authority of the Archon. The adjective formed from archive is archival.

History

The practice of keeping official documents is very old. Archaeologists have discovered archives of hundreds (and sometime thousands) of clay tablets going back to the third and second millennia BC in sites like Ebla, Mari, Amarna, Hattusas, Ugarit, and Pylos. These discoveries have been fundamental to know ancient alphabets, languages, literature, and politics. Archives were well developed by the ancient Chinese, the ancient Greeks, and ancient Romans (who called them Tabularia). However, they have been lost, since documents written on materials like papyrus and paper deteriorated at a faster pace, unlike their stone tablet counterparts. Archives of churches, kingdoms, and cities from the Middle Ages survive and have often kept their official status uninterruptedly until now. They are the basic tool for historical research on these ages.

England after 1066 developed archives and archival research methods. The Swiss developed archival systems after 1450. Modern archival thinking has many roots from the French Revolution. The French National Archives, who possess perhaps the largest archival collection in the world, with records going as far back as 625 A.D., were created in 1790 during the French Revolution from various government, religious, and private archives seized by the revolutionaries.

Users and institutions

Reading room of the Österreichisches Staatsarchiv (Austrian State Archive), in the Erdberg district of Vienna (2006) Historians, genealogists, lawyers, demographers, filmmakers, and others conduct research at archives. The research process at each archive is unique, and depends upon the institution that houses the archive. While there are many kinds of archives, the most recent census of archivists in the United States identifies five major types: academic, business (for profit), government, non-profit, and other. There are also four main areas of inquiry involved with archives: material technologies, organizing principles, geographic locations, and tangled embodiments of humans and non-humans. These areas help to further categorize what kind of archive is being created.

Charles Sturt University Regional Archives.

Archives in colleges, universities, and other educational facilities are typically housed within a library, and duties may be carried out by an archivist. Academic archives exist to preserve institutional history and serve the academic community. An academic archive may contain materials such as the institution's administrative records, personal and professional papers of former professors and presidents, memorabilia related to school organizations and activities, and items the academic library wishes to remain in a closed-stack setting, such as rare books or thesis copies. Access to the collections in these archives is usually by prior appointment only; some have posted hours for making inquiries. Users of academic archives can be undergraduates, graduate students, faculty and staff, scholarly researchers, and the general public. Many academic archives work closely with alumni relations departments or other campus institutions to help raise funds for their library or school. Qualifications for employment may vary. Entry-level positions usually require an undergraduate diploma, but typically archivists hold graduate degrees in history or library science (preferably certified by a body such as the American Library Association). Subject-area specialization becomes more common in higher ranking positions.

Business (for profit)

Archives located in for-profit institutions are usually those owned by a private business. Examples of prominent business archives in the United States include Coca-Cola (which also owns the separate museum World of Coca-Cola), Procter and Gamble, Motorola Heritage Services and Archives, and Levi Strauss & Co. These corporate archives maintain historic documents and items related to the history and administration of their companies. Business archives serve the purpose of helping their corporations maintain control over their brand by retaining memories of the company's past. Especially in business archives, records management is separate from the historic aspect of archives. Workers in these types of archives may have any combination of training and degrees, from either a history or library background. These archives are typically not open to the public and only used by workers of the owner company, though some allow approved visitors by appointment. Business archives are concerned with maintaining the integrity of their company, and are therefore selective of how their materials may be used.

Government

Government archives include those maintained by local and state government as well as those maintained by the national (or federal) government. Anyone may use a government archive, and frequent users include reporters, genealogists, writers, historians, students, and people seeking information on the history of their home or region. Many government archives are open to the public and no appointment is required to visit.

In the United States, National Archives and Records Administration (NARA) maintains central archival facilities in the District of Columbia and College Park, Maryland, with regional facilities distributed throughout the United States. Some city or local governments may have repositories, but their organization and accessibility varies widely. Similar to the library profession, certification requirements and education also varies widely, from state to state. Professional associations themselves encourage the need to professionalize. NARA offers the Certificate of Federal Records Management Training Program for professional development. The majority of state and local archives staff hold a bachelor's degree-increasingly repositories list advanced degrees (e.g. MA, MLS/MLIS, PhD) and certifications as a position requirement or preference.

In the UK, the National Archives (formerly known as the Public Record Office) is the government archive for England and Wales. The English Heritage Archive is the public archive of English Heritage. The National Archives of Scotland, located in Edinburgh, serve that country while the Public Record Office of Northern Ireland in Belfast is the government archive for Northern Ireland. A network of county record offices and other local authority-run archives exists throughout England, Wales, and Scotland and holds many important collections, including local government, landed estates, church, and business records. Many archives have contributed catalogues to the national "Access to Archives" programme and online searching across collections is possible.

In France, the French Archives Administration (Service interministériel des Archives de France) in the Ministry of Culture manages the National Archives (Archives nationales), which possess 406 km. (252 miles) of archives as of 2010 (the total length of occupied shelves put next to each other), with original records going as far back as A.D. 625, as well as the departmental archives (archives départementales), located in the préfectures of each of the 100 départements of France, which possess 2,297 km. (1,427 miles) of archives (as of 2010), and also the local city archives, about 600 in total, which possess 456 km. (283,4 miles) of archives (as of 2010). Put together, the total volume of archives under the supervision of the French Archives Administration is the largest in the world.

Most intergovernmental organisations keep their own historical archives. However, a number of European organisations, including the European Commission, choose to deposit their archives with the European University Institute in Florence.

Church

A prominent Church Archives is the Vatican Secret Archive. Archdioceses, dioceses, and parishes also have archives in the Roman Catholic and Anglican Churches. Very important are monastery archives, because of their antiquity, like the ones of Monte Cassino, Saint Gall, and Fulda. The records in these archives include manuscripts, papal records, local Church records, photographs, oral histories, audiovisual materials, and architectural drawings.

Most Protestant denominations have archives as well, including the Presbyterian U.S.A Historical Society, The Moravian Church Archives, The Southern Baptist Historical Library and Archives, the United Methodist Archives and History Center of the United Methodist Church, and the Christian Church (Disciples of Christ).

Non-profit

Non-profit archives include those in historical societies, not-for-profit businesses such as hospitals, and the repositories within foundations. Non-profit archives are typically set up with private funds from donors to preserve the papers and history of specific persons or places. Often these institutions rely on grant funding from the government as well as the private funds. Depending on the funds available, non-profit archives may be as small as the historical society in a rural town to as big as a state historical society that rivals a government archives. Users of this type of archive may vary as much as the institutions that hold them. Employees of non-profit archives may be professional archivists, para-professionals, or volunteers, as the education required for a position at a non-profit archive varies with the demands of the collection's user base.

Web archiving

Web archiving is the process of collecting portions of the World Wide Web and ensuring the collection is preserved in an archive, such as an archive site, for future researchers, historians, and the public. Due to the massive size of the Web, web archivists typically employ web crawlers for automated collection.

Similarly, software code and documentation can be archived on the web, as with the example of CPAN.

Other

Some archives defy categorization. There are tribal archives within the Native American nations in North America, and there are archives that exist within the papers of private individuals. Many museums keep archives in order to prove the provenance of their pieces. Any institution or persons wishing to keep their significant papers in an organized fashion that employs the most basic principles of archival science may have an archive. In the 2004 census of archivists taken in the United States, 2.7% of archivists were employed in institutions that defied categorization. This was a separate figure from the 1.3% that identified themselves as self-employed.

Another type of archive is the Public Secrets project. This is an interactive testimonial, in which women incarcerated in the California State Prison System describe what happened to them. The archive's mission is to gather stories from women who want to express themselves, and want their stories heard. This collection includes transcripts and an audio recording of the women telling their stories.

The archives of an individual may include letters, papers, photographs, computer files, scrapbooks, financial records, or diaries created or collected by the individual - regardless of media or format. The archives of an organization (such as a corporation or government) tend to contain other types of records, such as administrative files, business records, memos, official correspondence, and meeting minutes.

Standardization

The International Council on Archives (ICA) has developed a number of standards on archival description including the General International Standard Archival Description ISAD(G). ISAD(G) is meant to be used in conjunction with national standards or as a basis for nations to build their own standards. In the United States, ISAD(G) is implemented through Describing Archives: A Content Standard, popularly known as "DACS". In

Canada, ISAD(G) is implemented through the Council of Archives as the Rules for Archival Description, also known as "RAD".

ISO IS CURRENTLY WORKING ON STANDARDS.

The National Archives (TNA) is a non-ministerial government department. Its parent department is the Department for Digital, Culture, Media and Sport of the United Kingdom of Great Britain and Northern Ireland. It is the official archive of the UK government and for England and Wales; and "guardian of some of the nation's most iconic documents, dating back more than 1,000 years." There are separate national archives for Scotland (the National Records of Scotland) and Northern Ireland (the Public Record Office of Northern Ireland).

TNA was formerly four separate organisations: the Public Record Office (PRO), the Historical Manuscripts Commission, the Office of Public Sector Information (OPSI) and Her Majesty's Stationery Office (HMSO). The Public Record Office still exists as a legal entity, as the enabling legislation has not been modified, and documents held by the institution thus continue to be cited by many scholars as part of the PRO. Since 2008, TNA has also hosted the former UK Statute Law Database, now known as legislation.gov.uk.

It is institutional policy to include the definite article, with an initial capital letter, in its name (hence "The National Archives", abbreviated as TNA) but this practice is not always followed in the non-specialist media.

Location

The National Archives is based in Kew in the London Borough of Richmond upon Thames in south-west London. The building was opened in 1977 as an additional home for the public records, which were held in a building on Chancery Lane. The site was originally a World War I hospital, which was later used by several government departments. It is near to Kew Gardens Underground station.

Until its closure in March 2008, the Family Records Centre in Islington was run jointly by The National Archives and the General Register Office. The National Archives has an additional office in Norwich, which is primarily for former OPSI staff. There is also an additional record storage facility (DeepStore) in the worked-out parts of Winsford Rock Salt Mine, Winsford, Cheshire.

History

The National Archives was created in 2003 by combining the Public Record Office and the Historical Manuscripts Commission and is a non-ministerial department reporting to the Minister of State for digital policy.

On 31 October 2006, The National Archives merged with the Office of Public Sector Information (OPSI), which itself also contained Her Majesty's Stationery Office (HMSO) which was previously a part of the Cabinet Office. The name remained The National Archives.

Key roles

TNA claims it is "at the heart of information policy-setting standards and supporting innovation in information and records management across the UK, and providing a practical framework of best practice for opening up and encouraging the re-use of public sector information. This work helps inform today's decisions and ensure that they become tomorrow's permanent record." It has a number of key roles in information policy:

- Policy - advising government on information practice and policy, on issues from record creation through to its reuse
- Selection - selecting which documents to store
- Preservation - ensuring the documents remain in as good a condition as possible
- EAccess - providing the public with the opportunity to view the documents
- Advice - advising the public and other archives and archivists around the world on how to care for documents
- Intellectual property management - TNA (via OPSI and HMSO) manages crown copyright for the UK
- Regulation - ensuring that other public sector organisations adhere to both the public records act and the PSI reuse regulations.

SECTOR LEADERSHIP

The National Archives (and before it the Public Record Office) has long had a role of oversight and leadership for the entire archives sector and archives profession in the UK, including local government and non-governmental archives. Under the Public Records Act 1958 it is responsible for overseeing the appropriate custody of certain non-governmental public records in England and Wales. Under the 2003 Historical Manuscripts Commission Warrant it has responsibility for investigating and reporting on non-governmental records and archives of all kinds throughout the United Kingdom. In October 2011, when the Museums, Libraries and Archives Council was wound up, TNA took over its responsibilities in respect of archives in England, including providing information and advice to ministers on archives policy. The National Archives now sees this part of its role as being "to enhance the 'archival health of the nation'".

The National Archives is the UK government's official archive, "containing 1000 years of history from Domesday Book to the present", with records from parchment and paper scrolls through to digital files and archived websites. The material held at Kew includes the following:

- Documents from the central courts of law from the twelfth century onwards, including the Court of King's Bench, the Court of Common Pleas, the Court of Chancery, the Court of Exchequer, the Supreme Court of Judicature, the Central Criminal Court, Assizes, and many other courts
- Medieval, early modern and modern records of central government
- A large and disparate collection of maps, plans and architectural drawings
- Records for family historians including wills, naturalisation certificates and criminal records
- Service and operational records of the armed forces War Office, Admiralty etc.
- Foreign Office and Colonial Office correspondence and files
- Cabinet papers and Home Office records
- Statistics of the Board of Trade
- The surviving records of (mainly) the English railway companies, transferred from the British Railways Record Office

There is also a museum, which displays key documents such as Domesday Book and has exhibitions on various topics using material from the collections.

Researchers at the archive

The collections held by the National Archives can be searched using their online catalogue. Entrance to The National Archives is free. Anybody aged 16 or over can access the original documents at the Kew site, after producing two acceptable proofs of identity and being issued a free reader's ticket.

The reading room has terminals from which documents can be ordered up from secure storage areas by their reference number. The reference number is composed of three sections: the department code of up to four letters, such as WO for the War Office; a series or class number, for the "subcategory" or collection that the document comes from; and an individual document number. Documents can also be ordered in advance.

Once a document has been ordered, The National Archives aims to get it to the reader within 45 minutes (assuming it is kept at Kew rather than at their second repository, "Deep Store" - a former salt mine in Cheshire: it can take 2-3 days for files to be retrieved from the latter). Special arrangements are in place for readers wishing to retrieve large groups of files.

A reader's ticket is not needed to access records on microform or online. Frequently accessed documents such as the Abdication Papers have been put on microfilm, as have records for two million First World War soldiers. The originals of the latter were stored in a warehouse in London along with four million others, but incendiary bombs dropped on the warehouse in the Second World War started a fire in which most were destroyed. The surviving third were largely water or fire-damaged and thus acquired the colloquial name of the "Burnt Documents." Because they were mostly too fragile for public access, they were put on microfilm with the aid of the Heritage Lottery Fund. They have now also been digitised and are available on the Ancestry website.

Some of the most popular documents have now been digitised and are available to download from Discovery, for a fee of £3.50 per file, or through co-branded services called licensed Internet associates (LIA) as pay per view or part of their subscription service. A list of records online is available under the records, catalogues and online records menu on The National Archives' website.

All of the open census records have been digitised, and there are also significant other sources online, such as wills proved in the Prerogative Court of Canterbury, 1383-1858. Researchers are encouraged to check the online services first, to see if they can get what they want online. If a document is available online, The National Archives' policy is to encourage people to use the digital copy and not the original, even if they come to Kew, in order to protect the original from damage.

Storage

The documents are stored on mobile shelving - double-sided shelves, which are pushed together so that there is no aisle between them. A large handle on the end of each shelf allows them to be moved along tracks in the floor to create an aisle when needed.

They are generally stored in acid-free folders or boxes.

In the event of a fire The National Archives would be clearly unable to use sprinklers for fear of ruining its holdings, and so when the building is evacuated, argon gas is released into the air-tight repositories.

Other services

The National Archives also provides services to help users in their research and also find collections beyond those it holds.

Education

The National Archives' education web page is a free online resource for teaching and learning history, aimed at teachers and students. Users can select time periods they are interested in, from the medieval era to the present day. Each time period contains sub-topics with various materials that can be used as teaching tools for teachers. Resources for students focus primarily on tips for research and writing using archival materials.

"Access to Archives"

Access to Archives (also known as A2A) is a database containing details of archival collections held in many different archive repositories in England and Wales. As of March 2008, there are no more plans to add additional collections to A2A due to lack of funding from the Heritage Lottery Fund and the changing financial priorities of The National Archives, but existing entries can still be updated. The A2A database was transferred to The National Archives with a new platform with a simpler interface to ensure its availability.

A researcher at the archives

The National Register of Archives (NRA) is the central point for the collection and circulation of information about the content and nature of archival manuscripts relating to British history. It contains published and unpublished lists and catalogues describing archival collections in the UK and overseas: currently over 44,000 such catalogues are included. The register can be consulted in the National Archives reading room and the index used to be searchable as an online database on the National Archives web site.

The information is collected in a variety of ways. TNA is sent hard-copy catalogues from archive repositories holding records relating to British history. These are kept in the reading room at The National Archives and indexed in the online database. TNA conducts an annual survey of archive repositories and records all new accessions, and the accession lists are also available on TNA's website. Information is also obtained from surveys and guides to archival collections, and other publications. The Register includes name indexes to its contents (covering corporate names, personal names, family names, and place names); but not subject or thematic indexes. Where the catalogues are themselves available online the indexes provide direct electronic links; but many still exist in hard copy only (often as unpublished "grey literature"), and it remains necessary for the researcher to visit either TNA or the specific repository in order to consult them.

A separate National Register of Archives for Scotland is maintained at the National Archives of Scotland, but its contents are duplicated within the NRA at Kew.

ARCHON directory

ARCHON Directory is a database of contact details for archive repositories in the UK and institutions elsewhere in the world which have substantial collections of manuscripts relating to British history.

"Your Archives"

Your Archives is a wiki for the National Archives on-line community which was launched in May 2007; it was closed for editing on 30 September 2012 in preparation of archiving on the Government web archive. The contributions are made by users to give additional information to that which is available on the other services provided by the National Archives, including the catalogue, research guides, documentonline and National Register of Archive. Your Archives encourages users to create articles not only about historical records held by the National Archives, but those held in other archive repositories.

Databases

The National Archives also hosts several databases on types of records including hospital records; migration records; and manorial records. Working with the Wellcome Library, TNA has made hospital records available via the Hospital Records Database. The Hospital Records Database has not been updated since 2012, and there are no current updates occurring as of 2018.

The Manorial Documents Register includes records relating to manors located in England and Wales. Digitization of the records is on-going as of 2018.

Civil Pages

The National Archives operates the Civil Pages project on behalf of the Cabinet Office, operating as an online directory for the civil service, facilitating working together and providing a means of sharing knowledge securely between government departments.

Smartphone applications

In January 2011 The National Archives, in conjunction with historian Nick Barratt and smartphone applications development studio RevelMob, developed its first Old Money iPhone app, which uses historic price data from documents held at The National Archives to see what a sum of money from the past (from 1270) would be worth today and the spending power it would have commanded at the time. In September 2011, TNA's museum began using QRpedia codes, which can be scanned by smartphone users in order to retrieve information about exhibits from Wikipedia.

Blogs and Podcasts

TNA regularly posts blogs to its website. Posts cover a wide range of topics, from specific events and time periods to features on holdings in TNA, as well as information on the archive's operations. The "Archives Media Player" section holds videos and podcasts created and posted by TNA. Videos and audio are not posted as regularly as TNA's blog.

The Future: Archives Inspire 2015-19

Archives Inspire is a strategy document that sets out the goals and priorities of the organisation over four years, from 2015 onwards.

Forgeries discovered in 2005

In June 2005, journalist Ben Fenton of The Daily Telegraph received an email from a colleague asking him to investigate documents held at TNA that alleged that a British intelligence agent had, on the orders of Winston Churchill, murdered Heinrich Himmler, the head of the Nazi SS, in 1945. The three documents had come to prominence after being revealed by author Martin Allen in his book Himmler's Secret War.

On viewing photographs of the documents, Fenton's suspicions were immediately aroused by the fact that such a controversial policy was casually committed to paper, even to the extent of naming the assassin, and by the use of colourful language, unlike the civil service language of the 1940s used by senior Foreign Office officials John Wheeler-Bennett and Robert Bruce Lockhart. Viewing the original documents the next day, Fenton spotted what looked like pencil marks beneath the signature on one of them. This confirmed his suspicions and, along with his experience of analysing historic documents, it enabled him to persuade The Daily Telegraph to pay for forensic analysis.

TNA staff took four files, along with authenticated copies of the authors' handwriting, to Dr Audrey Giles, a former head of Scotland Yard's Questioned Documents Unit where she confirmed that the documents were certainly forgeries. One letter head had been printed on a laser printer, the earliest example of which was produced in 1977, and all had tear marks where they had been threaded on to the security tags. Further investigations by TNA staff revealed that the counterfeit documents contained errors, breaches of protocol and etiquette which their supposed authors would not have committed, prompting one expert to state that the inconsistencies in the papers "would lead any serious historian to question their veracity".

After his account of the deception appeared in the newspaper, Fenton was contacted by a German academic, Ernst Haiger, who informed him of his own suspicions over other TNA documents cited in an earlier Allen book. Examination by TNA experts led to more than a dozen documents being identified as suspicious and submitted to Home Office specialists for examination. When they, too, were declared forgeries, the TNA called in the police.

In the addendum to the later American edition of the book (which acknowledged that the papers were forged), Allen theorised that, some time after he saw the documents, they had been removed and replaced with clumsily forged replicas, to cast doubt upon his discoveries.

In all, twenty-nine forged documents were discovered, each typed on one of only four typewriters. They were placed in twelve separate files, and cited at least once in one or more of Allen's three books. According to the experts at TNA, documents now shown to be forgeries supported controversial arguments central to each of Allen's books: in Hidden

Agenda, five documents now known to be forged helped justify his claim that the Duke of Windsor betrayed military secrets to Hitler; in The Hitler/Hess Deception, thirteen forged papers supported.

Allen's contention that, in 1941, British intelligence used members of the Royal Family to fool the Nazis into thinking Britain was on the verge of a pro-German putsch; in Himmler's Secret War, twenty-two counterfeit papers also underpinned the book's core claims that British intelligence played mind games with Himmler to encourage him to betray Hitler from 1943 onwards, and that ultimately they murdered the SS chief.

In 2007 the Crown Prosecution Service announced that it was "not in the public interest" to prosecute the only suspect questioned by police. Allen's health problems had prevented the police questioning him for nine months, after which he told them he was wholly innocent. In a December 2007 response to questions from Norman Baker MP, the Solicitor-General said that the police investigation, guided by the opinion of a senior barrister, had produced "sufficient evidence for a realistic prospect of conviction" on charges of forgery, using a forged document and criminal damage but it had been decided that it was not in the public interest to proceed. In reaching that decision, "matters relating to Mr Allen's health and the surrounding circumstances were significant in deciding that a prosecution was not in the public interest". A well-planned attempt to corrupt the UK's primary source of historical information

MI5 Records in the News

MI5 records relating to British Prime Minister Margaret Thatcher's time in office have caused some questions and controversy regarding the transparency of the British government. In 2017, journalist Richard Norton-Taylor argued that MI5, and the British government by extension, was purposely withholding some information that the public deserves to know. Norton-Taylor specifically refers to Thatcher's reluctance to allow the publication of two books looking into the impact that intelligence organizations of Britain had on World War II, as well as her worries about British activities in Northern Ireland becoming known to the general public. Additional MI5 records relating to the blacklisting of government workers during Thatcher's time in office have also prompted questions after their release. In addition to government workers, the blacklists also targeted other groups, such as unions and minorities, that may not fall in line with conservative policies. Debates on the roles of MI5, Whitehall, and Thatcher's administration, have come up in light of these records at TNA and prompted questions of transparency as well as whether or not these blacklists had an effect on the careers of any individuals included. Questions also remain, as of 2018, whether or not there are still blacklists currently in effect and if these could affect government workers, unions, and other individuals possibly included in the blacklists.

4

ARCHIVAL RESEARCH

Archival research is a type of research which involves seeking out and extracting evidence from archival records. These records may be held either in collecting institutions, such as libraries and museums, or in the custody of the organization (whether a government body, business, family, or other agency) that originally generated or accumulated them, or in that of a successor body (transferring, or in-house archives). Archival research can be contrasted with (1) secondary research (undertaken in a library or online), which involves identifying and consulting secondary sources relating to the topic of enquiry; and (2) with other types of primary research and empirical investigation such as fieldwork and experiment.

HISTORY OF ARCHIVES ORGANIZATIONS

The oldest archives have been in existence for hundreds of years. For instance, the Vatican Secret Archives was started in the 17th century AD and contains state papers, papal account books, and papal correspondence dating back to the 8th century. Most archives that are still in existence do not claim collections that date back quite as far as the Vatican Archive. The Archives Nationales in France was founded in 1790 during the French Revolution and has holdings that date back to AD 625, and other European archives have a similar provenance. Archives in the modern world, while of more recent date, may also hold material going back several centuries, for example, the United States National Archives and Records Administration was established originally in 1934. The NARA contains records and collections dating back to the founding of the United States in the 18th century. Among the collections of the NARA are the Declaration of Independence, the Constitution of the United States, and an original copy of the Magna Carta. The British National Archives

(TNA) traces its history to the creation of the Public Record Office in 1838, while other state and national bodies were also formed in the late 19th and early 20th centuries.

Universities are another venue for archival holdings and manuscript collections. Most universities have archival holdings that chronicle the business of the university. Some universities also have archives or manuscript collections that focus on one aspect or another of the culture of the state or country in which the university is located. Schools and religious institutions, as well as local studies and history collections, museums and research institutions may all hold archives.

The reason for highlighting the breadth and depth of archives is to give some idea of the difficulties facing archival researchers. Some of these archives hold vast quantities of records. For example, the Vatican Secret Archive has upwards of 52 miles of archival shelving. An increasing number of archives are now accepting digital transfers, which can also present challenges for display and access.

Archival research methodologies

Archival research lies at the heart of most academic and other forms of original historical research; but it is frequently also undertaken (in conjunction with parallel research methodologies) in other disciplines within the humanities and social sciences, including literary studies, rhetoric, archaeology, sociology, human geography, anthropology, psychology, and organizational studies. It may also be important in other non-academic types of enquiry, such as the tracing of birth families by adoptees, and criminal investigations. Data held by archival institutions is also of use in scientific research and in establishing civil rights.

In addition to discipline, the kind of research methodology used in archival research can vary depending on its organization and its materials. For example, in an archives that has a large number of materials still unprocessed, a researcher may find consulting directly with archive staff who have a clear understanding of collections and their organization to be useful as they can be a source of information regarding unprocessed materials or of related materials in other archives and repositories. When an archive is not entirely oriented towards one or relevant to a single discipline, researchers, for example genealogists, may rely upon formal or informal networks to support research by sharing information about specific archives' organization and collections with each other.

Conducting research at an archive

The Hoover Institution Library and Archives Reading Room. A reading room is a space at an archive where users can consult materials under staff supervision. Archival research is generally more complex and time-consuming than secondary research, presenting challenges in identifying, locating and interpreting relevant documents. Although archives share similar features and characteristics they can also vary in significant ways. While publicly funded archives may have mandates that require them to be as accessible as possible other kinds, such as corporate, religious, or private archives, will have varying degrees of access and discoverability. Some materials may be restricted in other ways, such as on those containing sensitive or classified information, unpublished works, or imposed by agreements with the donor of materials. Furthermore, archival records are often unique, and the researcher must be prepared to travel to reach them. Even when materials are available in digital formats there may be restrictions on them that prohibit them from being accessed off-site.

Locating archival collections

Prior to online search, union catalogs were an important tool for finding materials in libraries and archives. In the United States, the National Union Catalog and the National Union Catalog of Manuscript Collections have been used by researchers to locate archives although much of its information has since been migrated to online systems.

An increasing number of archival institutions can be found via an online search. In addition, portals such as Europeana, the Digital Public Library of America and the National Library of Australia's Trove provide links to member institutions.

In the UK, JISC hosts the ArchivesHub, while the OCLC's ArchiveGrid provides an international portal for mostly library based institutions, which use MARC as a cataloguing tool for their holdings. The Association of Canadian Archivists (ACA) has partnered with the software company Artefactual to create ArchivesCanada, while the Australian Society of Archivists have used the same software for their Directory of Archives in Australia. Many other online search tools have been made available to facilitate search and discovery

If an archives cannot be found through online search or a publicly listed collection a researcher may have to track down its existence through other means, such as following other researcher's citations and references. This is particularly true for materials held by corporations or other organizations that may not employ an archivist and thus be unaware of the extent or contents of their materials.

In very restricted archives, access may be restricted only to individuals with certain credentials or affiliations with institutions like universities and then only to those of a certain level. Those lacking the necessary credentials may need to request letters of introduction from an individual or institution to provide to the archive.

Locating materials within archives

Archives usually contain unique materials and their organization may also be entirely unique or idiosyncratic to the institution or organization that maintains them. This is one important distinction with libraries where material is organized according to standardized classification systems. Traditionally, archives have followed the principle of respect des fonds in which the provenance and original order is maintained although some rearrangement, physical or intellectual, may be done by the archivist to facilitate its use. A basic guideline for archival description is the International Standard of Archival Description (General) (ISAD/G or ISAD), produced by the International Council on Archives (ICA). American institutions may also be guided by Describing Archives: a content standard (DACS) and in Canada by the Rules of Archival Description (RAD). Understanding how archival descriptions and finding aids are constructed is known as archival intelligence.

In addition to these standards and rules for creating hard copy and online listings and catalogues, archivists may also provide access to their catalogues through APIs or through the encoding standards EAD (Encoded archival description) (relating to the fonds, series, and items) and EAC (Encoded archival context)(the organisations and people that created the archives).

Finding aids are a common reference tool created by archivists for locating materials. They come in a variety of forms, such as registers, card catalogs, or inventories. Many finding aids to archival documents are now hosted online as web pages or uploaded as documents, such as at the Library of Congress' Rare Book & Special Collections. The level of detail in finding aids can vary from granular item-level descriptions to coarse collection-level descriptions. If an archive has a large backlog of unprocessed materials, there may not be any kind of finding aid at all. From around 2005, an ideology known as "More Product, Less Process", or MPLP, has been adopted by many North American collecting archives seeking to reduce processing time or alleviate backlogs to provide access to materials sooner, the results of which may be minimally described finding aids.

Although most archive repositories welcome researchers, and have professional staff tasked with assisting them, the large quantity of records means that finding aids may be of only limited usefulness: the researcher will need to hunt through large quantities of documents in search of material relevant to his or her particular enquiry. Some records may be closed to public access for reasons of confidentiality; and others may be written in archaic handwriting, in ancient or foreign languages, or in technical terminology. Archival documents were generally created for immediate practical or administrative purposes, not for the benefit of future researchers, and additional contextual research may be necessary to make sense of them. Many of these challenges are exacerbated when the records are still in the custody of the generating body or in private hands, where owners or custodians may be unwilling to provide access to external enquirers, and where finding aids may be even more rudimentary or non-existent.

CONSULTING ARCHIVAL MATERIALS

Reading Room of the Maritime Research Center, San Francisco. In the foreground, a user is seated at a table and is consulting materials stored in archival boxes which are brought to them by staff.

Archival materials are usually held in closed stacks and non-circulating. Users request to see specific materials from the archives and may only consult them on-site. After locating the relevant record location using a finding aid or other discovery tool a user may then have to submit the request to the archives, such as using a request form. If an archives has part of its holdings located in a separate building or facility, it make take days or weeks to retrieve materials, requiring a user to submit their requests in advance of an on-site consultation.

Reading room of the National Archives of Norway. In the foreground are overhead scanners. Since archival materials are unique, some archives may have equipment available for users to duplicate materials.

A reading room is a space, usually within or near the archive, where users can consult archival materials under staff supervision. The unique, fragile, or sensitive nature of some materials sometimes requires the certain kinds of restrictions on their use, handling, and/or duplication. Many archives restrict what kinds of items can be brought into a reading room from outside, such as pencils, notepads, bags, and even clothing, to guard against theft or risk of damage to materials. Further restrictions may be placed on the number of materials that can be consulted at any given time, such as limiting a user to one box at a time and requiring all materials to be laid flat and visible at all times. Some archives provide basic supplies including scrap paper and pencils or foam wedges for supporting unusually large materials. Duplication services may be available at the archive although the policies, costs, and time required can vary. Increasingly, archives also allow users to use their own devices, such as handheld cameras, cell phones, and even scanners, to duplicate materials.The use of white or any other glove, while popular in television programs, is not necessarily required for handling archival documents, due to concerns about fragility of pages and text. They may be required for handling volumes with poor bindings, if the gloves are removed for the internal pages to prevent transfer of dirt and other material, and should be used when handling photographs. Always check with the archivist as to whether gloves are required or not.

Archives may also provide access to content via microfilm (including fiche and other formats) due to the fragility or popularity of the original archive. Digital copies may also be provided for the same reason. Before asking for access to the original, make sure that the items that have been reformatted are suitable for the use you require. Reasons for asking for access to original content might included the need to view a colour image (architectural perspective and elevation drawings, maps and plans, etc) or for accessibility reasons (minor visual vertigo is usually not considered a reason for access to originals, as the effect can be mitigated by slower perusal of the film).

Some materials may contain information that concerns the privacy and confidentiality of living individuals, such as medical and student records, and demand special care. Materials that might contain personally identifiable information, such as social security numbers or names, must be handled appropriately, and an archive might provide redacted copies of materials or deny access to materials entirely due to privacy or other legislative concerns.

Off-site and electronic materials

More and more archival materials are being digitized or are born-digital enabling them to be accessed off-site through the internet or other networked services. Archives that have digital materials accessible to the public may make their holdings discoverable to internet search engines by sharing or exposing their electronic catalogs and/or metadata, using standards like the Open Archives Initiative Protocol for Metadata Harvesting (OAI-PMH). Some institutions have online portals where users can freely access digital materials that have been made available by the archive such as the Archives of the New York Public Library or the Smithsonian Institution Archives. Governments and their related institutions may use these "electronic", or "virtual", reading rooms to upload documents and materials that have been requested by the public such as through FOIA requests or in accordance with records disclosure policies.

Papyrus

Papyrus /ppars/ is a material similar to thick paper that was used in ancient times as a writing surface. It was made from the pith of the papyrus plant, Cyperus papyrus, a wetland sedge. Papyrus (plural: papyri) can also refer to a document written on sheets of such material, joined together side by side and rolled up into a scroll, an early form of a book.

An official letter on a papyrus of the 3rd century BCE

Papyrus is first known to have been used in Egypt (at least as far back as the First Dynasty), as the papyrus plant was once abundant across the Nile Delta. It was also used throughout the Mediterranean region and in the Kingdom of Kush. Apart from a writing material, ancient Egyptians employed papyrus in the construction of other artifacts, such as reed boats, mats, rope, sandals, and baskets.

Roman portraiture fresco of a young man with a papyrus scroll, from Herculaneum, 1st century AD Papyrus was first manufactured in Egypt as far back as the fourth millennium BCE. The earliest archaeological evidence of papyrus was excavated in 2012 and 2013 at

Wadi al-Jarf, an ancient Egyptian harbor located on the Red Sea coast. These documents date from c. 2560-2550 BCE (end of the reign of Khufu). The papyrus rolls describe the last years of building the Great Pyramid of Giza. In the first centuries BCE and CE, papyrus scrolls gained a rival as a writing surface in the form of parchment, which was prepared from animal skins. Sheets of parchment were folded to form quires from which book-form codices were fashioned. Early Christian writers soon adopted the codex form, and in the Græco-Roman world, it became common to cut sheets from papyrus rolls to form codices.

Codices were an improvement on the papyrus scroll, as the papyrus was not pliable enough to fold without cracking and a long roll, or scroll, was required to create large-volume texts. Papyrus had the advantage of being relatively cheap and easy to produce, but it was fragile and susceptible to both moisture and excessive dryness. Unless the papyrus was of perfect quality, the writing surface was irregular, and the range of media that could be used was also limited.

Papyrus was replaced in Europe by the cheaper, locally produced products parchment and vellum, of significantly higher durability in moist climates, though Henri Pirenne's connection of its disappearance with the Muslim conquest of Egypt is contested. Its last appearance in the Merovingian chancery is with a document of 692, though it was known in Gaul until the middle of the following century. The latest certain dates for the use of papyrus are 1057 for a papal decree (typically conservative, all papal bulls were on papyrus until 1022), under Pope Victor II, and 1087 for an Arabic document. Its use in Egypt continued until it was replaced by more inexpensive paper introduced by the Islamic world who originally learned of it from the Chinese. By the 12th century, parchment and paper were in use in the Byzantine Empire, but papyrus was still an option. Papyrus was made in several qualities and prices. Pliny the Elder and Isidore of Seville described six variations of papyrus which were sold in the Roman market of the day. These were graded by quality based on how fine, firm, white, and smooth the writing surface was. Grades ranged from the superfine Augustan, which was produced in sheets of 13 digits (10 inches) wide, to the least expensive and most coarse, measuring six digits (four inches) wide. Materials deemed unusable for writing or less than six digits were considered commercial quality and were pasted edge to edge to be used only for wrapping.

Until the middle of the 19th century, only some isolated documents written on papyrus were known, and that museums simply displayed them as curiosities. They did not contain literary works. The first modern discovery of papyri rolls was made at Herculaneum in 1752. Until then, the only papyri known had been a few surviving from medieval times. Scholarly investigations began with the Dutch historian Caspar Jacob Christiaan Reuvens (1793-1835). He wrote about the content of the Leyden papyrus, published in 1830. The first publication has been credited to the British scholar Charles Wycliffe Goodwin (1817-1878), who published for the Cambridge Antiquarian Society, one of the Papyri Graecae Magicae V, translated into English with commentary in 1853.

Etymology

The English word "papyrus" derives, via Latin, from Greek (papyros), a loanword of unknown (perhaps Pre-Greek) origin. Greek has a second word for it, (byblos, said to derive from the name of the Phoenician city of Byblos). The Greek writer Theophrastus, who flourished during the 4th century BCE, uses papyros when referring to the plant used as a foodstuff and byblos for the same plant when used for nonfood products, such as cordage, basketry, or writing surfaces. The more specific term biblos, which finds its way into English in such words as 'bibliography', 'bibliophile', and 'bible', refers to the inner bark of the papyrus plant. Papyrus is also the etymon of 'paper', a similar substance.

Documents written on papyrus

The word for the material papyrus is also used to designate documents written on sheets of it, often rolled up into scrolls. The plural for such documents is papyri. Historical papyri are given identifying names - generally the name of the discoverer, first owner or institution where they are kept-and numbered, such as "Papyrus Harris I". Often an abbreviated form is used, such as "pHarris I". These documents provide important information on ancient writings; they give us the only extant copy of Menander, the Egyptian Book of the Dead, Egyptian treatises on medicine (the Ebers Papyrus) and on surgery (the Edwin Smith papyrus), Egyptian mathematical treatises (the Rhind papyrus), and Egyptian folk tales (the Westcar papyrus). When, in the 18th century, a library of ancient papyri was found in Herculaneum, ripples of expectation spread among the learned men of the time. However, since these papyri were badly charred, their unscrolling and deciphering is still going on today.

Papyrus plants near Syracuse, Sicily

Papyrus is made from the stem of the papyrus plant, Cyperus papyrus. The outer rind is first removed, and the sticky fibrous inner pith is cut lengthwise into thin strips of about 40 cm (16 in) long. The strips are then placed side by side on a hard surface with their edges slightly overlapping, and then another layer of strips is laid on top at a right angle. The strips may have been soaked in water long enough for decomposition to begin, perhaps increasing adhesion, but this is not certain. The two layers possibly were glued together. While still moist, the two layers are hammered together, mashing the layers into a single sheet. The sheet is then dried under pressure. After drying, the sheet is polished with some rounded object, possibly a stone or seashell or round hardwood.

Sheets could be cut to fit the obligatory size or glued together to create a longer roll. A wooden stick would be attached to the last sheet in a roll, making it easier to handle. To form the long strip scrolls required, a number of such sheets were united, placed so all the horizontal fibres parallel with the roll's length were on one side and all the vertical fibres on the other. Normally, texts were first written on the recto, the lines following the fibres, parallel to the long edges of the scroll. Secondarily, papyrus was often reused, writing across the fibres on the verso. Pliny the Elder describes the methods of preparing papyrus in his Naturalis Historia.

In a dry climate, like that of Egypt, papyrus is stable, formed as it is of highly rot-resistant cellulose; but storage in humid conditions can result in molds attacking and destroying the material. Library papyrus rolls were stored in wooden boxes and chests made in the form of statues. Papyrus scrolls were organized according to subject or author, and identified with clay labels that specified their contents without having to unroll the scroll. In European conditions, papyrus seems to have lasted only a matter of decades; a 200-year-old papyrus was considered extraordinary. Imported papyrus once commonplace in Greece and Italy has since deteriorated beyond repair, but papyri are still being found in Egypt; extraordinary examples include the Elephantine papyri and the famous finds at Oxyrhynchus and Nag Hammadi. The Villa of the Papyri at Herculaneum, containing the library of Lucius Calpurnius Piso Caesoninus, Julius Caesar's father-in-law, was preserved by the eruption of Mount Vesuvius, but has only been partially excavated.

Sporadic attempts to revive the manufacture of papyrus have been made since the mid-18th century. Scottish explorer James Bruce experimented in the late 18th century with papyrus plants from the Sudan, for papyrus had become extinct in Egypt. Also in the 18th century, Sicilian Saverio Landolina manufactured papyrus at Syracuse, where papyrus plants had continued to grow in the wild. During the 1920s, when Egyptologist Battiscombe Gunn lived in Maadi, outside Cairo, he experimented with the manufacture of papyrus, growing the plant in his garden. He beat the sliced papyrus stalks between two layers of linen, and produced successful examples of papyrus, one of which was exhibited in the Egyptian Museum in Cairo. The modern technique of papyrus production used in Egypt for the tourist trade was developed in 1962 by the Egyptian engineer Hassan Ragab using plants that had been reintroduced into Egypt in 1872 from France. Both Sicily and Egypt have centres of limited papyrus production.

Papyrus is still used by communities living in the vicinity of swamps, to the extent that rural householders derive up to 75% of their income from swamp goods. Particularly in East and Central Africa, people harvest papyrus, which is used to manufacture items that are sold or used locally. Examples include baskets, hats, fish traps, trays or winnowing mats, and floor mats. Papyrus is also used to make roofs, ceilings, rope and fences. Although alternatives, such as eucalyptus, are increasingly available, papyrus is still used as fuel.

The Heracles Papyrus

This is a collection of William Tyssen-Amherst, 1st Baron Amherst of Hackney. It includes biblical manuscripts, early church fragments, and classical documents from the Ptolemaic, Roman, and Byzantine eras. The collection was edited by Bernard Grenfell and Arthur Hunt in 1900-1901. It is housed at the Pierpont Morgan Library (New York).

- Archduke Rainer Papyri: One of the world's largest collection of papyri (about 180,000 objects) in the Austrian National Library.
- Berlin Papyri: housed in the Egyptian Museum and Papyrus Collection.
- Berliner griechische Urkunden: BGU, a publishing project ongoing since 1895
- Bodmer Papyri: This collection was purchased by Martin Bodmer in 1955-1956. Currently it is housed in the Bibliotheca Bodmeriana in Cologny. It includes Greek and Coptic documents, classical texts, biblical books, and writing of the early churches.
- Brooklyn Papyrus: This papyrus focuses mainly on snakebites and its remedies. It speaks of remedial methods for poisons obtained from snakes, scorpions, and tarantulas. The Brooklyn Papyrus currently resides in the Brooklyn Museum.
- Chester Beatty Papyri: collection of 11 codices acquired by Alfred Chester Beatty in 1930-1931 and 1935. It is housed at the Chester Beatty Library. The collection was edited by Frederic G. Kenyon.
- Colt Papyri: it is housed at the Pierpont Morgan Library (New York).
- The Herculaneum papyri: These papyri were found in Herculaneum in the eighteenth century, carbonized by the eruption of Mount Vesuvius. After some tinkering, a method was found to unroll and to read them. Most of them are housed at the Naples National Archaeological Museum.
- The Heroninos Archive is a collection of around a thousand papyrus documents, dealing with the management of a large Roman estate, dating to the third century CE, found at the very end of the 19th century at Kasr El Harit, the site of ancient Theadelphia [de], in the Faiyum area of Egypt by Bernard Pyne Grenfell and Arthur Surridge Hunt. It is spread over many collections throughout the world.
- The Houghton's papyri: the collection at Houghton Library, Harvard University was acquired between 1901 and 1909 thanks to a donation from the Egypt Exploration Fund.
- Saite Oracle Papyrus: This papyrus located at the Brooklyn Museum records the petition of a man named Pemou on behalf of his father, Harsiese to ask their god for permission to change temples.

- Martin Schøyen Collection: biblical manuscripts in Greek and Coptic, Dead Sea Scrolls, classical documents
- Michigan Papyrus Collection: this collection contains above 10 000 papyri fragments. It is housed at the University of Michigan.
- Oxyrhynchus Papyri: these numerous papyri fragments were discovered by Grenfell and Hunt in and around Oxyrhynchus. The publication of these papyri is still in progress. A large part of the Oxyrhynchus papyri are housed at the Ashmolean Museum in Oxford, others in the British Museum in London, in the Egyptian Museum in Cairo, and many other places.
- Princeton Papyri: it is housed at the Princeton University
- Papiri della Società Italiana (PSI): a series, still in progress, published by the Società per la ricerca dei Papiri greci e latini in Egitto and from 1927 onwards by the succeeding Istituto Papirologico "G. Vitelli" in Florence. These papyri are situated at the institute itself and in the Biblioteca Laurenziana.
- Rylands Papyri: this collection contains above 700 papyri, with 31 ostraca and 54 codices. It is housed at the John Rylands University Library.
- Tebtunis Papyri: housed by the Bancroft Library at the University of California, Berkeley, this is a collection of more than 30,000 fragments dating from the 3rd century BCE through the 3rd century CE, found in the winter 1899-1900 at the site of ancient Tebtunis, Egypt, by an expedition team led by the British papyrologists Bernard P. Grenfell and Arthur S. Hunt.
- Washington University Papyri Collection: includes 445 manuscript fragments, dating from the first century BCE to the eighth century AD. Housed at the Washington University Libraries.
- Will of Naunakhte: found at Deir el-Medina and dating to the 20th dynasty, it is notable because it is a legal document for a non-noble woman.
- Yale Papyrus Collection: numbers over six thousand inventoried items and is cataloged, digitally scanned, and accessible online for close study. It is housed at the Beinecke

5

ICT AND ELECTRONIC DOCUMENTS

Information technology (IT) is the application of computers and internet to store, retrieve, transmit, and manipulate data, or information, often in the context of a business or other enterprise. IT is considered a subset of information and communications technology (ICT). In 2012, Zuppo proposed an ICT hierarchy where each hierarchy level "contain some degree of commonality in that they are related to technologies that facilitate the transfer of information and various types of electronically mediated communications." Business/IT was one level of the ICT hierarchy.

The term is commonly used as a synonym for computers and computer networks, but it also encompasses other informationdistribution technologies such as television and telephones. Several industries are associated with information technology, including computer hardware, software, electronics, semiconductors, internet, telecom equipment, engineering, healthcare, e-commerce, and computer services.

Humans have been storing, retrieving, manipulating, and communicating information since the Sumerians in Mesopotamiadeveloped writing in about 3000 BC, but the term information technology in its modern sense first appeared in a 1958 article published in the Harvard Business Review; authors Harold J. Leavitt and Thomas L. Whisler commented that "the new technology does not yet have a single established name. We shall call it information technology (IT)." Their definition consists of three categories: techniques for processing, the application of statistical and mathematical methods to decision-making, and the simulation of higher-order thinking through computer programs.

Based on the storage and processing technologies employed, it is possible to distinguish four distinct phases of IT development: pre-mechanical (3000 BC – 1450 AD), mechanical

(1450–1840), electromechanical (1840–1940), electronic (1940–present), and moreover, IT as a service. This article focuses on the most recent period (electronic), which began in about 1940.

HISTORY OF COMPUTER TECHNOLOGY

Devices have been used to aid computation for thousands of years, probably initially in the form of a tally stick. The Antikythera mechanism, dating from about the beginning of the first century BC, is generally considered to be the earliest known mechanical analog computer, and the earliest known geared mechanism. Comparable geared devices did not emerge in Europe until the 16th century, and it was not until 1645 that the first mechanical calculator capable of performing the four basic arithmetical operations was developed.

Electronic computers, using either relays or valves, began to appear in the early 1940s. The electromechanical Zuse Z3, completed in 1941, was the world's first programmable computer, and by modern standards one of the first machines that could be considered a complete computing machine. Colossus, developed during the Second World War to decrypt Germanmessages was the first electronic digital computer. Although it was programmable, it was not general-purpose, being designed to perform only a single task. It also lacked the ability to store its program in memory; programming was carried out using plugs and switches to alter the internal wiring. The first recognisably modern electronic digital stored-program computer was the Manchester Small-Scale Experimental Machine (SSEM), which ran its first program on 21 June 1948.

The development of transistors in the late 1940s at Bell Laboratories allowed a new generation of computers to be designed with greatly reduced power consumption. The first commercially available stored-program computer, the Ferranti Mark I, contained 4050 valves and had a power consumption of 25 kilowatts. By comparison the first transistorised computer, developed at the University of Manchester and operational by November 1953, consumed only 150 watts in its final version.

Data processing

Data Storage

Early electronic computers such as Colossus made use of punched tape, a long strip of paper on which data was represented by a series of holes, a technology now obsolete. Electronic data storage, which is used in modern computers, dates from World War II, when a form of delay line memory was developed to remove the clutter from radar signals, the first practical application of which was the mercury delay line. The first random-access digital storage device was the Williams tube, based on a standard cathode ray tube, but the information stored in it and delay line memory was volatile in that it had to be continuously refreshed, and thus was lost once power was removed. The earliest form of non-volatile computer storage was the magnetic drum, invented in 1932 and used in the Ferranti Mark 1, the world's first commercially available general-purpose electronic computer.

IBM introduced the first hard disk drive in 1956, as a component of their 305 RAMAC computer system. Most digital data today is still stored magnetically on hard disks, or optically on media such as CD-ROMs. Until 2002 most information was stored on analog devices, but that year digital storage capacity exceeded analog for the first time. As of 2007 almost 94% of the data stored worldwide was held digitally: 52% on hard disks, 28% on optical devices and 11% on digital magnetic tape. It has been estimated that the worldwide capacity to store information on electronic devices grew from less than 3 exabytes in 1986 to 295 exabytes in 2007, doubling roughly every 3 years.

Databases

Database management systems emerged in the 1960s to address the problem of storing and retrieving large amounts of data accurately and quickly. One of the earliest such systems was IBM's Information Management System (IMS), which is still widely deployed more than 40 years later. IMS stores data hierarchically, but in the 1970s Ted Codd proposed an alternative relational storage model based on set theory and predicate logic and the familiar concepts of tables, rows and columns. The first commercially available relational database management system (RDBMS) was available from Oracle in 1980.

All database management systems consist of a number of components that together allow the data they store to be accessed simultaneously by many users while maintaining its integrity. A characteristic of all databases is that the structure of the data they contain is defined and stored separately from the data itself, in a database schema.

The extensible markup language (XML) has become a popular format for data representation in recent years. Although XML data can be stored in normal file systems, it is commonly held in relational databases to take advantage of their "robust implementation verified by years of both theoretical and practical effort". As an evolution of the Standard Generalized Markup Language (SGML), XML's text-based structure offers the advantage of being both machine and human-readable.

Data retrieval

The relational database model introduced a programming-language independent Structured Query Language (SQL), based on relational algebra.

The terms "data" and "information" are not synonymous. Anything stored is data, but it only becomes information when it is organized and presented meaningfully. Most of the world's digital data is unstructured, and stored in a variety of different physical formats even within a single organization. Data warehouses began to be developed in the 1980s to integrate these disparate stores. They typically contain data extracted from various sources, including external sources such as the Internet, organized in such a way as to facilitate decision support systems (DSS).

Data transmission

Data transmission has three aspects: transmission, propagation, and reception. It can be broadly categorized as broadcasting, in which information is transmitted unidirectionally downstream, or telecommunications, with bidirectional upstream and downstream channels.

XML has been increasingly employed as a means of data interchange since the early 2000s, particularly for machine-oriented interactions such as those involved in web-oriented protocols such as SOAP, describing "data-in-transit rather than... data-at-rest". One of the challenges of such usage is converting data from relational databases into XML Document Object Model (DOM) structures.

Data manipulation

Hilbert and Lopez identify the exponential pace of technological change (a kind of Moore's law): machines' application-specific capacity to compute information per capita roughly doubled every 14 months between 1986 and 2007; the per capita capacity of the world's general-purpose computers doubled every 18 months during the same two decades; the global telecommunication capacity per capita doubled every 34 months; the world's storage capacity per capita required roughly 40 months to double (every 3 years); and per capita broadcast information has doubled every 12. 3 years.

Massive amounts of data are stored worldwide every day, but unless it can be analysed and presented effectively it essentially resides in what have been called data tombs: "data archives that are seldom visited". To address that issue, the field of data mining – "the process of discovering interesting patterns and knowledge from large amounts of data" – emerged in the late 1980s.

PERSPECTIVE

Academic Perspective

In an academic context, the Association for Computing Machinery defines IT as "undergraduate degree programs that prepare students to meet the computer technology needs of business, government, healthcare, schools, and other kinds of organizations.... IT specialists assume responsibility for selecting hardware and software products appropriate for an organization, integrating those products with organizational needs and infrastructure, and installing, customizing, and maintaining those applications for the organization's computer users."

Commercial and Employment Perspective

In a business context, the Information Technology Association of America has defined information technology as "the study, design, development, application, implementation, support or management of computer-based information systems". The responsibilities of those working in the field include network administration, software development and installation, and the planning and management of an organization's technology life cycle, by which hardware and software are maintained, upgraded and replaced.

The business value of information technology lies in the automation of business processes, provision of information for decision making, connecting businesses with their customers, and the provision of productivity tools to increase efficiency.

Review of Literature

A literature review is a text of a scholarly paper, which includes the current knowledge including substantive findings, as well as theoretical and methodological contributions to a particular topic. Literature reviews are secondary sources, and do not report new or original experimental work. Most often associated with academic-oriented literature, such reviews are found in academic journals, and are not to be confused with book reviews that may also appear in the same publication. Literature reviews are a basis for research in nearly every academic field. A narrow-scope literature review may be included as part of a peer-reviewed journal article presenting new research, serving to situate the current study within the body of the relevant literature and to provide context for the reader. In such a case, the review usually precedes the methodology and results sections of the work. Producing a literature review may also be part of graduate and post-graduate student work, including in the preparation of a thesis, dissertation, or a journal article. Literature reviews are also common in a research proposal or prospectus (the document that is approved before a student formally begins a dissertation or thesis).

Types

The main types of literature reviews are: evaluative, exploratory, and instrumental.

A fourth type, the systematic review, is often classified separately, but is essentially a literature review focused on a research question, trying to identify, appraise, select and synthesize all high-quality research evidence and arguments relevant to that question. A meta-analysis is typically a systematic review using statistical methods to effectively combine the data used on all selected studies to produce a more reliable result.

Process and Product

Shields and Rangarajan (2013) distinguish between the process of reviewing the literature and a finished work or product known as a literature review. :193–229 The process of reviewing the literature is often ongoing and informs many aspects of the empirical research project. All of the latest literature should inform a research project. Scholars need to be scanning the literature long after a formal literature review product appears to be completed.

A careful literature review is usually 15 to 30 pages and could be longer. The process of reviewing the literature requires different kinds of activities and ways of thinking. Shields and Rangarajan (2013) and Granello (2001) link the activities of doing a literature review with Benjamin Bloom's revised taxonomy of the cognitive domain (ways of thinking: remembering, understanding, applying, analyzing, evaluating, and creating).

The first category in Bloom's taxonomy is remembering. For a person doing a literature review this would include tasks such as recognition, retrieval and recollection of the relevant literature. During this stage relevant books, articles, monographs, dissertations, etc. are identified and read. Bloom's second category understanding occurs as the scholar comprehends the material they have collected and read. This step is critical because no one can write clearly about something they do not understand. Understanding may be challenging because the literature could introduce the scholar to new terminology, conceptual framework and methodology. Comprehension (particularly for new scholars) is often improved by taking careful notes. In Bloom's third category applying the scholar is able to make connections between the literature and his or her larger research project. This is particularly true if the literature review is to be a chapter in a future empirical study. The literature review begins to inform the research question, and methodological approaches. When scholars analyze (fourth category in Bloom's taxonomy) they are able to separate material into parts and figure out how the parts fit together. Analysis of the literature allows the scholar to develop frameworks for analysis and the ability to see the big picture and know how details from the literature fit within the big picture. Analysis facilitates the development of an outline (list). The books, articles and monographs read will be of different quality and value. When scholars use Bloom's fifth category evaluating they are able to see the strengths and weaknesses of the theories, arguments, methodology and findings of the literature they have collected and read. When scholars engage in creating the final category in Bloom's taxonomy, they bring creativity to the process of doing a literature review. In other words, they draw new and original insights from the literature. They may be able to find a fresh and original research question, identify a heretofore, unknown gap in the literature or make surprising connections. By understanding how ways of thinking connect to tasks of a literature review, a scholar is able to be self-reflective and bring metacognition to the process of reviewing the literature.

Most of these tasks occur before the writing even begins. The process of reviewing the literature and writing a literature review can be complicated and lengthy. It is helpful to bring a system of organization and planning to the task. When an orderly system can be designed, it is easier to keep track of the articles, books, materials read, notes, outlines and drafts.

ADVANTAGES OF USING ICT IN THE LIBRARY

Formation and Communication Technology (ICT) has transformed library services globally. Most current information are recorded in electronic format, ICT has also contributed immensely to the performance of librarians in the discharge of their duties such as in cataloguing, reference services, circulation management, serials control etc. ICT has contributed to the library in the following specific ways.

Library management softwares

Libraries utilize softwares designed to manage different library routines and processes. Most of these softwares are integrated and have modules for the different activities or tasks carried out in the library like cataloguing, statistics, acquisition processes, serials control etc. Some examples of such softwares are CDS/ISIS, GLAS, ALICE for Windows, X-Lib and SLAM. SLAM is used in the University Library FUTA and stands for (Strategic Library Automation Management).

OPAC: This means Online Public Access Catalogue and is the computerized version of the library catalogue or a database of the library holdings. The advantage of the OPAC over manual methods is ease of use and the fact that it saves space. It provides access to the catalogues of a library on the local intranet, extranet or even the internet.

Office Operations: Word processing, accounting,, database management and communication through e-mail are all enabled in the library through ICT.

Networking: Library users can access information of various types such as online databases, e-journals, e- books, government publications digitally through networked systems. Access may be allowed online remotely through the internet or intranets.

Electronic Document Delivery: Libraries may not rely anymore on postal services to send documents to users or carry out interlibrary lending. Libraries send documents through electronic networks that can deliver documents in various formats e. g PDF straight to users' desktops.

Online user education or tutorials: Libraries can use the internet or CD –ROMS to educate their users or carry out information literacy programmes. Virtual tours can be offered online making user education more convenient for all.

E-reference services: Some services such as SDI (Selective dissemination of information) or Current Awareness Services (CAS) and virtual reference desks, announcements of new acquisitions and other reader advisory services can be made easier through the internet.

Users can have online interaction with the reference staff. Library cooperation and resource sharing: A central union catalogue can be better managed through ICT, thus libraries can create and share bibliographic records and other information resources in digital format.

Institutional Repositories: Institutional repositories are publications that originate locally from within the university community such as theses, dissertations, reports, conference papers and seminar papers. ICT has made it possible not only to provide better access to these resources but also to ensure the preservation of the resources.

E- libraries: Digital libraries depend on information recorded on digital formats like CD-ROMS. Virtual libraries are libraries that do not exist in physical space or structure but can be accessed via networks. E. g. The Nigerian Virtual Library.

Social Media Networks: Social media networks like twitter, facebbok and linkedIn, are some interactive internet services that are presently serving as communication forum for librarians and their uses. These networks can be deployed for educational uses. Discussion groups, listserves and communities also assist library services

E- mails: This is a means of communication between the library and the users.

Library websites: A medium of communication for libraries to their users. It is also used to promote the library and publicise it.

Online searching: searching of of online databases like AGORA, ERIC. Browsing and surfing the internet through search engines, metasearch engines and subject directories to supplement library sources

Advantages of Using ICT in the library

- ICT makes library work easier, faster, cheaper and more effective.
- Helps to manage information overload as information retrieval is made easier in computerized systems.
- Remote access is enabled through networked systems
- Computerization saves space and reduces paper.

Challenges of using ICT in libraries

- Poor funding of ICT infrastructures
- Constant change of software and hardware
- Erratic power supply
- Insufficient bandwidth
- Lack of technical IT knowledge by library staff
- Copyright and intellectual property rights management

ICT Advantages & Disadvantages

ICTs stand for information and communication technologies and are defined, for the purposes, as a "diverse set of technological tools and resources used to communicate, and to create, disseminate, store, and manage information." These technologies include computers, the Internet, broad casting technologies (radio and television), and telephony.

The Effectiveness of ICTs in Education

ICTs are a potentially powerful tool for extending educational opportunities, both formal and non-for mal, to previously underserved constituencies—scattered and rural populations, groups traditionally excluded from education due to cultural or social reasons such as ethnic minorities, girls and women, persons with disabilities, and the elderly, as well as all others who for reasons of cost or because of time constraints are unable to enroll on campus.

- Anytime, anywhere. One defining feature of ICTs is their ability to transcend time and space. ICTs make possible asynchronous learning, or learning characterized by a time lag between the delivery of instruction and its reception by learners. Online course materials, for example, may be accessed 24 hours a day, 7 days a week. ICT-based educational delivery (e. g., educational programming broadcast over radio or television) also dispenses with the need for all learners and the instructor to be in one physical location. Additionally, certain types of ICTs, such as teleconferencing technologies, enable instruction to be received simultaneously by multiple, geographically dispersed learners (i. e., synchronous learning).
- Access to remote learning resources. Teachers and learners no longer have to rely solely on printed books and other materials in physical media housed in libraries (and available in limited quantities) for their educational needs. With the Internet and the World Wide Web, a wealth of learning materials in almost every subject and in a variety of media can now be accessed from anywhere at anytime of the day and by an unlimited number of people. This is particularly significant for many schools in developing countries, and even some in developed countries, that have limited and outdated library resources. ICTs also facilitate access to resource persons, mentors, experts, researchers, professionals, business leaders, and peers—all over the world.
- ICTs help prepare individuals for the workplace. One of the most commonly cited reasons for using ICTs in the classroom has been to better prepare the current generation of students for a workplace where ICTs, particularly computers, the Internet and related technologies, are becoming more and more ubiquitous.

Technological literacy, or the ability to use ICTs effectively and efficiently, is thus seen as representing a competitive edge in an increasingly globalizing job market.

Benefits/Advantages of ICT in Education

Here are some of the benefits which ICT brings to education according to recent research findings.

General benefits

- Greater efficiency throughout the school.
- Communication channels are increased through email, discussion groups and chat rooms
- Regular use of ICT across different curriculum subjects can have a beneficial motivational influence on students' learning.

Benefits for teachers

- ICT facilitates sharing of resources, expertise and advice
- Greater flexibility in when and where tasks are carried out
- Gains in ICT literacy skills, confidence and enthusiasm.
- Easier planning and preparation of lessons and designing materials
- Access to up-to-date pupil and school data, any time and anywhere.
- Enhancement of professional image projected to colleagues.
- Students are generally more 'on task' and express more positive feelings when they use computers than when they are given other tasks to do.
- Computer use during lessons motivated students to continue using learning outside school hours.

Benefits for students

- Higher quality lessons through greater collaboration between teachers in planning and preparing resources.
- More focused teaching, tailored to students' strengths and weaknesses, through better analysis of attainment data
- Improved pastoral care and behaviour management through better tracking of students
- Gains in understanding and analytical skills, including improvements in reading
- Comprehension.

- Development of writing skills (including spelling, grammar, punctuation, editing and re-drafting), also fluency, originality and elaboration.
- Encouragement of independent and active learning, and self-responsibility for learning.
- Flexibility of 'anytime, anywhere' access (Jacobsen and Kremer, 2000)
- Development of higher level learning styles.
- Students who used educational technology in school felt more successful in school, were more motivated to learn and have increased self-confidence and self-esteem
- Students found learning in a technology-enhanced setting more stimulating and student-centred than in a traditional classroom
- Broadband technology supports the reliable and uninterrupted downloading of web-hosted educational multimedia resources
- Opportunities to address their work to an external audience
- Opportunities to collaborate on assignments with people outside or inside school

Benefits for parents

- Easier communication with teachers
- Higher quality student reports – more legible, more detailed, better presented
- Greater access to more accurate attendance and attainment information
- Increased involvement in education for parents and, in some cases, improved self-esteem
- Increased knowledge of children's learning and capabilities, owing to increase in learning activity being situated in the home
- Parents are more likely to be engaged in the school community
- You will see that ICT can have a positive impact across a very wide range of aspects of school life.

ICT and Raising Standards

Recent research also points to ICT as a significant contributory factor in the raising of standards of achievement in schools.

- Schools judged by the school inspectors to have very good ICT resources achieved better results than schools with poor ICT.
- Schools that made good use of ICT within a subject tended to have better achievement in that subject than other schools.

- Socio-economic circumstances and prior performance of pupils were not found to be critical.
- Secondary schools with very good ICT resources achieved, on average, better results in English, Mathematics and Science than those with poor ICT resources.
- A range of research indicates the potential of ICT to support improvements in aspects of literacy, numeracy and science.
- Improved writing skills: grammar, presentation, spelling, word recognition and volume of work.
- Age-gains in mental calculations and enhanced number skills, for example the use of decimals.
- Better data handling skills and increased ability to read, interpret and sketch graphs Improvements in conceptual understanding of Mathematics (particularly problem solving) and Science (particularly through use of simulations)

The use of ICTs help improve the quality of education

ICTs can enhance the quality of education in several ways: by increasing learner motivation and engagement by facilitating the acquisition of basic skills, and by enhancing teacher training. ICTs are also transformational tools which, when used appropriately, can promote the shift to a learner-centered environment.

Motivating to learn. ICTs such as videos, television and multimedia computer software that combine text, sound, and colorful, moving images can be used to provide challenging and authentic content that will engage the student in the learning process. Interactive radio likewise makes use of sound effects, songs, dramatizations, comic skits, and other performance conventions to compel the students to listen and become involved in the lessons being delivered. More so than any other type of ICT, networked computers with Internet connectivity can increase learner motivation as it combines the media richness and interactivity of other ICTs with the opportunity to connect with real people and to participate in real world events.

Facilitating the acquisition of basic skills. The transmission of basic skills and concepts that are the foundation of higher order thinking skills and creativity can be facilitated by ICTs through drill and practice. Educational television programs such as Sesame Street use repetition and reinforcement to teach the alphabet, numbers, colors, shapes and other basic concepts. Most of the early uses of computers were for computer-based learning (also called computer-assisted instruction) that focused on mastery of skills and content through repetition and reinforcement.

Enhancing teacher training. ICTs have also been used to improve access to and the quality of teacher training. For example, At Indira Gandhi National Open University, satellite-based one-way video- and two-way audio-conferencing was held in 1996, supplemented by print-materials and recorded video, to train 910 primaryschool teachers and facilitators from 20 district training institutes in Karnataka State. The teachers interacted with remote lecturers by telephone and fax

Examples of ICT-based activities

What kind of classroom activities are suited to the use of ICT? The following is a brief guide to some of the most common uses of ICT in teaching and learning.

Finding out

Students can use ICT to find out information and to gain new knowledge in several ways. They may find information on the Internet or by using an ICT-based encyclopedia such as Microsoft Encarta. They may find information by extracting it from a document prepared by the teacher and made available to them via ICT, such as document created using Microsoft Word or a Microsoft PowerPoint slideshow. They may find out information by communicating with people elsewhere using email, such as students in a different school or even in a different country.

Processing knowledge

Students can use ICT as part of a creative process where they have to consider more carefully the information which they have about a given subject. They may need to carry out calculations (eg. by using Microsoft Excel), or to check grammar and spelling in a piece of writing (perhaps using Microsoft Word), or they may need to re-sequence a series of events (for example by re-ordering a series of Microsoft PowerPoint slides).

Sharing knowledge

Students can use ICT to present their work in a highly professional format. They can create documents and slideshows to demonstrate what they have learned, and then share this with other students, with their teacher, and even via email with people all around the world.

Computers and the Internet use for teaching and learning

There are three general approaches to the instructional use of computers and the Internet, namely:

1) Learning about computers and the Internet, in which technological literacy is the end goal;
2) Learning with computers and the Internet, in which the technology facilitates learning across the curriculum; and

3) Learning through computers and the Internet, integrating technological skills development with curriculum applications.

Learn about computers and the Internet

Learning about computers and the Internet focuses on developing technological literacy. It typically includes:

- Fundamentals: basic terms, concepts and operations
- Use of the keyboard and mouse
- Use of productivity tools such as word processing, spreadsheets, data base and graphics programs
- Use of research and collaboration tools such as search engines and email
- Basic skills in using programming and authoring applications such as Logo or HyperStudio
- Developing an awareness of the social impact of technological change.

Learning with computers and the Internet

Learning with the technology means focusing on how the technology can be the means to learning ends across the curriculum. It includes:

- Presentation, demonstration, and the manipulation of data using productivity tools
- Use of curriculum-specific applications types such as educational games, drill and practice, simulations, tutorials, virtual laboratories, visualizations and graphical representations of abstract concepts, musical composition, and expert systems
- Use of information and resources on CD-ROM or online such as encyclopedia, interactive mapsand atlases, electronic journals and other references.

Technological literacy is required for learning with technologies to be possible, implying a two-step process in which students learn about the technologies before they can actually use them to learn.

Learning through computers and the Internet mean

Learning through computers and the Internet combines learning about them with learning with them. It involves learning the technological skills "just-in-time" or when the learner needs to learn them as he or she engages in a curriculum-related activity.

Computers and the Internet used in distance education

Many higher educational institutions offering distance education courses have started to leverage the Internet to improve their programme's reach and quality.

Disadvantages of ICT

One of the major barriers for the cause of ICT not reaching its full potential in the foundation stage is teacher's attitude. According to Hara (2004), within the early years education attitudes towards ICT can vary considerably. Some see it as a potential tool to aid learning whereas others seem to disagree with the use of technology in early year settings. Blatchford and Whitebread (2003:16), suggests that the use of ICT in the foundation stage is "unhealthy and hinders learning". Other early years educators who are opposed to offering ICT experiences within the educational settings take a less extreme view than this and suggest that ICT is fine, but there are other more vital experiences that young children will benefit from, (Blatchford and Whitebread, 2003). In theory some people may have the opinion that the teachers who had not experienced ICT throughout their learning tend to have a negative attitude towards it, as they may lack the training in that area of the curriculum.

Another important drawback to using ICT in schools is the fact that computers are expensive. According to the IT learning exchange (2001), in most schools ICT will be the single largest curriculum budget cost. This may be seen as a good thing but on the other hand there will be little money left over for other significant costs.

Challenges of using ICT in libraries

Information and communications technology (ICT) is an extended term for information technology (IT) which stresses the role of unified communications and the integration of telecommunications (telephone lines and wireless signals), computers as well as necessary enterprise software, middleware, storage, and audio-visual systems, which enable users to access, store, transmit, and manipulate information.

The term ICT is also used to refer to the convergence of audio-visual and telephone networks with computer networks through a single cabling or link system. There are large economic incentives (huge cost savings due to elimination of the telephone network) to merge the telephone network with the computer network system using a single unified system of cabling, signal distribution and management.

However, ICT has no universal definition, as "the concepts, methods and applications involved in ICT are constantly evolving on an almost daily basis." The broadness of ICT covers any product that will store, retrieve, manipulate, transmit or receive information electronically in a digital form, e. g. personal computers, digital television, email, robots. For clarity, Zuppo provided an ICT hierarchy where all levels of the hierarchy "contain some degree of commonality in that they are related to technologies that facilitate the transfer of information and various types of electronically mediated communications". Skills Framework for the Information Age is one of many models for describing and managing competencies for ICT professionals for the 21st century.

Technology and LIS: a historical perspective

In his prophetic 1945 article As We May Think, Vannevar Bush envisioned a machine called a memex, a collective memory machine that would make knowledge more accessible. The author begins his argument by discussing the growing amount of information in the world. The increasing amount and complexity of information along with the time gap between creation and dissemination requires a new technology. Bush's technology would focus on greater usability in information retrieval, allowing users to create their own "sort of mechanized private file and library". Through the miniaturization of data using photocells or microfilm, great amounts of information could be stored in very little space. Traditionally information is stored in index or hierarchical form, but this is not how the brain stores information. The memex would arrange things associatively, mimicking the way the human brain stores and contextualizes information.

This memex is remarkably similar to a modern day computer, in that it would be a new technology designed for personal use that would allow for the creation, storage, and organization of different materials and data. This is a fascinating article as it explains how the need of a new way to store, organize and retrieve increasing amounts of data led to the idea of modern day computers. It is a particularly interesting article in the modern context, where information and data continue to expand at an exponential rate. What new technologies and changes in data organization will the future hold? How will libraries adapt to these changes?

Technology began to transform libraries in the 1950s with microfilm and in the mid-1960s with the Xerox machine. Computerized databases were developed in the 1970s and offered more information and better ways to search and obtain it. Networks such as OCLC and RLIN made it easier to share resources. Although this article predates widespread use of the Internet, it is correct in predicting that technology will continue to change the future of libraries. Technology has allowed greater access to information for more people, but it was too early for the author to accurately predict the digital divide. He argues that libraries must innovate to stay alive and that change is happening so quickly that it often appears "chaotic." The World Wide Web, however, is often described as chaotic, unorganized, and confusing, but its benefits greatly outweigh its risks. Because new technology often helps libraries keep people connected to information, libraries must strive to make sense out of the technological chaos. The author makes a strong case for businesses' need to compete but states that libraries' structure and rules "inhibit us from making the kind of innovation that is needed to compete and survive." The challenge, he concludes, is not in introducing new technology but in creating new management structures for libraries. This plan seems to push libraries toward behaving like businesses, but I think this would restrict access and introduce new economic, cultural, and political problems.

Implementing information technologies in libraries

According to John Bushman, the implementation of information technology requires librarians to ask two basic questions:

- Why is the technology good for libraries, librarians, or the public?
- Where will the technology lead us?

It is the librarian's duty to ask these questions and become involved in finding the answers. All technological advances need to be approached critically, with the knowledge that they may have both social and political consequences. Librarians need to be able to evaluate technologies to determine whether a given technology will harm or help the library and its community. Funding, getting the public involved with the change in technology, getting them to deal with the positive and negative effects of change, and making sure the librarians are able to handle the pressures are all ways of becoming involved with finding the answers about information technology and the future of libraries.

DIGITAL LIBRARIES AND SERVICES

Digital Libraries

The Digital Library Federation looked at what it sees as the major issues regarding digital libraries in the future. These are the five challenges the organization have outlined: architectural and systems in libraries, standards and practices, collection development, how communities will use a digital library, and long-term access to digital libraries. In terms of designing and implementing new technology, information sharing about new technology is vital because few employees in libraries actually manage technological change. Libraries need to have a plan so adopting technology and training employees and users is a smooth transition. The library is simultaneously a consumer and supplier of information and needs to have standards to critique itself. Issues involved in collection development include costs, copyright and licensing, all facets of computerizing, support services, and the impact on the rest of the library. How information is presented online can determine whether and to what extent it is used by the public. The sources of digital information are coming from all kinds of places and shared resources can help defray costs. Making the decision about what information to digitize and anticipating the costs of preserving the information is the last of these challenges.

The digital library service environment is defined as a network online information space in which users can discover, locate, acquire access to, and increasingly use information. There is no distinction about the information format. The identity of a digital library is the way the library discloses, provides access to, and supports the use of its increasingly virtual collection. Managing, administering, monitoring and ensuring fair use of its collection are a part of the mix, as well as keeping up with new technologies to support education and cultural engagement so that the library can evolve and sustain itself. The prospect of a completely virtual library still seems in the future, but we seem headed in that direction.

The National Digital Library Program was created by the Library of Congress so libraries, schools and homes will have access to original documents of American history and culture. The goal by the year 2000 was to digitize over 5 million items. The challenge is selecting from over 110 million items and converting to a technological format that will last. Some funding is coming from private donations. The article is descriptive, informative, but at the same time unclear about how the selection of information to be digitized was made. The Library of Congress is a leading repository of information. Is their selection of information for this digitizing project representative of the body of knowledge that Americans and world scholars can look to understand what has shaped American history? Should we be questioning whether American history is more important than other cultures that have been influential in world history? For instance, the book, In Search of the Cradle of Civilization, (Frawley, et al) places east Indian settlements earlier than Sumerian, Mesopotamian, and Babylonian societies. India, the largest democracy in the world today, has been ignored by the rest of the world. Books like In Search of the Cradle can be found at The Theosophical Society which has been a part of Wheaton's local history for over 100 years. A part of my role in the Olcott Library is to apply for a state grant that will digitize important elements of the collection that contribute to Illinois history.

Virtual reference

In an effort to reach patrons accessing the library via computers, many libraries and library consortia offer virtual reference services. These services can be either real-time or offset, and are offered via email, instant messaging, web form interfaces, SMS, and even virtual reality games. According to the Reference and User Services Association, "Virtual reference is responsive to patrons' need for convenient access to reference service."

Though virtual reference is a great convenience for library patrons, its implementation introduces several challenges for traditional libraries. Most individual institutions don't have the staffing levels necessary to monitor an IM service regularly enough for the service be attractive to users. For real-time virtual reference, many libraries are part of chat co-operatives or consortia, some of which are able to offer reference services 24 hours a day. However, this does mean that reference workers from other institutions, who may not be as familiar with the patrons' home institution's resources, may not be able to provide services of as high a quality as the home institution might. In his introduction to Digital Reference Service in the New Millennium: Planning, Management, and Evaluation, R. David Lankes examines the emerging field of digital reference, how it affects the traditional reference staff and service, and addresses two key issues, "scalability" and "ambiguity".

Lankes makes the argument that the availability and use of digital resources are fundamentally re-defining the role of reference services. According to Lankes, library reference staff are now becoming "information brokers", because of the nature of the digital environment and changing user expectations. He discusses two issues, scalability (the ability to service growth), and ambiguity (identifying resources needed to meet user's needs). He describes several differing initiatives that have been or could be brought into play to address these issues, both alterations of existing reference practices, and new methods of providing relevant reference services in a digital age.

His arguments are sound, and pose fundamental questions as to what defines a "Library" and "Reference Services", as one would expect in the introductory chapter of a book on the changing role the digital world plays in the reference field. Some of the questions and possible solutions, however, seem very radical and unrealistic given the fragmented standard reference environment based on local libraries, both from a funding and staffing perspective, and assumes that some "entity" (modeled on the private sector) will provide a more centralized construct more appropriate for the digital age.

Access to technology

Gordon Flagg explains how the FCC unanimously passed a new rule on May 7, 1997 that decreased the charges of telecommunication services to schools and libraries throughout the nation. The discounts range from 20-90% (the highest percent going to libraries and schools in low-income, rural, and high-cost communities). In order to raise the $2. 25 billion needed for this plan they increased fees ($1. 50 for residential and $3. 00 for business) and taxes on second phone lines. This decision was praised by the ALA because it allows more schools and libraries to access the internet where in the based it was too costly to do so. That way everyone has the opportunity to use this service even if they cannot afford it in their homes. Some experts feared that this reduction would be difficult to sustain in the long run, because it is such a big undertaking and that there may be legal challenges they might have to deal with.

Physical libraries in a cyber world

Rapidly-deteriorating materials create an urgent need to focus on preservation, particularly in research libraries. Preservation decisions often fall into two major categories: selection and medium.

- Problems of selection are best answered by a team of both librarians and scholars, who employ criteria that is three-fold: collection-, subject-, and usage-based.
- Problems of medium, on the other hand, are more subjective. Microfilm is quite stable and durable, but access is somewhat limited. Digitization, while alleviating access problems, poses concerns about cost, instability, and hardware and software change.

Abby Smith advocates a preservation strategy that includes a combination of microfilm and digital storage. To be sure, funding for this multi-pronged approach is unanswered, but Smith's ideas in action will help ensure the selection of a broad scope of scholarly works for preservation in forms that meet researchers' needs of integrity and accessibility. Since the publication of Smith's article, however, digital storage has gained more potential. For instance, some problems of cost and changing technology can be mitigated by storing documents on, say, a one-terabyte hard drive. Drive size has certainly come down in cost since 1999, and a hard drive will not become obsolete as quickly as many removable formats. Moreover, accessibility may be benefited by the sheer amount of works that can fit on a terabyte hard drive. Nonetheless, it is clear that the mediums used for preservation should be reevaluated as digitization expands.

Cost of adoption

Libraries have been transformed and modernized by the application of information technology. Users do not have to go to libraries, and have the opportunity to retrieve information via Internet. Because of all the new technology being introduced to libraries, library administrators are forced to break down the budget, in order to make wise decisions when it comes to long-term benefits for the library. If a library administrator follows a cost structure model, he/she will have more success determining the direct and indirect costs. Also, the library administrator will be able to understand the initial and recurring costs within the life cycle of implied information technologies. It is common for administrators to forget to include training and other necessary costs, which may hurt their long-term budget. It is essential for library administrators to analyze each part of the budget, so he/she does not end up wasting any money.

I agree with the author's statement about the "bigger picture" when it comes to a budget, and remembering the significance of keeping up with new technology offered. Chapter five brings up several great points about the importance of the growth of technology, and the awareness of people's right to privacy. Much of society is getting comfortable with technology, and requires the programs offered. It is the library's job to provide the programs to the public, and not go over the budget, while remembering the importance of an individual's privacy.

Monetary costs are not the only costs to adopting new technology. Author Nicholson Baker is a firm believer that adopting new technologies can come at the expense of preserving history. Libraries around the country, including those at academic institutions, have replaced many of their card catalogs with online access catalogs. They are throwing out their card catalogs, sometimes with fanfare. Despite some attempts to preserve data by microfilming the cards and proofing the new records, information is being lost because of errors and omissions.

Librarians rapidly adapted to technology to cope with a cataloging crisis caused by growing numbers of items to process. The author argues that they are overlooking their mission to preserve books. Instead of being archetype librarians, they want to be seen as technology specialists. Author Nicholson Baker contended that disposing of the card catalog was akin to tossing out history. The notations made on each card over decades, make the card catalog itself an artifact worthy of preservation. It is ironic that while the goal of libraries is to preserve information, they are keen to dispose of the catalog, which he sees as more than a finding aid. With humor, wit and irony Baker described the evolution of the library catalog. Accession dates, provenance and notes in some catalogs might be of value to scholars, but the nostalgia for well-thumbed faded cards with carefully written notes seems to be Baker's primary object.

Nicholson again critiqued libraries' adoption of technologies in his 2001 book Double fold: libraries and the assault on paper, Nicholson Baker presents a strongly-worded critique of libraries' digital reproduction of paper materials. In one of his most compelling case studies, he examines the case of the Syracuse Daily Standard newspaper, which in 1858, claimed to have been printed on paper "said to be taken from Egyptian [sic] mummies." When he attempted to find the actual newspapers, he discovered that the local public library had since discarded its paper copies of the newspaper, instead offering a microfilm copy to its patrons.

The book, which the New York Times described as a "blistering and thoroughly idiosyncratic attack", was strongly criticized by the library community. A major argument against Baker's book was that libraries build their collections based on both current and anticipated use, rather than strictly preserving anything they can. Not every item ever published can be collected and preserved in its original format, nor will every item ever published be useful to library patrons, especially if it has disintegrated extensively. A second major argument against the book was the impracticality of maintaining print items, particularly acidic ones, on a large scale. A third argument notes that digitization and microfilm tend to enable more people access to a particular item, as microforms can be shared via Interlibrary Loan much more feasibly than can decaying print resources, and since digitized materials can often be shared with anyone who can access the Internet. For a bibliography of reactions to Baker's book, see the of Research Library's exhaustive list.

Conclusion: Rutenbeck's "Five great challenges"

According to Jeff Rutenbeck, the continued growth of the digital world presents five major challenges to its users: malleability, selectivity, exclusivity, vulnerability, and superficiality.

Malleability

Malleability refers to the total impermanence of digital information, from data to pictures to even people's identities. Unlike print, digital information can be reconfigured in ways that print information cannot.

Selectivity

Selectivity addresses the preference by users to only consider information available online, dismissing information available only in print.

Exclusivity

The digital divide comes to the forefront with exclusivity, since new technology is being introduced constantly, but there is no universal way to bring everyone to the same levels of competence.

Vulnerability

Vulnerability highlights the inherent problems with our interconnectedness; while we enjoy the easy and constant flow of information and ideas, at the same time, we leave ourselves open to security breaches and systems failures.

Superficiality

What I feel is the greatest challenge in the digital age is superficiality. We have access to so much information, but there is no guarantee that what we see is accurate.

Conclusion

The author identifies the issues clearly, and offers suggestions as to how we can battle these challenges, but acknowledges that there is no clear cut answer to overcoming any of them. Most users, including myself, butt against these issues in our personal and business life, and struggle with how to reconcile them, since, as the author acknowledges, any answer leads to compromises.

6

NETWORKS AND SECURITY MEASURES

Network security is the security provided to a network from unauthorized access and risks. It is the duty of network administrators to adopt preventive measures to protect their networks from potential security threats. Computer networks that are involved in regular transactions and communication within the government, individuals, or business require security. The most common and simple way of protecting a network resource is by assigning it a unique name and a corresponding password.

TYPES OF NETWORK SECURITY DEVICES

Active Devices

These security devices block the surplus traffic. Firewalls, antivirus scanning devices, and content filtering devices are the examples of such devices.

Passive Devices

These devices identify and report on unwanted traffic, for example, intrusion detection appliances.

Preventative Devices

These devices scan the networks and identify potential security problems. For example, penetration testing devices and vulnerability assessment appliances.

Unified Threat Management (UTM)

These devices serve as all-in-one security devices. Examples include firewalls, content filtering, web caching, etc.

Firewalls

A firewall is a network security system that manages and regulates the network traffic based on some protocols. A firewall establishes a barrier between a trusted internal network and the internet. Firewalls exist both as software that run on a hardware and as hardware appliances. Firewalls that are hardware-based also provide other functions like acting as a DHCP server for that network.

Most personal computers use software-based firewalls to secure data from threats from the internet. Many routers that pass data between networks contain firewall components and conversely, many firewalls can perform basic routing functions.

Firewalls are commonly used in private networks or intranets to prevent unauthorized access from the internet. Every message entering or leaving the intranet goes through the firewall to be examined for security measures.

An ideal firewall configuration consists of both hardware and software based devices. A firewall also helps in providing remote access to a private network through secure authentication certificates and logins.

Hardware and Software Firewalls

Hardware firewalls are standalone products. These are also found in broadband routers. Most hardware firewalls provide a minimum of four network ports to connect other computers. For larger networks Š e. g., for business purpose Š business networking firewall solutions are available.

Software firewalls are installed on your computers. A software firewall protects your computer from internet threats.

Antivirus

An antivirus is a tool that is used to detect and remove malicious software. It was originally designed to detect and remove viruses from computers.

Modern antivirus software provide protection not only from virus, but also from worms, Trojan-horses, adwares, spywares, keyloggers, etc. Some products also provide protection from malicious URLs, spam, phishing attacks, botnets, DDoS attacks, etc.

Content Filtering

Content filtering devices screen unpleasant and offensive emails or webpages. These are used as a part of firewalls in corporations as well as in personal computers. These devices generate the message "Access Denied" when someone tries to access any unauthorized web page or email. Content is usually screened for pornographic content and also for violence- or hate-oriented content. Organizations also exclude shopping and job related contents.

Content filtering can be divided into the following categories:

- Web filtering
- Screening of Web sites or pages
- E-mail filtering
- Screening of e-mail for spam
- Other objectionable content

Intrusion Detection Systems

Intrusion Detection Systems, also known as Intrusion Detection and Prevention Systems, are the appliances that monitor malicious activities in a network, log information about such activities, take steps to stop them, and finally report them.

Intrusion detection systems help in sending an alarm against any malicious activity in the network, drop the packets, and reset the connection to save the IP address from any blockage. Intrusion detection systems can also perform the following actions "

- Correct Cyclic Redundancy Check (CRC) errors
- Prevent TCP sequencing issues
- Clean up unwanted transport and network layer options

Common security measures

Introduction to network security focuses on common security measures. It covers firewalls, intrusion detection systems, sniffers and more.

Firewalls

By far the most common security measure these days is a firewall. A lot of confusion surrounds the concept of a firewall, but it can basically be defined as any perimeter device that permits or denies traffic based on a set of rules configured by the administrator. Thus, a firewall may be as simple as a router with access lists or as complex as a set of modules distributed through the network controlled from one central location.

The firewall protects everything "behind" it from everything in "front" of it. Usually the "front" of the firewall is its Internet facing side, and the "behind" is the internal network. The way firewalls are designed to suit different types of networks is called the firewall topology.

These are packages meant for individual desktops and are fairly easy to use. The first thing they do is make the machine invisible to pings and other network probes. Most of them also let you choose what programs are allowed to access the Internet. Therefore, you can allow your browser and mail client, but if you see some suspicious program trying to access the network, you can disallow it. This is a form of egress filtering or outbound traffic filtering and provides very good protection against Trojan horse programs and worms.

However, firewalls are no cure-all solution to network security woes. A firewall is only as good as its rule set, and there are many ways an attacker can find common misconfigurations and errors in the rules. For example, if the firewall blocks all traffic except traffic originating from port 53 (DNS) so that everyone can resolve names, the attacker could then use this rule to his advantage. By changing the source port of his attack or scan to port 53, the firewall will allow all of his traffic through, because it assumes it is DNS traffic.

Bypassing firewalls is a whole study in itself and one which is very interesting (especially to those with a passion for networking), because it normally involves misusing the way TCP and IP are supposed to work. That said, firewalls today are becoming very sophisticated and a well-installed firewall can severely thwart a would-be attacker's plans. It is important to remember that the firewall does not look into the data section of the packet. Thus, if you have a Web server that is vulnerable to a CGI exploit and the firewall is set to allow traffic to it, there is no way the firewall can stop an attacker from attacking the Web server. It does not look at the data inside the packet. That would be the job of an intrusion-detection system (covered in part three).

Antivirus systems

Everyone is familiar with the desktop version of antivirus packages like Norton Antivirus and McAfee. The way these operate is fairly simple — when researchers find a new virus, they figure out some unique characteristic it has (maybe a registry key it creates or a file it replaces) and out of this they write the virus "signature."

The whole load of signatures for which your antivirus software scans is known as the virus "definitions." This is the reason why keeping your virus definitions up-to-date is very important. Many antivirus packages have an auto-update feature for you to download the latest definitions. The scanning ability of your software is only as good as the date of your definitions. In the enterprise, it is very common for administrators to install antivirus software on all machines, but there is no policy for regular updates of the definitions. This is meaningless protection and serves only to provide a false sense of security.

With the recent spread of e-mail viruses, antivirus software at the mail server is becoming increasingly popular. The mail server will automatically scan any e-mail it receives for viruses and quarantine the infections. The idea is that since all mail passes through the mail server, this is the logical point to scan for viruses. Given that most mail servers have a permanent connection to the Internet, they can regularly download the latest definitions. On the downside, these can be evaded quite simply. If you zip up the infected file or Trojan, or encrypt it, the antivirus system may not be able to scan it.

End users must be taught how to respond to antivirus alerts. This is especially true in the enterprise — an attacker doesn't need to try and bypass your fortress-like firewall if all he has to do is e-mail Trojans to a lot of people in the company. It takes just one uninformed user to open the infected package to allow the hacker a backdoor to the internal network. It is advisable that the IT department gives a brief seminar on how to handle e-mail from untrusted sources and how to deal with attachments. These are very common attack vectors, simply because you may harden a computer system as much as you like, but the weak point still remains the user who operates it. As crackers say, "The human is the path of least resistance into the network."

Intrusion-detection systems

There are basically two types of intrusion-detection systems (IDS):

- Host-based IDS
- Network-based IDS

Host-based IDS: These systems are installed on a particular important machine (usually a server or some important target) and are tasked with making sure that the system state matches a particular set baseline. For example, the popular file-integrity checker Tripwire is run on the target machine just after it has been installed. It creates a database of file signatures for the system and regularly checks the current system files against their known safe signatures. If a file has been changed, the administrator is alerted. This works very well because most attackers will replace a common system file with a trojaned version to give them backdoor access.

Network-based IDS: These systems are more popular and quite easy to install. Basically, they consist of a normal network sniffer running in promiscuous mode. (In this mode, the network card picks up all traffic even if it is not meant for it.) The sniffer is attached to a database of known attack signatures, and the IDS analyzes each packet that it picks up to check for known attacks. For example, a common Web attack might contain the string / system32/cmd. exe? in the URL. The IDS will have a match for this in the database and will alert the administrator.

Newer versions of IDS support active prevention of attacks. Instead of just alerting an administrator, the IDS can dynamically update the firewall rules to disallow traffic from the attacking IP address for some amount of time. Or the IDS can use "session sniping" to fool both sides of the connection into closing down so that the attack cannot be completed.

Unfortunately, IDS systems generate a lot of false positives. A false positive is basically a false alarm, where the IDS sees legitimate traffic and for some reason matches it against an attack pattern. This tempts a lot of administrators into turning them off or even worse — not bothering to read the logs. This may result in an actual attack being missed.

IDS evasion is also not all that difficult for an experienced attacker. The signature is based on some unique feature of the attack, and so the attacker can modify the attack so that the signature is not matched.

This might be totally missed by the IDS. Furthermore, an attacker could split the attack into many packets by fragmenting the packets. This means that each packet would only contain a small part of the attack, and the signature would not match. Even if the IDS is able to reassemble fragmented packets, this creates a time overhead and since the IDS has to run at near real-time status, they tend to drop packets while they are processing. IDS evasion is a topic for a paper on its own.

The advantage of a network-based IDS is that it is very difficult for an attacker to detect. The IDS itself does not need to generate any traffic, and, in fact, many of them have a broken TCP/IP stack so that they don't have an IP address. Thus the attacker does not know whether the network segment is being monitored or not.

NETWORK COMPONENTS

Computer networks share common devices, functions, and features including servers, clients, transmission media, shared data, shared printers and other hardware and software resources, network interface card(NIC), local operating system(LOS), and the network operating system (NOS).

Servers - Servers are computers that hold shared files, programs, and the network operating system. Servers provide access to network resources to all the users of the network. There are many different kinds of servers, and one server can provide several functions. For example, there are file servers, print servers, mail servers, communication servers, database servers, fax servers and web servers, to name a few.

Clients - Clients are computers that access and use the network and shared network resources. Client computers are basically the customers(users) of the network, as they request and receive services from the servers.

Transmission Media - Transmission media are the facilities used to interconnect computers in a network, such as twisted-pair wire, coaxial cable, and optical fiber cable. Transmission media are sometimes called channels, links or lines.

Shared data - Shared data are data that file servers provide to clients such as data files, printer access programs and e-mail.

Shared printers and other peripherals - Shared printers and peripherals are hardware resources provided to the users of the network by servers. Resources provided include data files, printers, software, or any other items used by clients on the network.

Network Interface Card - Each computer in a network has a special expansion card called a network interface card (NIC). The NIC prepares(formats) and sends data, receives data, and controls data flow between the computer and the network. On the transmit side, the NIC passes frames of data on to the physical layer, which transmits the data to the physical link. On the receiver's side, the NIC processes bits received from the physical layer and processes the message based on its contents.

Local Operating System - A local operating system allows personal computers to access files, print to a local printer, and have and use one or more disk and CD drives that are located on the computer. Examples are MS-DOS, Unix, Linux, Windows 2000, Windows 98, Windows XP etc.

Network Operating System - The network operating system is a program that runs on computers and servers, and allows the computers to communicate over the network.

Hub - Hub is a device that splits a network connection into multiple computers. It is like a distribution center. When a computer requests information from a network or a specific computer, it sends the request to the hub through a cable. The hub will receive the request and transmit it to the entire network. Each computer in the network should then figure out whether the broadcast data is for them or not.

Switch - Switch is a telecommunication device grouped as one of computer network components. Switch is like a Hub but built in with advanced features. It uses physical device addresses in each incoming messages so that it can deliver the message to the right destination or port.

Like a hub, switch doesn't broadcast the received message to entire network, rather before sending it checks to which system or port should the message be sent. In other words, switch connects the source and destination directly which increases the speed of the network. Both switch and hub have common features: Multiple RJ-45 ports, power supply and connection lights.

5. Router When we talk about computer network components, the other device that used to connect a LAN with an internet connection is called Router. When you have two distinct networks (LANs) or want to share a single internet connection to multiple computers, we use a Router. In most cases, recent routers also include a switch which in other words can be used as a switch. You don't need to buy both switch and router, particularly if you are installing small business and home networks. There are two types of Router: wired and wireless. The choice depends on your physical office/home setting, speed and cost.

Networking hardware

Networking hardware, also known as network equipment or computer networking devices, are physical devices which are required for communication and interaction between devices on a computer network. Specifically, they mediate data in a computer network. Units which are the last receiver or generate data are called hosts or data terminal equipment.

Range

Networking devices may include gateways, routers, network bridges, modems, wireless access points, networking cables, line drivers, switches, hubs, and repeaters; and may also include hybrid network devices such as multilayer switches, protocol converters, bridge routers, proxy servers, firewalls, network address translators, multiplexers, network interface controllers, wireless network interface controllers, ISDN terminal adapters and other related hardware. The most common kind of networking hardware today is a copper-based Ethernet adapter which is a standard inclusion on most modern computer systems. Wireless networking has become increasingly popular, especially for portable and handheld devices.

Other networking hardware used in computers includes data center equipment (such as file servers, database servers and storage areas), network services (such as DNS, DHCP, email, etc.) as well as devices which assure content delivery.

Taking a wider view, mobile phones, PDAs and even modern coffee machines may also be considered networking hardware. As technology advances and IP-based networks are integrated into building infrastructure and household utilities, network hardware will become an ambiguous term owing to the vastly increasing number of "network capable" endpoints.

Specific devices

- Gateway: an interface providing a compatibility between networks by converting transmission speeds, protocols, codes, or security measures.
- Router: a networking device that forwards data packets between computer networks. Routers perform the "traffic directing" functions on the Internet. A data packet is typically forwarded from one router to another through the networks that constitute the internetwork until it reaches its destination node. It works on OSI layer 3.
- Switch: a device that connects devices together on a computer network, by using packet switching to receive, process and forward data to the destination device. Unlike less advanced network hubs, a network switch forwards data only to one or multiple devices that need to receive it, rather than broadcasting the same data out of each of its ports. It works on OSI layer 2.
- Bridge: a device that connects multiple network segments. It works on OSI layers 1 and 2.

- Hub: for connecting multiple Ethernet devices together and making them act as a single network segment. It has multiple input/output (I/O) ports, in which a signal introduced at the input of any port appears at the output of every port except the original incoming. A hub works at the physical layer (layer 1) of the OSI model. Repeater hubs also participate in collision detection, forwarding a jam signal to all ports if it detects a collision. Hubs are now largely obsolete, having been replaced by network switches except in very old installations or specialized applications.
- Repeater: an electronic device that receives a signal and retransmits it at a higher level or higher power, or onto the other side of an obstruction, so that the signal can cover longer distances.

Hybrid network devices include:

- Multilayer switch: a switch that, in addition to switching on OSI layer 2, provides functionality at higher protocol layers.
- Protocol converter: a hardware device that converts between two different types of transmission, for interoperation.
- Bridge router (brouter): a device that works as a bridge and as a router. The brouter routes packets for known protocols and simply forwards all other packets as a bridge would.
- Hardware or software components which typically sit on the connection point of different networks (for example, between an internal network and an external network) include:
- Proxy server: computer network service which allows clients to make indirect network connections to other network services.
- Firewall: a piece of hardware or software put on the network to prevent some communications forbidden by the network policy. A firewall typically establishes a barrier between a trusted, secure internal network and another outside network, such as the Internet, that is assumed to not be secure or trusted.
- Network address translator (NAT): network service (provided as hardware or as software) that converts internal to external network addresses and vice versa.
- Other hardware devices used for establishing networks or dial-up connections include:
- Multiplexer: a device that selects only one signal from several electrical input signals.
- Network interface controller (NIC): a device connecting a computer to a wire-based computer network.

- Wireless network interface controller: a device connecting the attached computer to a radio-based computer network.
- Modem: device that modulates an analog "carrier" signal (such as sound) to encode digital information, and that also demodulates such a carrier signal to decode the transmitted information. Used (for example) when a computer communicates with another computer over a telephone network.
- ISDN terminal adapter (TA): a specialized gateway for ISDN.
- Line driver: a device to increase transmission distance by amplifying the signal; used in base-band networks only.

OPTICAL FIBERS

An optical fiber or optical fibre is a flexible, transparent fiber made by drawing glass (silica) or plastic to a diameter slightly thicker than that of a human hair. Optical fibers are used most often as a means to transmit light between the two ends of the fiber and find wide usage in fiber-optic communications, where they permit transmission over longer distances and at higher bandwidths (data rates) than wire cables. Fibers are used instead of metal wires because signals travel along them with lesser amounts of loss; in addition, fibers are also immune to electromagnetic interference, a problem from which metal wires suffer excessively. Fibers are also used for illumination, and are wrapped in bundles so that they may be used to carry images, thus allowing viewing in confined spaces, as in the case of a fiberscope. Specially designed fibers are also used for a variety of other applications, some of them being fiber optic sensors and fiber lasers.

Optical fibers typically include a transparent core surrounded by a transparent cladding material with a lower index of refraction. Light is kept in the core by the phenomenon of total internal reflection which causes the fiber to act as a waveguide. Fibers that support many propagation paths or transverse modes are called multi-mode fibers (MMF), while those that support a single mode are called single-mode fibers (SMF). Multi-mode fibers generally have a wider core diameter and are used for short-distance communication links and for applications where high power must be transmitted. Single-mode fibers are used for most communication links longer than 1, 000 meters (3, 300 ft).

Being able to join optical fibers with low loss is important in fiber optic communication. This is more complex than joining electrical wire or cable and involves careful cleaving of the fibers, precise alignment of the fiber cores, and the coupling of these aligned cores. For applications that demand a permanent connection a fusion splice is common. In this technique, an electric arc is used to melt the ends of the fibers together. Another common technique is a mechanical splice, where the ends of the fibers are held in contact by mechanical force. Temporary or semi-permanent connections are made by means of specialized optical fiber connectors.

The field of applied science and engineering concerned with the design and application of optical fibers is known as fiber optics. The term was coined by Indian physicist Narinder Singh Kapany who is widely acknowledged as the father of fiber optics.

History

Guiding of light by refraction, the principle that makes fiber optics possible, was first demonstrated by Daniel Colladon and Jacques Babinet in Paris in the early 1840s. John Tyndall included a demonstration of it in his public lectures in London, 12 years later. Tyndall also wrote about the property of total internal reflection in an introductory book about the nature of light in 1870:

When the light passes from air into water, the refracted ray is bent towards the perpendicular... When the ray passes from water to air it is bent from the perpendicular... If the angle which the ray in water encloses with the perpendicular to the surface be greater than 48 degrees, the ray will not quit the water at all: it will be totally reflected at the surface.... The angle which marks the limit where total reflection begins is called the limiting angle of the medium. For water this angle is 48°272, for flint glass it is 38°412, while for diamond it is 23°422.

Unpigmented human hairs have also been shown to act as an optical fiber.

Practical applications, such as close internal illumination during dentistry, appeared early in the twentieth century. Image transmission through tubes was demonstrated independently by the radio experimenter Clarence Hansell and the television pioneer John Logie Baird in the 1920s. The principle was first used for internal medical examinations by Heinrich Lamm in the following decade. Modern optical fibers, where the glass fiber is coated with a transparent cladding to offer a more suitable refractive index, appeared later in the decade. Development then focused on fiber bundles for image transmission. Harold Hopkins and Narinder Singh Kapany at Imperial College in London achieved low-loss light transmission through a 75 cm long bundle which combined several thousand fibers. Their article titled "A flexible fibrescope, using static scanning" was published in the journal Nature in 1954. The first fiber optic semi-flexible gastroscope was patented by Basil Hirschowitz, C. Wilbur Peters, and Lawrence E. Curtiss, researchers at the University of Michigan, in 1956. In the process of developing the gastroscope, Curtiss produced the first glass-clad fibers; previous optical fibers had relied on air or impractical oils and waxes as the low-index cladding material.

A variety of other image transmission applications soon followed. In 1880 Alexander Graham Bell and Sumner Tainter invented the Photophone at the Volta Laboratory in Washington, D. C., to transmit voice signals over an optical beam. It was an advanced form of telecommunications, but subject to atmospheric interferences and impractical until the secure transport of light that would be offered by fiber-optical systems. In the late 19th and early 20th centuries, light was guided through bent glass rods to illuminate body cavities. Jun-ichi Nishizawa, a Japanese scientist at Tohoku University, also proposed the use of optical fibers for communications in 1963, as stated in his book published in 2004 in India. Nishizawa invented other technologies that contributed to the development of optical fiber communications, such as the graded-index optical fiber as a channel for transmitting light from semiconductor lasers. The first working fiber-optical data transmission system was demonstrated by German physicist Manfred Börner at Telefunken Research Labs in Ulm in 1965, which was followed by the first patent application for this technology in 1966. NASA used fiber optics in the television cameras that were sent to the moon. At the time, the use in the cameras was classified confidential, and employees handling the cameras had to be supervised by someone with an appropriate security clearance.

Narinder Singh Kapany, a physicist working at the ordnance factory in Dehradun in the 1950s was experimenting with using right-angled prisms to bend light. He subsequently went on to first demonstrate successfully that light can be transmitted through bent glass fibres during his doctoral work at the Imperial College of Science in London in the early fifties, and published the findings in a paper in Nature in 1954. Since then, Kapany developed applications of fibre optics for endoscopy during the fifties and later coined the term 'Fibre Optics' in an article in Scientific American in 1960. For his body of work on the subject, he is known as the father of fiber-optics.

Charles K. Kao and George A. Hockham of the British company Standard Telephones and Cables (STC) were the first to promote the idea that the attenuation in optical fibers could be reduced below 20 decibels per kilometer (dB/km), making fibers a practical communication medium. They proposed that the attenuation in fibers available at the time was caused by impurities that could be removed, rather than by fundamental physical effects such as scattering. They correctly and systematically theorized the light-loss properties for optical fiber, and pointed out the right material to use for such fibers — silica glass with high purity. This discovery earned Kao the Nobel Prize in Physics in 2009.

The crucial attenuation limit of 20 dB/km was first achieved in 1970 by researchers Robert D. Maurer, Donald Keck, Peter C. Schultz, and Frank Zimar working for American glass maker Corning Glass Works. They demonstrated a fiber with 17 dB/km attenuation by doping silica glass with titanium. A few years later they produced a fiber with only 4 dB/km attenuation using germanium dioxide as the core dopant. In 1981, General Electric produced fused quartz ingots that could be drawn into strands 25 miles (40 km) long.

Robust modern optical fiber uses glass for both core and sheath, and is therefore less prone to aging. It was invented by Gerhard Bernsee of Schott Glass in Germany in 1973. Initially high-quality optical fibers could only be manufactured at 2 meters per second. Chemical engineer Thomas Mensah joined Corning in 1983 and increased the speed of manufacture to over 50 meters per second, making optical fiber cables cheaper than traditional copper ones. These innovations ushered in the era of optical fiber telecommunication.

The Italian research center CSELT worked with Corning to develop practical optical fiber cables, resulting in the first metropolitan fiber optic cable being deployed in Torino in 1977. CSELT also developed an early technique for splicing optical fibers, called Springroove.

Attenuation in modern optical cables is far less than in electrical copper cables, leading to long-haul fiber connections with repeater distances of 70–150 kilometers (43–93 mi). The erbium-doped fiber amplifier, which reduced the cost of long-distance fiber systems by reducing or eliminating optical-electrical-optical repeaters, was co-developed by teams led by David N. Payne of the University of Southampton and Emmanuel Desurvire at Bell Labs in 1986.

The emerging field of photonic crystals led to the development in 1991 of photonic-crystal fiber, which guides light by diffraction from a periodic structure, rather than by total internal reflection. The first photonic crystal fibers became commercially available in 2000. Photonic crystal fibers can carry higher power than conventional fibers and their wavelength-dependent properties can be manipulated to improve performance.

Record speeds

- 2006 – Nippon Telegraph and Telephone Corporation transferred 14 terabits per second over a single 160 km long optical fiber
- 2009 – Bell Labs in Villarceaux, France transferred 100 Gbit/s over 7000 km fiber
- 2010 – Bell Labs in Villarceaux, France transferred 100 petabits per second.
- 2010 – Nippon Telegraph and Telephone Corporation transferred 69. 1 Tbit/s over a single 240 km fiber multiplexing 432 channels, equating to 171 Gbit/s per channel
- 2012 – Nippon Telegraph and Telephone Corporation transferred 1 Petabit per second over 50 kilometers over a single fiber

USES

Communication

Optical fiber can be used as a medium for telecommunication and computer networking because it is flexible and can be bundled as cables. It is especially advantageous for long-distance communications, because light propagates through the fiber with little attenuation compared to electrical cables. This allows long distances to be spanned with few repeaters.

The per-channel light signals propagating in the fiber have been modulated at rates as high as 111 gigabits per second (Gbit/s) by NTT, although 10 or 40 Gbit/s is typical in deployed systems. In June 2013, researchers demonstrated transmission of 400 Gbit/s over a single channel using 4-mode orbital angular momentum multiplexing.

Each fiber can carry many independent channels, each using a different wavelength of light (wavelength-division multiplexing (WDM)). The net data rate (data rate without overhead bytes) per fiber is the per-channel data rate reduced by the FEC overhead, multiplied by the number of channels (usually up to eighty in commercial dense WDM systems as of 2008). As of 2011 the record for bandwidth on a single core was 101 Tbit/s (370 channels at 273 Gbit/s each). The record for a multi-core fiber as of January 2013 was 1. 05 petabits per second. In 2009, Bell Labs broke the 100 (petabit per second)×kilometer barrier (15. 5 Tbit/s over a single 7, 000 km fiber).

For short distance application, such as a network in an office building, fiber-optic cabling can save space in cable ducts. This is because a single fiber can carry much more data than electrical cables such as standard category 5 Ethernet cabling, which typically runs at 100 Mbit/s or 1 Gbit/s speeds. Fiber is also immune to electrical interference; there is no cross-talk between signals in different cables, and no pickup of environmental noise. Non-armored fiber cables do not conduct electricity, which makes fiber a good solution for protecting communications equipment in high voltage environments, such as power generation facilities, or metal communication structures prone to lightning strikes. They can also be used in environments where explosive fumes are present, without danger of ignition. Wiretapping (in this case, fiber tapping) is more difficult compared to electrical connections, and there are concentric dual-core fibers that are said to be tap-proof.

Fibers are often also used for short-distance connections between devices. For example, most high-definition televisions offer a digital audio optical connection. This allows the streaming of audio over light, using the TOSLINK protocol.

Advantages over copper wiring

The advantages of optical fiber communication with respect to copper wire systems are:

Broad bandwidth

A single optical fiber can carry over 3, 000, 000 full-duplex voice calls or 90, 000 TV channels.

Immunity to electromagnetic interference

Light transmission through optical fibers is unaffected by other electromagnetic radiation nearby. The optical fiber is electrically non-conductive, so it does not act as an antenna to pick up electromagnetic signals. Information traveling inside the optical fiber is immune to electromagnetic interference, even electromagnetic pulses generated by nuclear devices.

Low attenuation loss over long distances

Attenuation loss can be as low as 0. 2 dB/km in optical fiber cables, allowing transmission over long distances without the need for repeaters.

Electrical insulator

Optical fibers do not conduct electricity, preventing problems with ground loops and conduction of lightning. Optical fibers can be strung on poles alongside high voltage power cables.

Material cost and theft prevention

Conventional cable systems use large amounts of copper. Global copper prices experienced a boom in the 2000s, and copper has been a target of metal theft.

Security of information passed down the cable

Copper can be tapped with very little chance of detection.

Sensors

Fibers have many uses in remote sensing. In some applications, the sensor is itself an optical fiber. In other cases, fiber is used to connect a non-fiberoptic sensor to a measurement system. Depending on the application, fiber may be used because of its small size, or the fact that no electrical power is needed at the remote location, or because many sensors can be multiplexed along the length of a fiber by using different wavelengths of light for each sensor, or by sensing the time delay as light passes along the fiber through each sensor. Time delay can be determined using a device such as an optical time-domain reflectometer.

Optical fibers can be used as sensors to measure strain, temperature, pressure and other quantities by modifying a fiber so that the property to measure modulates the intensity, phase, polarization, wavelength, or transit time of light in the fiber. Sensors that vary the intensity of light are the simplest, since only a simple source and detector are required. A particularly useful feature of such fiber optic sensors is that they can, if required, provide distributed sensing over distances of up to one meter. In contrast, highly localized measurements can be provided by integrating miniaturized sensing elements with the tip of the fiber. These can be implemented by various micro- and nanofabrication technologies, such that they do not exceed the microscopic boundary of the fiber tip, allowing such applications as insertion into blood vessels via hypodermic needle.

Extrinsic fiber optic sensors use an optical fiber cable, normally a multi-mode one, to transmit modulated light from either a non-fiber optical sensor—or an electronic sensor connected to an optical transmitter. A major benefit of extrinsic sensors is their ability to reach otherwise inaccessible places. An example is the measurement of temperature inside aircraft jet engines by using a fiber to transmit radiation into a radiation pyrometer outside the engine. Extrinsic sensors can be used in the same way to measure the internal temperature of electrical transformers, where the extreme electromagnetic fields present make other measurement techniques impossible. Extrinsic sensors measure vibration, rotation, displacement, velocity, acceleration, torque, and twisting. A solid state version of the gyroscope, using the interference of light, has been developed. The fiber optic gyroscope (FOG) has no moving parts, and exploits the Sagnac effect to detect mechanical rotation.

Common uses for fiber optic sensors includes advanced intrusion detection security systems. The light is transmitted along a fiber optic sensor cable placed on a fence, pipeline, or communication cabling, and the returned signal is monitored and analyzed for disturbances. This return signal is digitally processed to detect disturbances and trip an alarm if an intrusion has occurred.

Optical fibers are widely used as components of optical chemical sensors and optical biosensors.

Power transmission

Optical fiber can be used to transmit power using a photovoltaic cell to convert the light into electricity. While this method of power transmission is not as efficient as conventional ones, it is especially useful in situations where it is desirable not to have a metallic conductor as in the case of use near MRI machines, which produce strong magnetic fields. Other examples are for powering electronics in high-powered antenna elements and measurement devices used in high-voltage transmission equipment.

Other uses

Optical fibers have a wide number of applications. They are used as light guides in medical and other applications where bright light needs to be shone on a target without a clear line-of-sight path. In some buildings, optical fibers route sunlight from the roof to other parts of the building. Optical fiber lamps are used for illumination in decorative applications, including signs, art, toys and artificial Christmas trees. Swarovski boutiques use optical fibers to illuminate their crystal showcases from many different angles while only employing one light source. Optical fiber is an intrinsic part of the light-transmitting concrete building product, LiTraCon.

Optical fiber is also used in imaging optics. A coherent bundle of fibers is used, sometimes along with lenses, for a long, thin imaging device called an endoscope, which is used to view objects through a small hole. Medical endoscopes are used for minimally invasive exploratory or surgical procedures. Industrial endoscopes are used for inspecting anything hard to reach, such as jet engine interiors. Many microscopes use fiber-optic light sources to provide intense illumination of samples being studied.

In spectroscopy, optical fiber bundles transmit light from a spectrometer to a substance that cannot be placed inside the spectrometer itself, in order to analyze its composition. A spectrometer analyzes substances by bouncing light off and through them. By using fibers, a spectrometer can be used to study objects remotely.

An optical fiber doped with certain rare earth elements such as erbium can be used as the gain medium of a laser or optical amplifier. Rare-earth-doped optical fibers can be used to provide signal amplification by splicing a short section of doped fiber into a regular (undoped) optical fiber line. The doped fiber is optically pumped with a second laser wavelength that is coupled into the line in addition to the signal wave. Both wavelengths of light are transmitted through the doped fiber, which transfers energy from the second pump wavelength to the signal wave. The process that causes the amplification is stimulated emission.

Optical fiber is also widely exploited as a nonlinear medium. The glass medium supports a host of nonlinear optical interactions, and the long interaction lengths possible in fiber facilitate a variety of phenomena, which are harnessed for applications and fundamental investigation. Conversely, fiber nonlinearity can have deleterious effects on optical signals, and measures are often required to minimize such unwanted effects. Optical fibers doped with a wavelength shifter collect scintillation light in physics experiments.

Fiber optic sights for handguns, rifles, and shotguns use pieces of optical fiber to improve visibility of markings on the sight.

Principle of operation

An optical fiber is a cylindrical dielectric waveguide (nonconducting waveguide) that transmits light along its axis, by the process of total internal reflection. The fiber consists of a core surrounded by a cladding layer, both of which are made of dielectric materials. To confine the optical signal in the core, the refractive index of the core must be greater than that of the cladding. The boundary between the core and cladding may either be abrupt, in step-index fiber, or gradual, in graded-index fiber.

Index of refraction

The index of refraction (or refractive index) is a way of measuring the speed of light in a material. Light travels fastest in a vacuum, such as in outer space. The speed of light in a vacuum is about 300, 000 kilometers (186, 000 miles) per second. The refractive index of a medium is calculated by dividing the speed of light in a vacuum by the speed of light in that medium. The refractive index of a vacuum is therefore 1, by definition. A typical singlemode fiber used for telecommunications has a cladding made of pure silica, with an index of 1. 444 at 1, 500 nm, and a core of doped silica with an index around 1. 4475. The larger the index of refraction, the slower light travels in that medium. From this information, a simple rule of thumb is that a signal using optical fiber for communication will travel at around 200, 000 kilometers per second. To put it another way, the signal will take 5 milliseconds to travel 1, 000 kilometers in fiber. Thus a phone call carried by fiber between Sydney and New York, a 16, 000-kilometer distance, means that there is a minimum delay of 80 millisecondsbetween when one caller speaks and the other hears. (The fiber in this case will probably travel a longer route, and there will be additional delays due to communication equipment switching and the process of encoding and decoding the voice onto the fiber).

Total internal reflection

When light traveling in an optically dense medium hits a boundary at a steep angle (larger than the critical angle for the boundary), the light is completely reflected. This is called total internal reflection. This effect is used in optical fibers to confine light in the core. Light travels through the fiber core, bouncing back and forth off the boundary between the core and cladding. Because the light must strike the boundary with an angle greater than the critical angle, only light that enters the fiber within a certain range of angles can travel down the fiber without leaking out. This range of angles is called the acceptance cone of the fiber. The size of this acceptance cone is a function of the refractive index difference between the fiber's core and cladding.

In simpler terms, there is a maximum angle from the fiber axis at which light may enter the fiber so that it will propagate, or travel, in the core of the fiber. The sine of this maximum angle is the numerical aperture (NA) of the fiber. Fiber with a larger NA requires less precision to splice and work with than fiber with a smaller NA. Single-mode fiber has a small NA.

Multi-mode fiber

Fiber with large core diameter (greater than 10 micrometers) may be analyzed by geometrical optics. Such fiber is called multi-mode fiber, from the electromagnetic analysis. In a step-index multi-mode fiber, rays of light are guided along the fiber core by total internal reflection. Rays that meet the core-cladding boundary at a high angle (measured relative to a line normal to the boundary), greater than the critical angle for this boundary, are completely reflected. The critical angle (minimum angle for total internal reflection) is determined by the difference in index of refraction between the core and cladding materials. Rays that meet the boundary at a low angle are refracted from the core into the cladding, and do not convey light and hence information along the fiber. The critical angle determines the acceptance angle of the fiber, often reported as a numerical aperture. A high numerical aperture allows light to propagate down the fiber in rays both close to the axis and at various angles, allowing efficient coupling of light into the fiber. However, this high numerical aperture increases the amount of dispersion as rays at different angles have different path lengths and therefore take different times to traverse the fiber.

In graded-index fiber, the index of refraction in the core decreases continuously between the axis and the cladding. This causes light rays to bend smoothly as they approach the cladding, rather than reflecting abruptly from the core-cladding boundary. The resulting curved paths reduce multi-path dispersion because high angle rays pass more through the lower-index periphery of the core, rather than the high-index center. The index profile is chosen to minimize the difference in axial propagation speeds of the various rays in the fiber. This ideal index profile is very close to a parabolic relationship between the index and the distance from the axis.

Single-mode fiber

Fiber with a core diameter less than about ten times the wavelength of the propagating light cannot be modeled using geometric optics. Instead, it must be analyzed as an electromagnetic structure, by solution of Maxwell's equations as reduced to the electromagnetic wave equation. The electromagnetic analysis may also be required to understand behaviors such as speckle that occur when coherent light propagates in multi-mode fiber. As an optical waveguide, the fiber supports one or more confined transverse modes by which light can propagate along the fiber. Fiber supporting only one mode is called single-mode or mono-mode fiber. The behavior of larger-core multi-mode fiber can also be modeled using the wave equation, which shows that such fiber supports more than one mode of propagation (hence the name). The results of such modeling of multi-mode fiber approximately agree with the predictions of geometric optics, if the fiber core is large enough to support more than a few modes.

The waveguide analysis shows that the light energy in the fiber is not completely confined in the core. Instead, especially in single-mode fibers, a significant fraction of the energy in the bound mode travels in the cladding as an evanescent wave.

The most common type of single-mode fiber has a core diameter of 8–10 micrometers and is designed for use in the near infrared. The mode structure depends on the wavelength of the light used, so that this fiber actually supports a small number of additional modes at visible wavelengths. Multi-mode fiber, by comparison, is manufactured with core diameters as small as 50 micrometers and as large as hundreds of micrometers. The normalized frequency V for this fiber should be less than the first zero of the Bessel function J0(approximately 2. 405).

SPECIAL-PURPOSE FIBER

Some special-purpose optical fiber is constructed with a non-cylindrical core and/or cladding layer, usually with an elliptical or rectangular cross-section. These include polarization-maintaining fiber and fiber designed to suppress whispering gallery mode propagation. Polarization-maintaining fiber is a unique type of fiber that is commonly used in fiber optic sensors due to its ability to maintain the polarization of the light inserted into it.

Photonic-crystal fiber is made with a regular pattern of index variation (often in the form of cylindrical holes that run along the length of the fiber). Such fiber uses diffraction effects instead of or in addition to total internal reflection, to confine light to the fiber's core. The properties of the fiber can be tailored to a wide variety of applications.

Mechanisms of attenuation

Attenuation in fiber optics, also known as transmission loss, is the reduction in intensity of the light beam (or signal) as it travels through the transmission medium. Attenuation coefficients in fiber optics usually use units of dB/km through the medium due to the relatively high quality of transparency of modern optical transmission media. The medium is usually a fiber of silica glass that confines the incident light beam to the inside. Attenuation is an important factor limiting the transmission of a digital signal across large distances. Thus, much research has gone into both limiting the attenuation and maximizing the amplification of the optical signal. Empirical research has shown that attenuation in optical fiber is caused primarily by both scattering and absorption. Single-mode optical fibers can be made with extremely low loss. Corning's SMF-28 fiber, a standard single-mode fiber for telecommunications wavelengths, has a loss of 0. 17 dB/km at 1550 nm. For example, an 8 km length of SMF-28 transmits nearly 75% of light at 1, 550 nm. It has been noted that if ocean water was as clear as fiber, one could see all the way to the bottom even of the Marianas Trench in the Pacific Ocean, a depth of 36, 000 feet.

Light scattering

The propagation of light through the core of an optical fiber is based on total internal reflection of the lightwave. Rough and irregular surfaces, even at the molecular level, can cause light rays to be reflected in random directions. This is called diffuse reflection or scattering, and it is typically characterized by wide variety of reflection angles.

Light scattering depends on the wavelength of the light being scattered. Thus, limits to spatial scales of visibility arise, depending on the frequency of the incident light-wave and the physical dimension (or spatial scale) of the scattering center, which is typically in the form of some specific micro-structural feature. Since visible light has a wavelength of the order of one micrometer (one millionth of a meter) scattering centers will have dimensions on a similar spatial scale. Thus, attenuation results from the incoherent scattering of light at internal surfaces and interfaces. In (poly)crystalline materials such as metals and ceramics, in addition to pores, most of the internal surfaces or interfaces are in the form of grain boundaries that separate tiny regions of crystalline order. It has recently been shown that when the size of the scattering center (or grain boundary) is reduced below the size of the wavelength of the light being scattered, the scattering no longer occurs to any significant extent. This phenomenon has given rise to the production of transparent ceramic materials.

Similarly, the scattering of light in optical quality glass fiber is caused by molecular level irregularities (compositional fluctuations) in the glass structure. Indeed, one emerging school of thought is that a glass is simply the limiting case of a polycrystalline solid. Within this framework, "domains" exhibiting various degrees of short-range order become the building blocks of both metals and alloys, as well as glasses and ceramics. Distributed both between and within these domains are micro-structural defects that provide the most ideal locations for light scattering. This same phenomenon is seen as one of the limiting factors in the transparency of IR missile domes.

At high optical powers, scattering can also be caused by nonlinear optical processes in the fiber.

UV-Vis-IR absorption

In addition to light scattering, attenuation or signal loss can also occur due to selective absorption of specific wavelengths, in a manner similar to that responsible for the appearance of color. Primary material considerations include both electrons and molecules as follows:

- At the electronic level, it depends on whether the electron orbitals are spaced (or "quantized") such that they can absorb a quantum of light (or photon) of a specific wavelength or frequency in the ultraviolet (UV) or visible ranges. This is what gives rise to color.
- At the atomic or molecular level, it depends on the frequencies of atomic or molecular vibrations or chemical bonds, how close-packed its atoms or molecules are, and whether or not the atoms or molecules exhibit long-range order. These factors will determine the capacity of the material transmitting longer wavelengths in the infrared (IR), far IR, radio and microwave ranges.

The design of any optically transparent device requires the selection of materials based upon knowledge of its properties and limitations. The Lattice absorption characteristics observed at the lower frequency regions (mid IR to far-infrared wavelength range) define the long-wavelength transparency limit of the material. They are the result of the interactive coupling between the motions of thermally induced vibrations of the constituent atoms and molecules of the solid lattice and the incident light wave radiation. Hence, all materials are bounded by limiting regions of absorption caused by atomic and molecular vibrations (bond-stretching)in the far-infrared (>10 μm).

Thus, multi-phonon absorption occurs when two or more phonons simultaneously interact to produce electric dipole moments with which the incident radiation may couple. These dipoles can absorb energy from the incident radiation, reaching a maximum coupling with the radiation when the frequency is equal to the fundamental vibrational mode of the molecular dipole (e. g. Si-O bond) in the far-infrared, or one of its harmonics. The selective absorption of infrared (IR) light by a particular material occurs because the selected frequency of the light wave matches the frequency (or an integer multiple of the frequency) at which the particles of that material vibrate. Since different atoms and molecules have different natural frequencies of vibration, they will selectively absorb different frequencies (or portions of the spectrum) of infrared (IR) light.

Reflection and transmission of light waves occur because the frequencies of the light waves do not match the natural resonant frequencies of vibration of the objects. When IR light of these frequencies strikes an object, the energy is either reflected or transmitted.

Manufacturing

Materials

Glass optical fibers are almost always made from silica, but some other materials, such as fluorozirconate, fluoroaluminate, and chalcogenide glasses as well as crystalline materials like sapphire, are used for longer-wavelength infrared or other specialized applications. Silica and fluoride glasses usually have refractive indices of about 1. 5, but some materials such as the chalcogenides can have indices as high as 3. Typically the index difference between core and cladding is less than one percent.

Plastic optical fibers (POF) are commonly step-index multi-mode fibers with a core diameter of 0. 5 millimeters or larger. POF typically have higher attenuation coefficients than glass fibers, 1 dB/m or higher, and this high attenuation limits the range of POF-based systems.

Silica

Silica exhibits fairly good optical transmission over a wide range of wavelengths. In the near-infrared (near IR) portion of the spectrum, particularly around 1. 5 ìm, silica can have extremely low absorption and scattering losses of the order of 0. 2 dB/km. Such remarkably low losses are possible only because ultra-pure silicon is available, it being essential for manufacturing integrated circuits and discrete transistors. A high transparency in the 1. 4-ìm region is achieved by maintaining a low concentration of hydroxyl groups (OH). Alternatively, a high OH concentration is better for transmission in the ultraviolet (UV) region. Silica can be drawn into fibers at reasonably high temperatures, and has a fairly broad glass transformation range. One other advantage is that fusion splicing and cleaving of silica fibers is relatively effective. Silica fiber also has high mechanical strength against both pulling and even bending, provided that the fiber is not too thick and that the surfaces have been well prepared during processing. Even simple cleaving (breaking) of the ends of the fiber can provide nicely flat surfaces with acceptable optical quality. Silica is also relatively chemically inert. In particular, it is not hygroscopic (does not absorb water).

Silica glass can be doped with various materials. One purpose of doping is to raise the refractive index (e. g. with germanium dioxide (GeO2) or aluminium oxide (Al2O3)) or to lower it (e. g. with fluorine or boron trioxide (B2O3)). Doping is also possible with laser-active ions (for example, rare earth-doped fibers) in order to obtain active fibers to be used, for example, in fiber amplifiers or laser applications. Both the fiber core and cladding are typically doped, so that the entire assembly (core and cladding) is effectively the same compound (e. g. an aluminosilicate, germanosilicate, phosphosilicate or borosilicate glass).

Particularly for active fibers, pure silica is usually not a very suitable host glass, because it exhibits a low solubility for rare earth ions. This can lead to quenching effects due to clustering of dopant ions. Aluminosilicates are much more effective in this respect. Silica fiber also exhibits a high threshold for optical damage. This property ensures a low tendency for laser-induced breakdown. This is important for fiber amplifiers when utilized for the amplification of short pulses.

Because of these properties silica fibers are the material of choice in many optical applications, such as communications (except for very short distances with plastic optical fiber), fiber lasers, fiber amplifiers, and fiber-optic sensors. Large efforts put forth in the development of various types of silica fibers have further increased the performance of such fibers over other materials.

Fluoride glass

Fluoride glass is a class of non-oxide optical quality glasses composed of fluorides of various metals. Because of their low viscosity, it is very difficult to completely avoid crystallization while processing it through the glass transition (or drawing the fiber from the melt). Thus, although heavy metal fluoride glasses (HMFG) exhibit very low optical attenuation, they are not only difficult to manufacture, but are quite fragile, and have poor resistance to moisture and other environmental attacks. Their best attribute is that they lack the absorption band associated with the hydroxyl (OH) group (3, 200–3, 600 cm”1; i. e., 2, 777–3, 125 nm or 2. 78–3. 13 ìm), which is present in nearly all oxide-based glasses.

An example of a heavy metal fluoride glass is the ZBLAN glass group, composed of zirconium, barium, lanthanum, aluminium, and sodium fluorides. Their main technological application is as optical waveguides in both planar and fiber form. They are advantageous especially in the mid-infrared (2, 000–5, 000 nm) range.

HMFGs were initially slated for optical fiber applications, because the intrinsic losses of a mid-IR fiber could in principle be lower than those of silica fibers, which are transparent only up to about 2 ìm. However, such low losses were never realized in practice, and the fragility and high cost of fluoride fibers made them less than ideal as primary candidates. Later, the utility of fluoride fibers for various other applications was discovered. These include mid-IR spectroscopy, fiber optic sensors, thermometry, and imaging. Also, fluoride fibers can be used for guided lightwave transmission in media such as YAG (yttrium aluminium garnet) lasers at 2. 9 ìm, as required for medical applications (e. g. ophthalmology and dentistry).

Phosphate glass

Phosphate glass constitutes a class of optical glasses composed of metaphosphates of various metals. Instead of the SiO4 tetrahedra observed in silicate glasses, the building block for this glass former is phosphorus pentoxide (P2O5), which crystallizes in at least four different forms. The most familiar polymorph comprises molecules of P4O10.

Phosphate glasses can be advantageous over silica glasses for optical fibers with a high concentration of doping rare earth ions. A mix of fluoride glass and phosphate glass is fluorophosphate glass.

Chalcogenide glass

The chalcogens—the elements in group 16 of the periodic table—particularly sulfur (S), selenium (Se) and tellurium (Te)—react with more electropositive elements, such as silver, to form chalcogenides. These are extremely versatile compounds, in that they can be crystalline or amorphous, metallic or semiconducting, and conductors of ions or electrons. Glass containing chalcogenides can be used to make fibers for far infrared transmission.

PROCESS

Preform

Standard optical fibers are made by first constructing a large-diameter "preform" with a carefully controlled refractive index profile, and then "pulling" the preform to form the long, thin optical fiber. The preform is commonly made by three chemical vapor deposition methods: inside vapor deposition, outside vapor deposition, and vapor axial deposition.

With inside vapor deposition, the preform starts as a hollow glass tube approximately 40 centimeters (16 in) long, which is placed horizontally and rotated slowly on a lathe. Gases such as silicon tetrachloride (SiCl4) or germanium tetrachloride (GeCl4) are injected with oxygen in the end of the tube. The gases are then heated by means of an external hydrogen burner, bringing the temperature of the gas up to 1, 900 K (1, 600 °C, 3, 000 °F), where the tetrachlorides react with oxygen to produce silica or germania (germanium dioxide) particles. When the reaction conditions are chosen to allow this reaction to occur in the gas phase throughout the tube volume, in contrast to earlier techniques where the reaction occurred only on the glass surface, this technique is called modified chemical vapor deposition (MCVD).

The oxide particles then agglomerate to form large particle chains, which subsequently deposit on the walls of the tube as soot. The deposition is due to the large difference in temperature between the gas core and the wall causing the gas to push the particles outwards (this is known as thermophoresis). The torch is then traversed up and down the length of the tube to deposit the material evenly. After the torch has reached the end of the tube, it is then brought back to the beginning of the tube and the deposited particles are then melted to form a solid layer. This process is repeated until a sufficient amount of material has been deposited. For each layer the composition can be modified by varying the gas composition, resulting in precise control of the finished fiber's optical properties.

In outside vapor deposition or vapor axial deposition, the glass is formed by flame hydrolysis, a reaction in which silicon tetrachloride and germanium tetrachloride are oxidized by reaction with water (H2O) in an oxyhydrogen flame. In outside vapor deposition the glass is deposited onto a solid rod, which is removed before further processing. In vapor axial deposition, a short seed rod is used, and a porous preform, whose length is not limited by the size of the source rod, is built up on its end. The porous preform is consolidated into a transparent, solid preform by heating to about 1, 800 K (1, 500 °C, 2, 800 °F).

Typical communications fiber uses a circular preform. For some applications such as double-clad fibers another form is preferred. In fiber lasers based on double-clad fiber, an asymmetric shape improves the filling factor for laser pumping. Because of the surface tension, the shape is smoothed during the drawing process, and the shape of the resulting fiber does not reproduce the sharp edges of the preform. Nevertheless, careful polishing of the preform is important, since any defects of the preform surface affect the optical and mechanical properties of the resulting fiber. In particular, the preform for the test-fiber shown in the figure was not polished well, and cracks are seen with the confocal optical microscope.

Drawing

The preform, however constructed, is placed in a device known as a drawing tower, where the preform tip is heated and the optical fiber is pulled out as a string. By measuring the resultant fiber width, the tension on the fiber can be controlled to maintain the fiber thickness.

Coatings

The light is guided down the core of the fiber by an optical cladding with a lower refractive index that traps light in the core through total internal reflection.

The cladding is coated by a buffer that protects it from moisture and physical damage. The buffer coating is what gets stripped off the fiber for termination or splicing. These coatings are UV-cured urethane acrylate composite or polyimide materials applied to the outside of the fiber during the drawing process. The coatings protect the very delicate strands of glass fiber—about the size of a human hair—and allow it to survive the rigors of manufacturing, proof testing, cabling and installation.

Today's glass optical fiber draw processes employ a dual-layer coating approach. An inner primary coating is designed to act as a shock absorber to minimize attenuation caused by microbending. An outer secondary coating protects the primary coating against mechanical damage and acts as a barrier to lateral forces, and may be colored to differentiate strands in bundled cable constructions.

These fiber optic coating layers are applied during the fiber draw, at speeds approaching 100 kilometers per hour (60 mph). Fiber optic coatings are applied using one of two methods: wet-on-dry and wet-on-wet. In wet-on-dry, the fiber passes through a primary coating application, which is then UV cured—then through the secondary coating application, which is subsequently cured. In wet-on-wet, the fiber passes through both the primary and secondary coating applications, then goes to UV curing.

Fiber optic coatings are applied in concentric layers to prevent damage to the fiber during the drawing application and to maximize fiber strength and microbend resistance. Unevenly coated fiber will experience non-uniform forces when the coating expands or contracts, and is susceptible to greater signal attenuation. Under proper drawing and coating processes, the coatings are concentric around the fiber, continuous over the length of the application and have constant thickness.

Fiber optic coatings protect the glass fibers from scratches that could lead to strength degradation. The combination of moisture and scratches accelerates the aging and deterioration of fiber strength. When fiber is subjected to low stresses over a long period, fiber fatigue can occur. Over time or in extreme conditions, these factors combine to cause microscopic flaws in the glass fiber to propagate, which can ultimately result in fiber failure. Three key characteristics of fiber optic waveguides can be affected by environmental conditions: strength, attenuation and resistance to losses caused by microbending. External optical fiber cable jackets and buffer tubes protect glass optical fiber from environmental conditions that can affect the fiber's performance and long-term durability. On the inside, coatings ensure the reliability of the signal being carried and help minimize attenuation due to microbending.

PRACTICAL ISSUES

Cable construction

In practical fibers, the cladding is usually coated with a tough resin coating and an additional buffer layer, which may be further surrounded by a jacket layer, usually plastic. These layers add strength to the fiber but do not contribute to its optical wave guide properties. Rigid fiber assemblies sometimes put light-absorbing ("dark") glass between the fibers, to prevent light that leaks out of one fiber from entering another. This reduces cross-talk between the fibers, or reduces flare in fiber bundle imaging applications.

Modern cables come in a wide variety of sheathings and armor, designed for applications such as direct burial in trenches, high voltage isolation, dual use as power lines, installation in conduit, lashing to aerial telephone poles, submarine installation, and insertion in paved streets. Multi-fiber cable usually uses colored coatings and/or buffers to identify each strand. The cost of small fiber-count pole-mounted cables has greatly decreased due to the high demand for fiber to the home (FTTH) installations in Japan and South Korea.

Fiber cable can be very flexible, but traditional fiber's loss increases greatly if the fiber is bent with a radius smaller than around 30 mm. This creates a problem when the cable is bent around corners or wound around a spool, making FTTX installations more complicated. "Bendable fibers", targeted towards easier installation in home environments, have been standardized as ITU-T G. 657. This type of fiber can be bent with a radius as low as 7. 5 mm without adverse impact. Even more bendable fibers have been developed. Bendable fiber may also be resistant to fiber hacking, in which the signal in a fiber is surreptitiously monitored by bending the fiber and detecting the leakage.

Another important feature of cable is cable's ability to withstand horizontally applied force. It is technically called max tensile strength defining how much force can be applied to the cable during the installation period.

Some fiber optic cable versions are reinforced with aramid yarns or glass yarns as intermediary strength member. In commercial terms, usage of the glass yarns are more cost effective while no loss in mechanical durability of the cable. Glass yarns also protect the cable core against rodents and termites.

Termination and splicing

Optical fibers are connected to terminal equipment by optical fiber connectors. These connectors are usually of a standard type such as FC, SC, ST, LC, MTRJ, or SMA. Optical fibers may be connected to each other by connectors or by splicing, that is, joining two fibers together to form a continuous optical waveguide. The generally accepted splicing method is arc fusion splicing, which melts the fiber ends together with an electric arc. For quicker fastening jobs, a "mechanical splice" is used. Fusion splicing is done with a specialized instrument. The fiber ends are first stripped of their protective polymer coating (as well as the more sturdy outer jacket, if present). The ends are cleaved (cut) with a precision cleaver to make them perpendicular, and are placed into special holders in the fusion splicer. The splice is usually inspected via a magnified viewing screen to check the cleaves before and after the splice. The splicer uses small motors to align the end faces together, and emits a small spark between electrodes at the gap to burn off dust and moisture. Then the splicer generates a larger spark that raises the temperature above the melting point of the glass, fusing the ends together permanently. The location and energy of the spark is carefully controlled so that the molten core and cladding do not mix, and this minimizes optical loss. A splice loss estimate is measured by the splicer, by directing light through the cladding on one side and measuring the light leaking from the cladding on the other side. A splice loss under 0. 1 dB is typical. The complexity of this process makes fiber splicing much more difficult than splicing copper wire.

Mechanical fiber splices are designed to be quicker and easier to install, but there is still the need for stripping, careful cleaning and precision cleaving. The fiber ends are aligned and held together by a precision-made sleeve, often using a clear index-matching gel that enhances the transmission of light across the joint. Such joints typically have higher optical loss and are less robust than fusion splices, especially if the gel is used. All splicing techniques involve installing an enclosure that protects the splice.

Fibers are terminated in connectors that hold the fiber end precisely and securely. A fiber-optic connector is basically a rigid cylindrical barrel surrounded by a sleeve that holds the barrel in its mating socket. The mating mechanism can be push and click, turn and latch (bayonet mount), or screw-in (threaded). The barrel is typically free to move within the sleeve, and may have a key that prevents the barrel and fiber from rotating as the connectors are mated.

A typical connector is installed by preparing the fiber end and inserting it into the rear of the connector body. Quick-set adhesive is usually used to hold the fiber securely, and a strain relief is secured to the rear. Once the adhesive sets, the fiber's end is polished to a mirror finish. Various polish profiles are used, depending on the type of fiber and the application. For single-mode fiber, fiber ends are typically polished with a slight curvature that makes the mated connectors touch only at their cores. This is called a physical contact (PC) polish. The curved surface may be polished at an angle, to make an angled physical contact (APC) connection. Such connections have higher loss than PC connections, but greatly reduced back reflection, because light that reflects from the angled surface leaks out of the fiber core. The resulting signal strength loss is called gap loss. APC fiber ends have low back reflection even when disconnected.

In the 1990s, terminating fiber optic cables was labor-intensive. The number of parts per connector, polishing of the fibers, and the need to oven-bake the epoxy in each connector made terminating fiber optic cables difficult. Today, many connectors types are on the market that offer easier, less labor-intensive ways of terminating cables. Some of the most popular connectors are pre-polished at the factory, and include a gel inside the connector. Those two steps help save money on labor, especially on large projects. A cleave is made at a required length, to get as close to the polished piece already inside the connector. The gel surrounds the point where the two pieces meet inside the connector for very little light loss. Long term performance of the gel is a design consideration, so for the most demanding installations, factory pre-polished pigtails of sufficient length to reach the first fusion splice enclosure is normally the safest approach that minimizes on-site labor.

Free-space coupling

It is often necessary to align an optical fiber with another optical fiber, or with an optoelectronic device such as a light-emitting diode, a laser diode, or a modulator. This can involve either carefully aligning the fiber and placing it in contact with the device, or can use a lens to allow coupling over an air gap. Typically the size of the fiber mode is much larger than the size of the mode in a laser diode or a silicon optical chip. In this case a tapered or lensed fiber is used to match the fiber mode field distribution to that of the other element. The lens on the end of the fiber can be formed using polishing, laser cutting or fusion splicing.

In a laboratory environment, a bare fiber end is coupled using a fiber launch system, which uses a microscope objective lens to focus the light down to a fine point. A precision translation stage (micro-positioning table) is used to move the lens, fiber, or device to allow the coupling efficiency to be optimized. Fibers with a connector on the end make this process much simpler: the connector is simply plugged into a pre-aligned fiberoptic collimator, which contains a lens that is either accurately positioned with respect to the fiber, or is adjustable. To achieve the best injection efficiency into single-mode fiber, the direction, position, size and divergence of the beam must all be optimized. With good beams, 70 to 90% coupling efficiency can be achieved.

With properly polished single-mode fibers, the emitted beam has an almost perfect Gaussian shape—even in the far field—if a good lens is used. The lens needs to be large enough to support the full numerical aperture of the fiber, and must not introduce aberrations in the beam. Aspheric lenses are typically used.

Fiber fuse

At high optical intensities, above 2 megawatts per square centimeter, when a fiber is subjected to a shock or is otherwise suddenly damaged, a fiber fuse can occur. The reflection from the damage vaporizes the fiber immediately before the break, and this new defect remains reflective so that the damage propagates back toward the transmitter at 1–3 meters per second (4–11 km/h, 2–8 mph). The open fiber control system, which ensures laser eye safety in the event of a broken fiber, can also effectively halt propagation of the fiber fuse. In situations, such as undersea cables, where high power levels might be used without the need for open fiber control, a "fiber fuse" protection device at the transmitter can break the circuit to keep damage to a minimum.

CHROMATIC DISPERSION

The refractive index of fibers varies slightly with the frequency of light, and light sources are not perfectly monochromatic. Modulation of the light source to transmit a signal also slightly widens the frequency band of the transmitted light. This has the effect that, over long distances and at high modulation speeds, the different frequencies of light can take different times to arrive at the receiver, ultimately making the signal impossible to discern, and requiring extra repeaters. This problem can be overcome in a number of ways, including the use of a relatively short length of fiber that has the opposite refractive index gradient.

Ethernet

Ethernet is a family of computer networking technologies commonly used in local area networks (LAN), metropolitan area networks (MAN) and wide area networks (WAN). It was commercially introduced in 1980 and first standardized in 1983 as IEEE 802. 3, and has since been refined to support higher bit rates and longer link distances. Over time, Ethernet has largely replaced competing wired LAN technologies such as token ring, FDDI and ARCNET.

The original 10BASE5 Ethernet uses coaxial cable as a shared medium, while the newer Ethernet variants use twisted pair and fiber optic links in conjunction with hubs or switches. Over the course of its history, Ethernet data transfer rates have been increased from the original 2. 94 megabits per second (Mbit/s) to the latest 100 gigabits per second (Gbit/s). The Ethernet standards comprise several wiring and signaling variants of the OSI physical layer in use with Ethernet.

Systems communicating over Ethernet divide a stream of data into shorter pieces called frames. Each frame contains source and destination addresses, and error-checking data so that damaged frames can be detected and discarded; most often, higher-layer protocols trigger retransmission of lost frames. As per the OSI model, Ethernet provides services up to and including the data link layer.

Since its commercial release, Ethernet has retained a good degree of backward compatibility. Features such as the 48-bit MAC address and Ethernet frame format have influenced other networking protocols. The primary alternative for some uses of contemporary LANs is Wi-Fi, a wireless protocol standardized as IEEE 802. 11.

History

Ethernet was developed at Xerox PARC between 1973 and 1974. It was inspired by ALOHAnet, which Robert Metcalfe had studied as part of his PhD dissertation. The idea was first documented in a memo that Metcalfe wrote on May 22, 1973, where he named it after the disproven luminiferous ether as an "omnipresent, completely-passive medium for the propagation of electromagnetic waves". In 1975, Xerox filed a patent application listing Metcalfe, David Boggs, Chuck Thacker, and Butler Lampson as inventors. In 1976, after the system was deployed at PARC, Metcalfe and Boggs published a seminal paper.

Metcalfe left Xerox in June 1979 to form 3Com. He convinced Digital Equipment Corporation (DEC), Intel, and Xerox to work together to promote Ethernet as a standard. The so-called "DIX" standard, for "Digital/Intel/Xerox", specified 10 Mbit/s Ethernet, with 48-bit destination and source addresses and a global 16-bit Ethertype-type field. It was published on September 30, 1980 as "The Ethernet, A Local Area Network. Data Link Layer and Physical Layer Specifications". Version 2 was published in November, 1982 and defines what has become known as Ethernet II. Formal standardization efforts proceeded at the same time and resulted in the publication of IEEE 802. 3 on June 23, 1983. Ethernet initially competed with two largely proprietary systems, Token Ring and Token Bus. Because Ethernet was able to adapt to market realities and shift to inexpensive and ubiquitous twisted pair wiring, these proprietary protocols soon found themselves competing in a market inundated by Ethernet products, and, by the end of the 1980s, Ethernet was clearly the dominant network technology. In the process, 3Com became a major company. 3Com shipped its first 10 Mbit/s Ethernet 3C100 NIC in March 1981, and that year started selling adapters for PDP-11s and VAXes, as well as Multibus-based Intel and Sun Microsystems computers. :9 This was followed quickly by DEC's Unibus to Ethernet adapter, which DEC sold and used internally to build its own corporate network, which reached over 10, 000 nodes by 1986, making it one of the largest computer networks in the world at that time. An Ethernet adapter card for the IBM PC was released in 1982, and, by 1985, 3Com had sold 100, 000. Parallel port based Ethernet adapters were produced for a time, with drivers for DOS and Windows. By the early 1990s, Ethernet became so prevalent that it was a must-have feature for modern computers, and Ethernet ports began to appear on some PCs and most workstations. This process was greatly sped up with the introduction of 10BASE-T and its relatively small modular connector, at which point Ethernet ports appeared even on low-end motherboards.

Since then, Ethernet technology has evolved to meet new bandwidth and market requirements. In addition to computers, Ethernet is now used to interconnect appliances and other personal devices. It is used in industrial applications and is quickly replacing legacy data transmission systems in the world's telecommunications networks. By 2010, the market for Ethernet equipment amounted to over $16 billion per year.

Standardization

In February 1980, the Institute of Electrical and Electronics Engineers (IEEE) started project 802 to standardize local area networks (LAN). The "DIX-group" with Gary Robinson (DEC), Phil Arst (Intel), and Bob Printis (Xerox) submitted the so-called "Blue Book" CSMA/CD specification as a candidate for the LAN specification. In addition to CSMA/CD, Token Ring (supported by IBM) and Token Bus (selected and henceforward supported by General Motors) were also considered as candidates for a LAN standard. Competing proposals and broad interest in the initiative led to strong disagreement over which technology to standardize. In December 1980, the group was split into three subgroups, and standardization proceeded separately for each proposal.

Delays in the standards process put at risk the market introduction of the Xerox Star workstation and 3Com's Ethernet LAN products. With such business implications in mind, David Liddle (General Manager, Xerox Office Systems) and Metcalfe (3Com) strongly supported a proposal of Fritz Röscheisen (Siemens Private Networks) for an alliance in the emerging office communication market, including Siemens' support for the international standardization of Ethernet (April 10, 1981). Ingrid Fromm, Siemens' representative to IEEE 802, quickly achieved broader support for Ethernet beyond IEEE by the establishment of a competing Task Group "Local Networks" within the European standards body ECMA TC24. On March 1982, ECMA TC24 with its corporate members reached an agreement on a standard for CSMA/CD based on the IEEE 802 draft. :8 Because the DIX proposal was most technically complete and because of the speedy action taken by ECMA which decisively contributed to the conciliation of opinions within IEEE, the IEEE 802. 3 CSMA/CD standard was approved in December 1982. IEEE published the 802. 3 standard as a draft in 1983 and as a standard in 1985.

Approval of Ethernet on the international level was achieved by a similar, cross-partisan action with Fromm as the liaison officer working to integrate with International Electrotechnical Commission (IEC) Technical Committee 83 (TC83) and International Organization for Standardization (ISO) Technical Committee 97 Sub Committee 6 (TC97SC6). The ISO 8802-3 standard was published in 1989.

Evolution

Ethernet evolved to include higher bandwidth, improved media access control methods, and different physical media. The coaxial cable was replaced with point-to-point links connected by Ethernet repeaters or switches.

Ethernet stations communicate by sending each other data packets: blocks of data individually sent and delivered. As with other IEEE 802 LANs, each Ethernet station is given a 48-bit MAC address. The MAC addresses are used to specify both the destination and the source of each data packet. Ethernet establishes link level connections, which can be defined using both the destination and source addresses. On reception of a transmission, the receiver uses the destination address to determine whether the transmission is relevant to the station or should be ignored. Network interfaces normally do not accept packets addressed to other Ethernet stations. Adapters come programmed with a globally unique address.

An EtherType field in each frame is used by the operating system on the receiving station to select the appropriate protocol module (e. g., an Internet Protocol version such as IPv4). Ethernet frames are said to be self-identifying, because of the frame type. Self-identifying frames make it possible to intermix multiple protocols on the same physical network and allow a single computer to use multiple protocols together. Despite the evolution of Ethernet technology, all generations of Ethernet (excluding early experimental versions) use the same frame formats. Mixed-speed networks can be built using Ethernet switches and repeaters supporting the desired Ethernet variants. Due to the ubiquity of Ethernet, the ever-decreasing cost of the hardware needed to support it, and the reduced panel space needed by twisted pair Ethernet, most manufacturers now build Ethernet interfaces directly into PC motherboards, eliminating the need for installation of a separate network card.

SHARED MEDIA

Ethernet was originally based on the idea of computers communicating over a shared coaxial cable acting as a broadcast transmission medium. The methods used were similar to those used in radio systems, with the common cable providing the communication channel likened to the Luminiferous aether in 19th century physics, and it was from this reference that the name "Ethernet" was derived.

Original Ethernet's shared coaxial cable (the shared medium) traversed a building or campus to every attached machine. A scheme known as carrier sense multiple access with collision detection (CSMA/CD) governed the way the computers shared the channel. This scheme was simpler than the competing token ring or token bus technologies. Computers are connected to an Attachment Unit Interface (AUI) transceiver, which is in turn connected to the cable (with thin Ethernet the transceiver is integrated into the network adapter). While a simple passive wire is highly reliable for small networks, it is not reliable for large extended networks, where damage to the wire in a single place, or a single bad connector, can make the whole Ethernet segment unusable.

Through the first half of the 1980s, Ethernet's 10BASE5 implementation used a coaxial cable 0. 375 inches (9. 5 mm) in diameter, later called "thick Ethernet" or "thicknet". Its successor, 10BASE2, called "thin Ethernet" or "thinnet", used the RG-58 coaxial cable. The emphasis was on making installation of the cable easier and less costly. :57

Since all communications happen on the same wire, any information sent by one computer is received by all, even if that information is intended for just one destination. The network interface card interrupts the CPU only when applicable packets are received: The card ignores information not addressed to it. Use of a single cable also means that the bandwidth is shared, such that, for example, available bandwidth to each device is halved when two stations are simultaneously active.

Collisions happen when two stations attempt to transmit at the same time. They corrupt transmitted data and require stations to retransmit. The lost data and retransmissions reduce throughput. In the worst case where multiple active hosts connected with maximum allowed cable length attempt to transmit many short frames, excessive collisions can reduce throughput dramatically. However, a Xerox report in 1980 studied performance of an existing Ethernet installation under both normal and artificially generated heavy load. The report claims that 98% throughput on the LAN was observed. This is in contrast with token passing LANs (token ring, token bus), all of which suffer throughput degradation as each new node comes into the LAN, due to token waits. This report was controversial, as modeling showed that collision-based networks theoretically became unstable under loads as low as 37% of nominal capacity. Many early researchers failed to understand these results. Performance on real networks is significantly better.

In a modern Ethernet, the stations do not all share one channel through a shared cable or a simple repeater hub; instead, each station communicates with a switch, which in turn forwards that traffic to the destination station. In this topology, collisions are only possible if station and switch attempt to communicate with each other at the same time, and collisions are limited to this link. Furthermore, the 10BASE-T standard introduced a full duplex mode of operation which became common with Fast Ethernet and the de facto standard with Gigabit Ethernet. In full duplex, switch and station can send and receive simultaneously, and therefore modern Ethernets are completely collision-free.

Repeaters and hubs

For signal degradation and timing reasons, coaxial Ethernet segments have a restricted size. Somewhat larger networks can be built by using an Ethernet repeater. Early repeaters had only two ports, allowing, at most, a doubling of network size. Once repeaters with more than two ports became available, it was possible to wire the network in a star topology. Early experiments with star topologies (called "Fibernet") using optical fiber were published by 1978.

Shared cable Ethernet is always hard to install in offices because its bus topology is in conflict with the star topology cable plans designed into buildings for telephony. Modifying Ethernet to conform to twisted pair telephone wiring already installed in commercial buildings provided another opportunity to lower costs, expand the installed base, and leverage building design, and, thus, twisted-pair Ethernet was the next logical development in the mid-1980s.

Ethernet on unshielded twisted-pair cables (UTP) began with StarLAN at 1 Mbit/s in the mid-1980s. In 1987 SynOptics introduced the first twisted-pair Ethernet at 10 Mbit/s in a star-wired cabling topology with a central hub, later called LattisNet. These evolved into 10BASE-T, which was designed for point-to-point links only, and all termination was built into the device. This changed repeaters from a specialist device used at the center of large networks to a device that every twisted pair-based network with more than two machines had to use. The tree structure that resulted from this made Ethernet networks easier to maintain by preventing most faults with one peer or its associated cable from affecting other devices on the network.

Despite the physical star topology and the presence of separate transmit and receive channels in the twisted pair and fiber media, repeater-based Ethernet networks still use half-duplex and CSMA/CD, with only minimal activity by the repeater, primarily generation of the jam signal in dealing with packet collisions. Every packet is sent to every other port on the repeater, so bandwidth and security problems are not addressed. The total throughput of the repeater is limited to that of a single link, and all links must operate at the same speed.

Bridging and switching

While repeaters can isolate some aspects of Ethernet segments, such as cable breakages, they still forward all traffic to all Ethernet devices. This creates practical limits on how many machines can communicate on an Ethernet network. The entire network is one collision domain, and all hosts have to be able to detect collisions anywhere on the network. This limits the number of repeaters between the farthest nodes. Segments joined by repeaters have to all operate at the same speed, making phased-in upgrades impossible.

To alleviate these problems, bridging was created to communicate at the data link layer while isolating the physical layer. With bridging, only well-formed Ethernet packets are forwarded from one Ethernet segment to another; collisions and packet errors are isolated. At initial startup, Ethernet bridges (and switches) work somewhat like Ethernet repeaters, passing all traffic between segments. By observing the source addresses of incoming frames, the bridge then builds an address table associating addresses to segments. Once an address is learned, the bridge forwards network traffic destined for that address only to the associated segment, improving overall performance. Broadcast traffic is still forwarded to all network segments. Bridges also overcome the limits on total segments between two hosts and allow the mixing of speeds, both of which are critical to deployment of Fast Ethernet. In 1989, the networking company Kalpana (acquired by Cisco Systems, Inc. in 1994) introduced their EtherSwitch, the first Ethernet switch. This works somewhat differently from an Ethernet bridge, where only the header of the incoming packet is examined before it is either dropped or forwarded to another segment. This greatly reduces the forwarding latency and the processing load on the network device. One drawback of this cut-through switching method is that packets that have been corrupted are still propagated through the network, so a jabbering station can continue to disrupt the entire network. The eventual remedy for this was a return to the original store and forward approach of bridging, where the packet would be read into a buffer on the switch in its entirety, verified against its checksum and then forwarded, but using more powerful application-specific integrated circuits. Hence, the bridging is then done in hardware, allowing packets to be forwarded at full wire speed.

When a twisted pair or fiber link segment is used and neither end is connected to a repeater, full-duplex Ethernet becomes possible over that segment. In full-duplex mode, both devices can transmit and receive to and from each other at the same time, and there is no collision domain. This doubles the aggregate bandwidth of the link and is sometimes advertised as double the link speed (for example, 200 Mbit/s). The elimination of the collision domain for these connections also means that all the link's bandwidth can be used by the two devices on that segment and that segment length is not limited by the need for correct collision detection.

Since packets are typically delivered only to the port they are intended for, traffic on a switched Ethernet is less public than on shared-medium Ethernet. Despite this, switched Ethernet should still be regarded as an insecure network technology, because it is easy to subvert switched Ethernet systems by means such as ARP spoofing and MAC flooding.

The bandwidth advantages, the improved isolation of devices from each other, the ability to easily mix different speeds of devices and the elimination of the chaining limits inherent in non-switched Ethernet have made switched Ethernet the dominant network technology.

ADVANCED NETWORKING

Simple switched Ethernet networks, while a great improvement over repeater-based Ethernet, suffer from single points of failure, attacks that trick switches or hosts into sending data to a machine even if it is not intended for it, scalability and security issues with regard to switching loops, broadcast radiation and multicast traffic, and bandwidth choke points where a lot of traffic is forced down a single link.

Advanced networking features in switches use shortest path bridging (SPB) or the spanning-tree protocol (STP) to maintain a loop-free, meshed network, allowing physical loops for redundancy (STP) or load-balancing (SPB). Advanced networking features also ensure port security, provide protection features such as MAC lockdown and broadcast radiation filtering, use virtual LANs to keep different classes of users separate while using the same physical infrastructure, employ multilayer switching to route between different classes, and use link aggregation to add bandwidth to overloaded links and to provide some redundancy.

IEEE 802. 1aq (shortest path bridging) includes the use of the link-state routing protocol IS-IS to allow larger networks with shortest path routes between devices. In 2012, it was stated by David Allan and Nigel Bragg, in 802. 1aq Shortest Path Bridging Design and Evolution: The Architect's Perspective that shortest path bridging is one of the most significant enhancements in Ethernet's history. Ethernet has replaced InfiniBand as the most popular system interconnect of TOP500 supercomputers.

ERROR CONDITIONS

Jabber

A node that is sending longer than the maximum transmission window for an Ethernet packet is considered to be jabbering. Depending on the physical topology, jabber detection and remedy differ somewhat.

- An MAU is required to detect and stop abnormally long transmission from the DTE in order to prevent permanent network disruption.
- On an electrically shared medium (10BASE5, 10BASE2, 1BASE5), jabber can only be detected by each end node, stopping reception. No further remedy is possible.
- A repeater/repeater hub uses a jabber timer that ends retransmission to the other ports when it expires. The timer runs for 40, 000 to 75, 000 bit times for 10 and 100 Mbit/s, 25, 000 to 50, 000 bit times for 1 Mbit/s, and 80, 000 to 150, 000 bit times for 1 Gbit/s. Jabbering ports are partitioned off the network until a carrier is no longer detected.
- End nodes utilizing a MAC layer will usually detect an oversized Ethernet frame and cease receiving. A bridge/switch will not forward the frame.
- A non-uniform frame size configuration in the network using jumbo frames may be detected as jabber by end nodes.
- A packet detected as jabber by an upstream repeater and subsequently cut off has an invalid frame check sequence and is dropped.

Runt frames

- Runts are packets or frames smaller than the minimum allowed size. They are dropped and not propagated.

Varieties of Ethernet

The Ethernet physical layer evolved over a considerable time span and encompasses coaxial, twisted pair and fiber-optic physical media interfaces, with speeds from 10 Mbit/s to 100 Gbit/s, with 400 Gbit/s expected by 2018. The first introduction of twisted-pair CSMA/CD was StarLAN, standardized as 802. 3 1BASE5; while 1BASE5 had little market penetration, it defined the physical apparatus (wire, plug/jack, pin-out, and wiring plan) that would be carried over to 10BASE-T.

The most common forms used are 10BASE-T, 100BASE-TX, and 1000BASE-T. All three utilize twisted pair cables and 8P8C modular connectors. They run at 10 Mbit/s, 100 Mbit/s, and 1 Gbit/s, respectively. Fiber optic variants of Ethernet offer high performance, better electrical isolation and longer distance (tens of kilometers with some versions). In general, network protocol stack software will work similarly on all varieties.

Frame structure

In IEEE 802. 3, a datagram is called a packet or frame. Packet is used to describe the overall transmission unit and includes the preamble, start frame delimiter (SFD) and carrier extension (if present). The frame begins after the start frame delimiter with a frame header featuring source and destination MAC addresses and a field giving either the protocol type for the payload protocol or the length of the payload. The middle section of the frame consists of payload data including any headers for other protocols (for example, Internet Protocol) carried in the frame. The frame ends with a 32-bit cyclic redundancy check, which is used to detect corruption of data in transit. :sections 3. 1. 1 and 3. 2 Notably, Ethernet packets have no time-to-live field, leading to possible problems in the presence of a switching loop.

Autonegotiation

Autonegotiation is the procedure by which two connected devices choose common transmission parameters, e. g. speed and duplex mode. Autonegotiation is an optional feature, first introduced with 100BASE-TX, while it is also backward compatible with 10BASE-T. Autonegotiation is mandatory for 1000BASE-T.

Network Interface Card

A network interface controller (NIC, also known as a network interface card, network adapter, LAN adapter or physical network interface, and by similar terms) is a computer hardware component that connects a computer to a computer network.

Early network interface controllers were commonly implemented on expansion cards that plugged into a computer bus. The low cost and ubiquity of the Ethernet standard means that most newer computers have a network interface built into the motherboard.

Modern network interface controllers offer advanced features such as interrupt and DMA interfaces to the host processors, support for multiple receive and transmit queues, partitioning into multiple logical interfaces, and on-controller network traffic processing such as the TCP offload engine.

Purpose

The network controller implements the electronic circuitry required to communicate using a specific physical layer and data link layer standard such as Ethernet, Fibre Channel, Wi-Fi or Token Ring. This provides a base for a full network protocol stack, allowing communication among small groups of computers on the same local area network (LAN) and large-scale network communications through routable protocols, such as Internet Protocol (IP).

The NIC allows computers to communicate over a computer network, either by using cables or wirelessly. The NIC is both a physical layer and data link layer device, as it provides physical access to a networking medium and, for IEEE 802 and similar networks, provides a low-level addressing system through the use of MAC addresses that are uniquely assigned to network interfaces.

Although other network technologies exist, IEEE 802 networks including the Ethernet variants have achieved near-ubiquity since the mid-1990s.

Implementation

Whereas network controllers used to operate on expansion cards that plugged into a computer bus, the low cost and ubiquity of the Ethernet standard means that most new computers have a network interface built into the motherboard. Newer server motherboards may even have dual network interfaces built-in. The Ethernet capabilities are either integrated into the motherboard chipset or implemented via a low-cost dedicated Ethernet chip, connected through the PCI (or the newer PCI Express) bus. A separate network card is not required unless additional interfaces are needed or some other type of network is used.

The NIC may use one or more of the following techniques to indicate the availability of packets to transfer:

- Polling is where the CPU examines the status of the peripheral under program control.
- Interrupt-driven I/O is where the peripheral alerts the CPU that it is ready to transfer data.

Also, NICs may use one or more of the following techniques to transfer packet data:

- Programmed input/output is where the CPU moves the data to or from the NIC to memory.

- Direct memory access (DMA) is where some other device other than the CPU assumes control of the system bus to move data to or from the NIC to memory. This removes load from the CPU but requires more logic on the card. In addition, a packet buffer on the NIC may not be required and latency can be reduced. There are two types of DMA: third-party DMA in which a DMA controller other than the NIC performs transfers, and bus mastering where the NIC itself performs transfers.

An Ethernet network controller typically has an 8P8C socket where the network cable is connected. Older NICs also supplied BNC, or AUI connections. A few LEDs inform the user of whether the network is active, and whether or not data transmission occurs. Ethernet network controllers typically support 10 Mbit/s Ethernet, 100 Mbit/s Ethernet, and 1000 Mbit/s Ethernet varieties. Such controllers are designated as "10/100/1000", meaning that they can support a notional maximum transfer rate of 10, 100 or 1000 Mbit/s. 10 Gigabit Ethernet NICs are also available, and, as of November 2014, are beginning to be available on computer motherboards.

PERFORMANCE AND ADVANCED FUNCTIONALITY

Multiqueue NICs provide multiple transmit and receive queues, allowing packets received by the NIC to be assigned to one of its receive queues. Each receive queue is assigned to a separate interrupt; by routing each of those interrupts to different CPUs/cores, processing of the interrupt requests triggered by the network traffic received by a single NIC can be distributed among multiple cores, bringing additional performance improvements in interrupt handling. Usually, a NIC distributes incoming traffic between the receive queues using a hash function, while separate interrupts can be routed to different CPUs/cores either automatically by the operating system, or manually by configuring the IRQ affinity.

The hardware-based distribution of the interrupts, described above, is referred to as receive-side scaling (RSS). :82 Purely software implementations also exist, such as the receive packet steering (RPS) and receive flow steering (RFS). Further performance improvements can be achieved by routing the interrupt requests to the CPUs/cores executing the applications which are actually the ultimate destinations for network packets that generated the interrupts. That way, taking the application locality into account results in higher overall performance, reduced latency and better hardware utilization, resulting from the higher utilization of CPU caches and fewer required context switches. Examples of such implementations are the RFS and Intel Flow Director.

With multiqueue NICs, additional performance improvements can be achieved by distributing outgoing traffic among different transmit queues. By assigning different transmit queues to different CPUs/cores, various operating system's internal contentions can be avoided; this approach is usually referred to as transmit packet steering (XPS).

Some NICs support transmit and receive queues without kernel support allowing the NIC to execute even when the functionality of the operating system of a critical system has been severely compromised. Those NICs support:

1. Accessing local and remote memory without involving the remote CPU.
2. Accessing local and remote I/O devices without involving local/remote CPU. This capability is supported by device-to-device communication over the I/O bus, present in switched-based I/O interconnects.
3. Controlling access to local resources such as control registers and memory.

Some products feature NIC partitioning (NPAR, also known as port partitioning) that uses SR-IOV to divide a single 10 Gigabit Ethernet NIC into multiple discrete virtual NICs with dedicated bandwidth, which are presented to the firmware and operating system as separate PCI device functions. TCP offload engine is a technology used in some NICs to offload processing of the entire TCP/IP stack to the network controller. It is primarily used with high-speed network interfaces, such as Gigabit Ethernet and 10 Gigabit Ethernet, for which the processing overhead of the network stack becomes significant.

Some NICs offer integrated field-programmable gate arrays (FPGAs) for user-programmable processing of network traffic before it reaches the host computer, allowing for significantly reduced latencies in time-sensitive workloads. Moreover, some NICs offer complete low-latency TCP/IP stacks running on integrated FPGAs in combination with userspace libraries that intercept networking operations usually performed by the operating system kernel; Solarflare's open-source OpenOnload network stack that runs on Linux is an example. This kind of functionality is usually referred to as user-level networking.

Hub

Hub is a concept in network science which refers to a node with a number of links that greatly exceeds the average. Emergence of hubs is a consequence of a scale-free property of networks. While hubs cannot be observed in a random network, they are expected to emerge in scale- free networks. Uprise of hubs in scale-free networks is associated with power- law distribution. Hubs have a significant impact on the network topology. Hubs can be found in many real networks, such as Brain Network or Internet.

Definition

A hub is a component of a network with a high- degree node. Hubs have a significantly larger number of links in comparison with other nodes in the network. The number of links (degrees) for a hub in a scale-free network is much higher than for the biggest node in a random network, keeping the size N of the network and average degree <k> constant. The existence of hubs is the biggest difference between random networks and scale-free networks. In random networks the degree k is comparable for every node and therefore it is not possible for hubs to emerge. In scale-free networks a few nodes (hubs) have a high degree k while the other nodes have a small number of links.

EMERGENCE

Emergence of hubs can be explained by difference between scale-free networks and random networks. Scale-free networks (Barabási–Albert model) are different from random networks (Erdős–Rényi model) in two aspects (a) growth, (b) preferential attachment.

- (a) Scale-free networks assume a continuous growth of the number of nodes N, compared to random networks which assume a fixed number of nodes. In scale-free networks the degree of the largest hub rises polynomially with the size of the network. Therefore, the degree of a hub can be high in a scale-free network. In random networks the degree of the largest node rises logaritmically (or slower) with N, thus the hub number will be small even in a very large network.
- (b) A new node in a scale-free network has a tendency to link to a node with a higher degree, compared to a new node in a random network which links itself to a random node. This process is called preferential attachment. The tendency of a new node to link to a node with a high degree k is characterized by power- law distribution (also known as rich-gets-richer process). This idea was introduced by Vilfredo Pareto and it explained why a small percentage of the population earns most of the money. This process is present in networks as well, for example 80 percent of web links point to 15 percent of webpages. The emergence of scale-free networks is not typical only of networks created by human action, but also of such networks as metabolic networks or illness networks. This phenomenon may be explained by the example of hubs on the World Wide Web such as Facebook or Google. These webpages are very well known and therefore the tendency of other webpages pointing to them is much higher than linking to random small webpages.

Emergence of hubs in networks is also related to time. In scale-free networks, nodes which emerged earlier have a higher chance of becoming a hub than latecomers. This phenomenon is called first-mover advantage and it explains why some nodes become hubs and some do not. However, in a real network, the time of emergence is not the only factor that influences the size of the hub. For example, Facebook emerged 8 years later after Google became the largest hub on the World Wide Web and yet in 2011 Facebook became the largest hub of WWW. Therefore, in real networks the growth and the size of a hub depends also on various attributes such as popularity, quality or the aging of a node.

Attributes

There are several attributes of Hubs in a scale-free networks. Shortening the path lengths in a network. The more observable hubs are in a network, the more they shrink a distances between nodes. In a scale-free networks hubs serve as bridges between the small degree nodes. Since the distance of two random nodes in a scale-free networks is small, we refer to scale-free networks as "small" or "ultra small". While a difference between path distance in a various small networks may not be noticeable, the difference in a path distance between large random network and scale-free network is remarkable.

Aging of hubs (nodes)

The phenomenon present in a real networks, when older hubs are shadowed in a network. This phenomenon is responsible for changes in evolution and topology of networks. The example of aging phenomenon may be the case of Facebook overtaking the position of the largest hub on the Web where Google was the largest node since 2000.

Robustness and Attack Tolerance

During the random failure of nodes or targeted attack hubs are key components of the network. During the random failure of nodes in network hubs are responsible for exceptional robustness of network. The chance that a random failure would delete the hub is very small, because hubs coexists with a large number of small degree nodes. The removal of small degree nodes does not have a large effect on integrity of network. Even though the random removal would hit the hub, the chance of fragmantation of network is very small because the remaining hubs would hold the network together. In this case, hubs are the strength of a scale-free networks.

During the targeted attack on hubs, the integrity of network would fall apart relatively fast. Since small nodes are predominantly linked to hubs the targeted attack on the largest hubs would result in destruction of network in a short period of time. The financial market meltdown in 2008 is an example of such a network failure, when bankrupt of the largest players (hubs) led to a continuous breakdown of the whole system. On the other hand, it may has a possitive effect when removing hubs in a terrorist network may destroy the whole terrorist group. The attack tolerance of network may be increased by connecting its peripheral nodes, however it requires to double the number of links.

Degree correlation

The perfect degree correlation means that each degree-k node is connected only to the same degree-k nodes. Such connectivity of nodes decide the topology of networks, which has an effect on robustness of network, the attribute discussed above. If the number of links between the hubs is the same as would be expected by chance, we refer to this network as Neutral Network. If hubs tend to connected to each other while avoiding linking to small-degree nodes we refer to this network as Assortative Network. This network is relatively resistant against attacks, because hubs form a core group, which is more reduntant against hub removal. If hubs avoid connecting to each other while linking to small-degree nodes, we refer to this network as Disassortative Network. This network has a hub-and-spoke character. Therefore, if we remove the hub in this type of network, it may damage or destroy the whole network.

Spreading phenomenon

The hubs are also responsible for effective spreading of material on network. In an analysis of disease spreading or information flow, hubs are referred to as super-spreaders. Super-spreaders may have a positive impact, such as effective information flow, but also devastating in a case of epidemic spreading such as H1N1 or AIDS. The mathematical models such as model of H1H1 Epidemic prediction may allow us to predict the spread of diseases based on human mobility networks, infectiousness, or social interactions among humans. Hubs are also important in the eradication of disease. In a scale-free network hubs are most likely to be infected, because of the large number of connections they have. After the hub is infected, it broadcasts the disease to the nodes it is linked to. Therefore, the selective immunization of hubs may be the cost- effective strategy in eradication of spreading disease.

Router

A router is a networking device that forwards data packets between computer networks. Routers perform the traffic directing functions on the Internet. A data packet is typically forwarded from one router to another router through the networks that constitute the internetwork until it reaches its destination node.

A router is connected to two or more data lines from different networks. When a data packet comes in on one of the lines, the router reads the address information in the packet to determine the ultimate destination. Then, using information in its routing table or routing policy, it directs the packet to the next network on its journey. This creates an overlay internetwork.

The most familiar type of routers are home and small office routers that simply pass IP packets between the home computers and the Internet. An example of a router would be the owner's cable or DSL router, which connects to the Internet through an Internet service provider (ISP). More sophisticated routers, such as enterprise routers, connect large business or ISP networks up to the powerful core routers that forward data at high speed along the optical fiber lines of the Internet backbone. Though routers are typically dedicated hardware devices, software-based routers also exist.

Applications

When multiple routers are used in interconnected networks, the routers can exchange information about destination addresses using a dynamic routing protocol. Each router builds up a routing table listing the preferred routes between any two systems on the interconnected networks.

A router may have interfaces for different physical types of network connections, such as copper cables, fibre optic, or wireless transmission. Its firmware can also support different networking communications protocol standards. Each network interface is used by this specialized computer software to enable data packets to be forwarded from one protocol transmission system to another. Routers may also be used to connect two or more logical groups of computer devices known as subnets, each with a different network prefix. The network prefixes recorded in the routing table do not necessarily map directly to the physical interface connections.

A router has two stages of operation called planes:

- Control plane: A router maintains a routing table that lists which route should be used to forward a data packet, and through which physical interface connection. It does this using internal pre-configured directives, called static routes, or by learning routes using a dynamic routing protocol. Static and dynamic routes are stored in the Routing Information Base (RIB). The control-plane logic then strips non-essential directives from the RIB and builds a Forwarding Information Base (FIB) to be used by the forwarding-plane.
- Forwarding plane: The router forwards data packets between incoming and outgoing interface connections. It routes them to the correct network type using information that the packet header contains. It uses data recorded in the routing table control plane.

Routers may provide connectivity within enterprises, between enterprises and the Internet, or between internet service providers' (ISPs) networks. The largest routers (such as the Cisco CRS-1 or Juniper T1600) interconnect the various ISPs, or may be used in large enterprise networks. Smaller routers usually provide connectivity for typical home and office networks. Other networking solutions may be provided by a backbone Wireless Distribution System (WDS), which avoids the costs of introducing networking cables into buildings.

All sizes of routers may be found inside enterprises. The most powerful routers are usually found in ISPs, academic and research facilities. Large businesses may also need more powerful routers to cope with ever increasing demands of intranet data traffic. A three-layer model is in common use, not all of which need be present in smaller networks.

Access

Access routers, including 'small office/home office' (SOHO) models, are located at customer sites such as branch offices that do not need hierarchical routing of their own. Typically, they are optimized for low cost. Some SOHO routers are capable of running alternative free Linux-based firmwares like Tomato, OpenWrt or DD-WRT.

Distribution

Distribution routers aggregate traffic from multiple access routers, either at the same site, or to collect the data streams from multiple sites to a major enterprise location. Distribution routers are often responsible for enforcing quality of service across a wide area network (WAN), so they may have considerable memory installed, multiple WAN interface connections, and substantial onboard data processing routines. They may also provide connectivity to groups of file servers or other external networks.

Security

External networks must be carefully considered as part of the overall security strategy. A router may include a firewall, VPN handling, and other security functions, or these may be handled by separate devices. Many companies produced security-oriented routers, including Cisco PIX series, Cisco Meraki MX series, Juniper NetScreen, and WatchGuard. Routers also commonly perform network address translation, (which allows multiple devices on a network to share a single public IP address) and stateful packet inspection. Some experts argue that open source routers are more secure and reliable than closed source routers because open source routers allow mistakes to be quickly found and corrected.

Core

In enterprises, a core router may provide a "collapsed backbone" interconnecting the distribution tier routers from multiple buildings of a campus, or large enterprise locations. They tend to be optimized for high bandwidth, but lack some of the features of edge routers.

Internet connectivity and internal use

Routers intended for ISP and major enterprise connectivity usually exchange routing information using the Border Gateway Protocol (BGP). RFC 4098 standard defines the types of BGP routers according to their functions:

- Edge router: Also called a provider edge router, is placed at the edge of an ISP network. The router uses External BGP to EBGP routers in other ISPs, or a large enterprise Autonomous System.

- Subscriber edge router: Also called a Customer Edge router, is located at the edge of the subscriber's network, it also uses EBGP to its provider's Autonomous System. It is typically used in an (enterprise) organization.
- Inter-provider border router: Interconnecting ISPs, is a BGP router that maintains BGP sessions with other BGP routers in ISP Autonomous Systems.
- Core router: A core router resides within an Autonomous System as a back bone to carry traffic between edge routers.
- Within an ISP: In the ISP's Autonomous System, a router uses internal BGP to communicate with other ISP edge routers, other intranet core routers, or the ISP's intranet provider border routers.
- "Internet backbone:" The Internet no longer has a clearly identifiable backbone, unlike its predecessor networks. See default-free zone (DFZ). The major ISPs' system routers make up what could be considered to be the current Internet backbone core. ISPs operate all four types of the BGP routers described here. An ISP "core" router is used to interconnect its edge and border routers. Core routers may also have specialized functions in virtual private networks based on a combination of BGP and Multi-Protocol Label Switching protocols.
- Port forwarding: Routers are also used for port forwarding between private Internet-connected servers.
- Voice/Data/Fax/Video Processing Routers: Commonly referred to as access servers or gateways, these devices are used to route and process voice, data, video and fax traffic on the Internet. Since 2005, most long-distance phone calls have been processed as IP traffic (VOIP) through a voice gateway. Use of access server type routers expanded with the advent of the Internet, first with dial-up access and another resurgence with voice phone service.
- Larger networks commonly use multilayer switches, with layer 3 devices being used to simply interconnect multiple subnets within the same security zone, and higher layer switches when filtering, translation, load balancing or other higher level functions are required, especially between zones.

HISTORICAL AND TECHNICAL INFORMATION

The very first device that had fundamentally the same functionality as a router does today was the Interface Message Processor (IMP); IMPs were the devices that made up the ARPANET, the first TCP/IP network. The idea for a router (called "gateways" at the time) initially came about through an international group of computer networking researchers called the International Network Working Group (INWG). Set up in 1972 as an informal group to consider the technical issues involved in connecting different networks, later that year it became a subcommittee of the International Federation for Information Processing. These devices were different from most previous packet switching schemes in two ways. First, they connected dissimilar kinds of networks, such as serial lines and local area networks. Second, they were connectionless devices, which had no role in assuring that traffic was delivered reliably, leaving that entirely to the hosts.

The idea was explored in more detail, with the intention to produce a prototype system as part of two contemporaneous programs. One was the initial DARPA-initiated program, which created the TCP/IP architecture in use today. The other was a program at Xerox PARC to explore new networking technologies, which produced the PARC Universal Packet system; due to corporate intellectual property concerns it received little attention outside Xerox for years. Some time after early 1974, the first Xerox routers became operational. The first true IP router was developed by Virginia Strazisar at BBN, as part of that DARPA-initiated effort, during 1975-1976. By the end of 1976, three PDP-11-based routers were in service in the experimental prototype Internet.

The first multiprotocol routers were independently created by staff researchers at MIT and Stanford in 1981; the Stanford router was done by William Yeager, and the MIT one by Noel Chiappa; both were also based on PDP-11s. Virtually all networking now uses TCP/IP, but multiprotocol routers are still manufactured. They were important in the early stages of the growth of computer networking when protocols other than TCP/IP were in use. Modern Internet routers that handle both IPv4 and IPv6 are multiprotocol but are simpler devices than routers processing AppleTalk, DECnet, IP and Xerox protocols.

From the mid-1970s and in the 1980s, general-purpose mini-computers served as routers. Modern high-speed routers are highly specialized computers with extra hardware added to speed both common routing functions, such as packet forwarding, and specialised functions such as IPsec encryption. There is substantial use of Linux and Unix software based machines, running open source routing code, for research and other applications. Cisco's operating system was independently designed. Major router operating systems, such as those from Juniper Networks and Extreme Networks, are extensively modified versions of Unix software.

Forwarding

The main purpose of a router is to connect multiple networks and forward packets destined either for its own networks or other networks. A router is considered a layer-3 device because its primary forwarding decision is based on the information in the layer-3 IP packet, specifically the destination IP address. When a router receives a packet, it searches its routing table to find the best match between the destination IP address of the packet and one of the addresses in the routing table. Once a match is found, the packet is encapsulated in the layer-2 data link frame for the outgoing interface indicated in the table entry. A router typically does not look into the packet payload, but only at the layer-3 addresses to make a forwarding decision, plus optionally other information in the header for hints on, for example, quality of service (QoS). For pure IP forwarding, a router is designed to minimize the state information associated with individual packets. Once a packet is forwarded, the router does not retain any historical information about the packet.

The routing table itself can contain information derived from a variety of sources, such as a default or static routes that are configured manually, or dynamic routing protocols where the router learns routes from other routers. A default route is one that is used to route all traffic whose destination does not otherwise appear in the routing table; this is common – even necessary – in small networks, such as a home or small business where the default route simply sends all non-local traffic to the Internet service provider. The default route can be manually configured (as a static route), or learned by dynamic routing protocols, or be obtained by DHCP.

A router can run more than one routing protocol at a time, particularly if it serves as an autonomous system border router between parts of a network that run different routing protocols; if it does so, then redistribution may be used (usually selectively) to share information between the different protocols running on the same router.

Besides making a decision as to which interface a packet is forwarded to, which is handled primarily via the routing table, a router also has to manage congestion when packets arrive at a rate higher than the router can process. Three policies commonly used in the Internet are tail drop, random early detection (RED), and weighted random early detection (WRED). Tail drop is the simplest and most easily implemented; the router simply drops new incoming packets once the length of the queue exceeds the size of the buffers in the router. RED probabilistically drops datagrams early when the queue exceeds a pre-configured portion of the buffer, until a pre-determined max, when it becomes tail drop. WRED requires a weight on the average queue size to act upon when the traffic is about to exceed the pre-configured size, so that short bursts will not trigger random drops.

Another function a router performs is to decide which packet should be processed first when multiple queues exist. This is managed through QoS, which is critical when Voice over IP is deployed, so as not to introduce excessive latency.

Yet another function a router performs is called policy-based routing where special rules are constructed to override the rules derived from the routing table when a packet forwarding decision is made.

Router functions may be performed through the same internal paths that the packets travel inside the router. Some of the functions may be performed through an application-specific integrated circuit (ASIC) to avoid overhead of scheduling CPU time to process the packets. Others may have to be performed through the CPU as these packets need special attention that cannot be handled by an ASIC.

Wi-Fi or WiFi is a technology for wireless local area networking with devices based on the IEEE 802. 11 standards. Wi-Fi is a trademark of the Wi-Fi Alliance, which restricts the use of the term Wi-Fi Certified to products that successfully complete interoperability certification testing.

Devices that can use Wi-Fi technology include personal computers, video-game consoles, smartphones, digital cameras, tablet computers, digital audio players and modern printers. Wi-Fi compatible devices can connect to the Internet via a WLAN network and a wireless access point. Such an access point (or hotspot) has a range of about 20 meters (66 feet) indoors and a greater range outdoors. Hotspot coverage can be as small as a single room with walls that block radio waves, or as large as many square kilometres achieved by using multiple overlapping access points.

Wi-Fi most commonly uses the 2. 4 gigahertz (12 cm) UHF and 5 gigahertz (6 cm) SHF ISM radio bands. Having no physical connections, it is more vulnerable to attack than wired connections, such as Ethernet.

History

In 1971, ALOHAnet connected the Hawaiian Islands with a UHF wireless packet network. ALOHAnet and the ALOHA protocol were early forerunners to Ethernet, and later the IEEE 802. 11 protocols, respectively.

A 1985 ruling by the U. S. Federal Communications Commission released the ISM band for unlicensed use. These frequency bands are the same ones used by equipment such as microwave ovens and are subject to interference.

In 1991, NCR Corporation with AT&T Corporation invented the precursor to 802. 11, intended for use in cashier systems. The first wireless products were under the name WaveLAN. They are the ones credited with inventing Wi-Fi.

The Australian radio-astronomer John O'Sullivan with his colleagues Terence Percival, Graham Daniels, Diet Ostry, John Deane developed a key patent used in Wi-Fi as a by-product of a Commonwealth Scientific and Industrial Research Organisation (CSIRO) research project, "a failed experiment to detect exploding mini black holes the size of an atomic particle". In 1992 and 1996, CSIRO obtained patents for a method later used in Wi-Fi to "unsmear" the signal.

The first version of the 802. 11 protocol was released in 1997, and provided up to 2 Mbit/s link speeds. This was updated in 1999 with 802. 11b to permit 11 Mbit/s link speeds, and this proved to be popular. In 1999, the Wi-Fi Alliance formed as a trade association to hold the Wi-Fi trademark under which most products are sold.

Wi-Fi uses a large number of patents held by many different organizations. In April 2009, 14 technology companies agreed to pay CSIRO $250 million for infringements on CSIRO patents. This led to Australia labeling Wi-Fi as an Australian invention, though this has been the subject of some controversy. CSIRO won a further $220 million settlement for Wi-Fi patent-infringements in 2012 with global firms in the United States required to pay the CSIRO licensing rights estimated to be worth an additional $1 billion in royalties. In 2016, the wireless local area network Test Bed was chosen as Australia's contribution to the exhibition A History of the World in 100 Objects held in the National Museum of Australia.

Etymology

The name Wi-Fi, commercially used at least as early as August 1999, was coined by the brand-consulting firm Interbrand. The Wi-Fi Alliance had hired Interbrand to create a name that was "a little catchier than 'IEEE 802. 11b Direct Sequence. ' "Phil Belanger, a founding member of the Wi-Fi Alliance who presided over the selection of the name "Wi-Fi," has stated that Interbrand invented Wi-Fi as a pun upon the word hi-fi.

Interbrand also created the Wi-Fi logo. The yin-yang Wi-Fi logo indicates the certification of a product for interoperability.

The Wi-Fi Alliance used the nonsense advertising slogan"The Standard for Wireless Fidelity" for a short time after the brand name was created, leading to the misconception that Wi-Fi was an abbreviation of "Wireless Fidelity." The name was however never officially "Wireless Fidelity". Nevertheless, the Wi-Fi Alliance was also called the "Wireless Fidelity Alliance Inc" in some publications and the IEEE's own website has stated "WiFi is a short name for Wireless Fidelity".

Non-Wi-Fi technologies intended for fixed points, such as Motorola Canopy, are usually described as fixed wireless. Alternative wireless technologies include mobile phone standards, such as 2G, 3G, 4G, and LTE.

The name is often written as WiFi, Wifi, or wifi, but these are not approved by the Wi-Fi Alliance.

Wi-Fi ad-hoc mode

Wi-Fi nodes operating in ad-hoc mode refers to devices talking directly to each other without the need to first talk to an access point (also known as base station). Ad-hoc mode was first invented and realized by Chai K. Toh in his 1996 invention of Wi-Fi ad-hoc routing, implemented on Lucent WaveLAN 802. 11a wireless on IBM ThinkPads over a size nodes scenario spanning a region of over a mile. The success was recorded in Mobile Computing magazine and later published formally in IEEE Transactions on Wireless Communications.

Wi-Fi certification

The IEEE does not test equipment for compliance with their standards. The non-profit Wi-Fi Alliance was formed in 1999 to fill this void — to establish and enforce standards for interoperability and backward compatibility, and to promote wireless local-area-network technology. As of 2010, the Wi-Fi Alliance consisted of more than 375 companies from around the world. The Wi-Fi Alliance enforces the use of the Wi-Fi brand to technologies based on the IEEE 802. 11 standards from the IEEE. This includes wireless local area network (WLAN) connections, device to device connectivity (such as Wi-Fi Peer to Peer aka Wi-Fi Direct), Personal area network (PAN), local area network (LAN) and even some limited wide area network (WAN) connections. Manufacturers with membership in the Wi-Fi Alliance, whose products pass the certification process, gain the right to mark those products with the Wi-Fi logo.

Specifically, the certification process requires conformance to the IEEE 802. 11 radio standards, the WPA and WPA2 security standards, and the EAP authentication standard. Certification may optionally include tests of IEEE 802. 11 draft standards, interaction with cellular-phone technology in converged devices, and features relating to security set-up, multimedia, and power-saving.

Not every Wi-Fi device is submitted for certification. The lack of Wi-Fi certification does not necessarily imply that a device is incompatible with other Wi-Fi devices. The Wi-Fi Alliance may or may not sanction derivative terms, such as Super Wi-Fi, coined by the US Federal Communications Commission (FCC) to describe proposed networking in the UHF TV band in the US.

IEEE 802. 11 standard

The IEEE 802. 11 standard is a set of media access control (MAC) and physical layer (PHY) specifications for implementing wireless local area network (WLAN) computer communication in the 2. 4, 3. 6, 5, and 60 GHz frequency bands. They are created and maintained by the IEEE LAN/MAN Standards Committee (IEEE 802). The base version of the standard was released in 1997, and has had subsequent amendments. The standard and amendments provide the basis for wireless network products using the Wi-Fi brand. While each amendment is officially revoked when it is incorporated in the latest version of the standard, the corporate world tends to market to the revisions because they concisely denote capabilities of their products. As a result, in the market place, each revision tends to become its own standard.

Uses

To connect to a Wi-Fi LAN, a computer has to be equipped with a wireless network interface controller. The combination of computer and interface controller is called a station. For all stations that share a single radio frequency communication channel, transmissions on this channel are received by all stations within range. The transmission is not guaranteed to be delivered and is therefore a best-effort delivery mechanism. A carrier wave is used to transmit the data. The data is organised in packets on an Ethernet link, referred to as "Ethernet frames".

Internet access

Wi-Fi technology may be used to provide Internet access to devices that are within the range of a wireless network that is connected to the Internet. The coverage of one or more interconnected access points (hotspots) can extend from an area as small as a few rooms to as large as many square kilometres. Coverage in the larger area may require a group of access points with overlapping coverage. For example, public outdoor Wi-Fi technology has been used successfully in wireless mesh networks in London, UK. An international example is Fon.

Wi-Fi provides service in private homes, businesses, as well as in public spaces at Wi-Fi hotspots set up either free-of-charge or commercially, often using a captive portal webpage for access. Organizations and businesses, such as airports, hotels, and restaurants, often provide free-use hotspots to attract customers. Enthusiasts or authorities who wish to provide services or even to promote business in selected areas sometimes provide free Wi-Fi access.

Routers that incorporate a digital subscriber line modem or a cable modem and a Wi-Fi access point, often set up in homes and other buildings, provide Internet access and internetworking to all devices connected to them, wirelessly or via cable.

Similarly, battery-powered routers may include a cellular Internet radiomodem and Wi-Fi access point. When subscribed to a cellular data carrier, they allow nearby Wi-Fi stations to access the Internet over 2G, 3G, or 4G networks using the tethering technique. Many smartphones have a built-in capability of this sort, including those based on Android, BlackBerry, Bada, iOS (iPhone), Windows Phone and Symbian, though carriers often disable the feature, or charge a separate fee to enable it, especially for customers with unlimited data plans. "Internet packs" provide standalone facilities of this type as well, without use of a smartphone; examples include the MiFi- and WiBro-branded devices. Some laptops that have a cellular modem card can also act as mobile Internet Wi-Fi access points.

Wi-Fi also connects places that normally don't have network access, such as kitchens and garden sheds.

City-wide Wi-Fi

In the early 2000s, many cities around the world announced plans to construct citywide Wi-Fi networks. There are many successful examples; in 2004, Mysore became India's first Wi-Fi-enabled city. A company called WiFiyNet has set up hotspots in Mysore, covering the complete city and a few nearby villages.

In 2005, St. Cloud, Florida and Sunnyvale, California, became the first cities in the United States to offer citywide free Wi-Fi (from MetroFi). Minneapolis has generated $1. 2 million in profit annually for its provider.

In May 2010, London, UK, Mayor Boris Johnson pledged to have London-wide Wi-Fi by 2012. Several boroughs including Westminster and Islington already had extensive outdoor Wi-Fi coverage at that point.

Officials in South Korea's capital are moving to provide free Internet access at more than 10, 000 locations around the city, including outdoor public spaces, major streets and densely populated residential areas. Seoul will grant leases to KT, LG Telecom and SK Telecom. The companies will invest $44 million in the project, which was to be completed in 2015.

Campus-Wide Wi-Fi

Many traditional university campuses in the developed world provide at least partial Wi-Fi coverage. Carnegie Mellon University built the first campus-wide wireless Internet network, called Wireless Andrew, at its Pittsburgh campus in 1993 before Wi-Fi branding originated. By February 1997 the CMU Wi-Fi zone was fully operational. Many universities collaborate in providing Wi-Fi access to students and staff through the Eduroam international authentication infrastructure.

Direct computer-to-computer communications

Wi-Fi also allows communications directly from one computer to another without an access point intermediary. This is called ad hoc Wi-Fi transmission. This wireless ad hoc network mode has proven popular with multiplayer handheld game consoles, such as the Nintendo DS, PlayStation Portable, digital cameras, and other consumer electronics devices. Some devices can also share their Internet connection using ad hoc, becoming hotspots or "virtual routers".

Similarly, the Wi-Fi Alliance promotes the specification Wi-Fi Direct for file transfers and media sharing through a new discovery- and security-methodology. Wi-Fi Direct launched in October 2010. Another mode of direct communication over Wi-Fi is Tunneled Direct Link Setup (TDLS), which enables two devices on the same Wi-Fi network to communicate directly, instead of via the access point.

Wi-Fi radio spectrum

802. 11b and 802. 11g use the 2. 4 GHz ISM band, operating in the United States under Part 15 Rules and Regulations. Because of this choice of frequency band, 802. 11b and g equipment may occasionally suffer interference from microwave ovens, cordless telephones, and Bluetooth devices.

Spectrum assignments and operational limitations are not consistent worldwide: Australia and Europe allow for an additional two channels (12, 13) beyond the 11 permitted in the United States for the 2. 4 GHz band, while Japan has three more (12–14). In the US and other countries, 802. 11a and 802. 11g devices may be operated without a license, as allowed in Part 15 of the FCC Rules and Regulations.

A Wi-Fi signal occupies five channels in the 2. 4 GHz band. Any two channel numbers that differ by five or more, such as 2 and 7, do not overlap. The oft-repeated adage that channels 1, 6, and 11 are the only non-overlapping channels is, therefore, not accurate. Channels 1, 6, and 11 are the only group of three non-overlapping channels in North America and the United Kingdom. In Europe and Japan using Channels 1, 5, 9, and 13 for 802. 11g and 802. 11n is recommended.

802. 11a uses the 5 GHz U-NII band, which, for much of the world, offers at least 23 non-overlapping channels rather than the 2. 4 GHz ISM frequency band, where adjacent channels overlap.

Interference

Wi-Fi connections can be disrupted or the Internet speed lowered by having other devices in the same area. Many 2. 4 GHz 802. 11b and 802. 11g access-points default to the same channel on initial startup, contributing to congestion on certain channels. Wi-Fi pollution, or an excessive number of access points in the area, especially on the neighboring channel, can prevent access and interfere with other devices' use of other access points, caused by overlapping channels in the 802. 11g/b spectrum, as well as with decreased signal-to-noise ratio (SNR) between access points. This can become a problem in high-density areas, such as large apartment complexes or office buildings with many Wi-Fi access points. It is advised to only use channel 1-6-11.

Additionally, other devices use the 2. 4 GHz band: microwave ovens, ISM band devices, security cameras, ZigBee devices, Bluetooth devices, video senders, cordless phones, baby monitors, and, in some countries, amateur radio, all of which can cause significant additional interference. It is also an issue when municipalities or other large entities (such as universities) seek to provide large area coverage.

Service set identifier (SSID)

In addition to running on different channels, multiple Wi-Fi networks can share channels.

A service set is the set of all the devices associated with a particular Wi-Fi network. The service set can be local, independent, extended or mesh.

Each service set has an associated identifier, the 32-byte Service Set Identifier (SSID), which identifies the particular network. The SSID is configured within the devices that are considered part of the network, and it is transmitted in the packets. Receivers ignore wireless packets from networks with a different SSID.

Throughput

As the 802. 11 specifications evolved to support higher throughput, the bandwidth requirements also increased to support them. 802. 11n uses double the radio spectrum/ bandwidth (40 MHz) compared to 802. 11a or 802. 11g (20 MHz). 76 This means there can be only one 802. 11n network on the 2. 4 GHz band at a given location, without interference to/from other WLAN traffic. 802. 11n can also be set to limit itself to 20 MHz bandwidth to prevent interference in dense community. Many newer consumer devices support the latest 802. 11ac standard, which uses the 5 GHz band exclusively and is capable of multi-station WLAN throughput of at least 1 gigabit per second. According to a study, devices with the 802. 11ac specification were expected to be common by 2015 with an estimated one billion spread around the world.

Hardware

Wi-Fi allows cheaper deployment of local area networks (LANs). Also, spaces where cables cannot be run, such as outdoor areas and historical buildings, can host wireless LANs. However, building walls of certain materials, such as stone with high metal content, can block Wi-Fi signals. Manufacturers are building wireless network adapters into most laptops. The price of chipsets for Wi-Fi continues to drop, making it an economical networking option included in even more devices.

Different competitive brands of access points and client network-interfaces can inter-operate at a basic level of service. Products designated as “Wi-Fi Certified” by the Wi-Fi Alliance are backward compatible. Unlike mobile phones, any standard Wi-Fi device will work anywhere in the world.

Standard devices

A wireless access point (WAP) connects a group of wireless devices to an adjacent wired LAN. An access point resembles a network hub, relaying data between connected wireless devices in addition to a (usually) single connected wired device, most often an Ethernet hub or switch, allowing wireless devices to communicate with other wired devices.

Wireless adapters allow devices to connect to a wireless network. These adapters connect to devices using various external or internal interconnects such as PCI, miniPCI, USB, ExpressCard, Cardbus and PC Card. As of 2010, most newer laptop computers come equipped with built in internal adapters.

Wireless routers integrate a Wireless Access Point, Ethernet switch, and internal router firmware application that provides IP routing, NAT, and DNS forwarding through an integrated WAN-interface. A wireless router allows wired and wireless Ethernet LAN devices to connect to a (usually) single WAN device such as a cable modem or a DSL modem. A wireless router allows all three devices, mainly the access point and router, to be configured through one central utility. This utility is usually an integrated web server that is accessible to wired and wireless LAN clients and often optionally to WAN clients. This utility may also be an application that is run on a computer, as is the case with as Apple's AirPort, which is managed with the AirPort Utility on Mac OS X and iOS.

Wireless network bridges connect a wired network to a wireless network. A bridge differs from an access point: an access point connects wireless devices to a wired network at the data-link layer. Two wireless bridges may be used to connect two wired networks over a wireless link, useful in situations where a wired connection may be unavailable, such as between two separate homes or for devices which do not have wireless networking capability (but have wired networking capability), such as consumer entertainment devices; alternatively, a wireless bridge can be used to enable a device which supports a wired connection to operate at a wireless networking standard which is faster than supported by the wireless network connectivity feature (external dongle or inbuilt) supported by the device (e. g. enabling Wireless-N speeds (up to the maximum supported speed on the wired Ethernet port on both the bridge and connected devices including the wireless access point) for a device which only supports Wireless-G). A dual-band wireless bridge can also be used to enable 5 GHz wireless network operation on a device which only supports 2. 4 GHz wireless networking functionality and has a wired Ethernet port.

Wireless range-extenders or wireless repeaters can extend the range of an existing wireless network. Strategically placed range-extenders can elongate a signal area or allow for the signal area to reach around barriers such as those pertaining in L-shaped corridors. Wireless devices connected through repeaters will suffer from an increased latency for each hop, as well as from a reduction in the maximum data throughput that is available. In addition, the effect of additional users using a network employing wireless range-extenders is to consume the available bandwidth faster than would be the case where but a single user migrates around a network employing extenders. For this reason, wireless range-extenders work best in networks supporting very low traffic throughput requirements, such as for cases where but a single user with a Wi-Fi equipped tablet migrates around the combined extended and non-extended portions of the total connected network. Additionally, a wireless device connected to any of the repeaters in the chain will have a data throughput that is also limited by the "weakest link" existing in the chain between where the connection originates and where the connection ends. Networks employing wireless extenders are also more prone to degradation from interference from neighboring access points that border portions of the extended network and that happen to occupy the same channel as the extended network.

The security standard, Wi-Fi Protected Setup, allows embedded devices with limited graphical user interface to connect to the Internet with ease. Wi-Fi Protected Setup has 2 configurations: The Push Button configuration and the PIN configuration. These embedded devices are also called The Internet of Things and are low-power, battery-operated embedded systems. A number of Wi-Fi manufacturers design chips and modules for embedded Wi-Fi, such as GainSpan.

EMBEDDED SYSTEMS

Increasingly in the last few years (particularly as of 2007), embedded Wi-Fi modules have become available that incorporate a real-time operating system and provide a simple means of wirelessly enabling any device which has and communicates via a serial port. This allows the design of simple monitoring devices. An example is a portable ECG device monitoring a patient at home. This Wi-Fi-enabled device can communicate via the Internet. These Wi-Fi modules are designed by OEMs so that implementers need only minimal Wi-Fi knowledge to provide Wi-Fi connectivity for their products.

In June 2014 Texas Instruments introduced the first ARM Cortex-M4 microcontroller with an onboard dedicated Wi-Fi MCU, the SimpleLink CC3200. It makes embedded systems with Wi-Fi connectivity possible to build as single-chip devices, which reduces their cost and minimum size, making it more practical to build wireless-networked controllers into inexpensive ordinary objects.

Range

The Wi-Fi signal range depends on the frequency band, radio power output, antenna gain and antenna type as well as the modulation technique. Line-of-sight is the thumbnail guide but reflection and refraction can have a significant impact.

An access point compliant with either 802. 11b or 802. 11g, using the stock antenna might have a range of 100 m (330 ft). The same radio with an external semi parabolic antenna (15 dB gain) might have a range over 20 miles.

Higher gain rating (dBi) indicates further deviation (generally toward the horizontal) from a theoretical, perfect isotropic radiator, and therefore the further the antenna can project a usable signal, as compared to a similar output power on a more isotropic antenna. For example, an 8 dBi antenna used with a 100 mW driver will have a similar horizontal range to a 6 dBi antenna being driven at 500 mW. Note that this assumes that radiation in the vertical is lost; this may not be the case in some situations, especially in large buildings or within a waveguide. In the above example, a directional waveguide could cause the low power 6 dBi antenna to project much further in a single direction than the 8 dBi antenna which is not in a waveguide, even if they are both being driven at 100 mW.

IEEE 802. 11n, however, can more than double the range. Range also varies with frequency band. Wi-Fi in the 2. 4 GHz frequency block has slightly better range than Wi-Fi in the 5 GHz frequency block used by 802. 11a (and optionally by 802. 11n). On wireless routers with detachable antennas, it is possible to improve range by fitting upgraded antennas which have higher gain in particular directions. Outdoor ranges can be improved to many kilometers through the use of high gain directional antennas at the router and remote device(s). In general, the maximum amount of power that a Wi-Fi device can transmit is limited by local regulations, such as FCC Part 15 in the US. Equivalent isotropically radiated power (EIRP) in the European Union is limited to 20 dBm (100 mW).

To reach requirements for wireless LAN applications, Wi-Fi has fairly high power consumption compared to some other standards. Technologies such as Bluetooth (designed to support wireless personal area network (PAN) applications) provide a much shorter propagation range between 1 and 100 m and so in general have a lower power consumption. Other low-power technologies such as ZigBee have fairly long range, but much lower data rate. The high power consumption of Wi-Fi makes battery life in mobile devices a concern.

Researchers have developed a number of "no new wires" technologies to provide alternatives to Wi-Fi for applications in which Wi-Fi's indoor range is not adequate and where installing new wires (such as CAT-6) is not possible or cost-effective. For example, the ITU-T G. hn standard for high speed local area networks uses existing home wiring (coaxial cables, phone lines and power lines). Although G. hn does not provide some of the advantages of Wi-Fi (such as mobility or outdoor use), it is designed for applications (such as IPTV distribution) where indoor range is more important than mobility.

For the best performance, a number of people only recommend using wireless networking as a supplement to wired networking.

Due to the complex nature of radio propagation at typical Wi-Fi frequencies, particularly the effects of signal reflection off trees and buildings, algorithms can only approximately predict Wi-Fi signal strength for any given area in relation to a transmitter. This effect does not apply equally to long-range Wi-Fi, since longer links typically operate from towers that transmit above the surrounding foliage. The practical range of Wi-Fi essentially confines mobile use to such applications as inventory-taking machines in warehouses or in retail spaces, barcode-reading devices at check-out stands, or receiving/ shipping stations. [–] Mobile use of Wi-Fi over wider ranges is limited, for instance, to uses such as in an automobile moving from one hotspot to another. Other wireless technologies are more suitable for communicating with moving vehicles.

Distance records

Distance records (using non-standard devices) include 382 km (237 mi) in June 2007, held by Ermanno Pietrosemoli and EsLaRed of Venezuela, transferring about 3 MB of data between the mountain-tops of El Águila and Platillon. The Swedish Space Agency transferred data 420 km (260 mi), using 6 watt amplifiers to reach an overhead stratospheric balloon.

Multiple access points

Increasing the number of Wi-Fi access points provides network redundancy, better range, support for fast roaming and increased overall network-capacity by using more channels or by defining smaller cells. Except for the smallest implementations (such as home or small office networks), Wi-Fi implementations have moved toward "thin" access points, with more of the network intelligence housed in a centralized network appliance, relegating individual access points to the role of "dumb" transceivers. Outdoor applications may use mesh topologies. When multiple access points are deployed they are often configured with the same SSID and security settings to form an "extended service set". Wi-Fi client devices will typically connect to the access point that can provide the strongest signal within that service set.

Network security

The main issue with wireless network security is its simplified access to the network compared to traditional wired networks such as Ethernet. With wired networking, one must either gain access to a building (physically connecting into the internal network), or break through an external firewall. To enable Wi-Fi, one merely needs to be within the range of the Wi-Fi network. Most business networks protect sensitive data and systems by attempting to disallow external access. Enabling wireless connectivity reduces security if the network uses inadequate or no encryption. An attacker who has gained access to a Wi-Fi network router can initiate a DNS spoofing attack against any other user of the network by forging a response before the queried DNS server has a chance to reply.

Data security risks

The most common wireless encryption-standard, Wired Equivalent Privacy (WEP), has been shown to be easily breakable even when correctly configured. Wi-Fi Protected

Access (WPA and WPA2) encryption, which became available in devices in 2003, aimed to solve this problem. Wi-Fi access points typically default to an encryption-free (open) mode. Novice users benefit from a zero-configuration device that works out-of-the-box, but this default does not enable any wireless security, providing open wireless access to a LAN. To turn security on requires the user to configure the device, usually via a software graphical user interface (GUI). On unencrypted Wi-Fi networks connecting devices can monitor and record data (including personal information). Such networks can only be secured by using other means of protection, such as a VPN or secure Hypertext Transfer Protocol over Transport Layer Security (HTTPS).

Wi-Fi Protected Access encryption (WPA2) is considered secure, provided a strong passphrase is used. A proposed modification to WPA2 is WPA-OTP or WPA3, which stores an on-chip optically generated onetime pad on all connected devices which is periodically updated via strong encryption then hashed with the data to be sent or received. This would be unbreakable using any (even quantum) computer system as the hashed data is essentially random and no pattern can be detected if it is implemented properly. Main disadvantage is that it would need multi-GB storage chips so would be expensive for the consumers.

Securing methods

A common measure to deter unauthorized users involves hiding the access point's name by disabling the SSID broadcast. While effective against the casual user, it is ineffective as a security method because the SSID is broadcast in the clear in response to a client SSID query. Another method is to only allow computers with known MAC addresses to join the network, but determined eavesdroppers may be able to join the network by spoofing an authorized address.

Wired Equivalent Privacy (WEP) encryption was designed to protect against casual snooping but it is no longer considered secure. Tools such as AirSnort or Aircrack-ng can quickly recover WEP encryption keys. Because of WEP's weakness the Wi-Fi Alliance approved Wi-Fi Protected Access (WPA) which uses TKIP. WPA was specifically designed to work with older equipment usually through a firmware upgrade. Though more secure than WEP, WPA has known vulnerabilities.

The more secure WPA2 using Advanced Encryption Standard was introduced in 2004 and is supported by most new Wi-Fi devices. WPA2 is fully compatible with WPA.

A flaw in a feature added to Wi-Fi in 2007, called Wi-Fi Protected Setup, allows WPA and WPA2 security to be bypassed and effectively broken in many situations. The only remedy as of late 2011 is to turn off Wi-Fi Protected Setup, which is not always possible.

Virtual Private Networks are often used to secure Wi-Fi.

Piggybacking

Piggybacking refers to access to a wireless Internet connection by bringing one's own computer within the range of another's wireless connection, and using that service without the subscriber's explicit permission or knowledge.

During the early popular adoption of 802. 11, providing open access points for anyone within range to use was encouraged to cultivate wireless community networks, particularly since people on average use only a fraction of their downstream bandwidth at any given time.

Recreational logging and mapping of other people's access points has become known as wardriving. Indeed, many access points are intentionally installed without security turned on so that they can be used as a free service. Providing access to one's Internet connection in this fashion may breach the Terms of Service or contract with the ISP. These activities do not result in sanctions in most jurisdictions; however, legislation and case law differ considerably across the world. A proposal to leave graffiti describing available services was called warchalking. A Florida court case determined that owner laziness was not to be a valid excuse.

Piggybacking often occurs unintentionally – a technically unfamiliar user might not change the default "unsecured" settings to their access point and operating systems can be configured to connect automatically to any available wireless network. A user who happens to start up a laptop in the vicinity of an access point may find the computer has joined the network without any visible indication. Moreover, a user intending to join one network may instead end up on another one if the latter has a stronger signal. In combination with automatic discovery of other network resources this could possibly lead wireless users to send sensitive data to the wrong middle-man when seeking a destination. For example, a user could inadvertently use an unsecure network to log in to a website, thereby making the login credentials available to anyone listening, if the website uses an unsecure protocol such as plain HTTP without TLS (HTTPS).

An unauthorized user can obtain security information (factory preset passphrase and/or Wi-Fi Protected Setup PIN) from a label on a wireless access point can use this information (or connect by the Wi-Fi Protected Setup pushbutton method) to commit unauthorized and/or unlawful activities.

Safety

The World Health Organization (WHO) says "no health effects are expected from exposure to RF fields from base stations and wireless networks", but notes that they promote research into effects from other RF sources. Although the WHO's International Agency for Research on Cancer (IARC) later classified radiofrequency electromagnetic fields as "possibly carcinogenic to humans (Group 2B)" (a category used when "a causal association is considered credible, but when chance, bias or confounding cannot be ruled out with reasonable confidence"), this was based on risks associated with wireless phone use rather than Wi-Fi networks.

The United Kingdom's Health Protection Agency reported in 2007 that exposure to Wi-Fi for a year results in the "same amount of radiation from a 20-minute mobile phone call". A review of studies involving 725 people who claimed electromagnetic hypersensitivity, "... suggests that 'electromagnetic hypersensitivity' is unrelated to the presence of EMF, although more research into this phenomenon is required."

Internet security

Internet security is a branch of computer security specifically related to the Internet, often involving browser security but also network security on a more general level as it applies to other applications or operating systems on a whole. Its objective is to establish rules and measures to use against attacks over the Internet. The Internet represents an insecure channel for exchanging information leading to a high risk of intrusion or fraud, such as phishing. Different methods have been used to protect the transfer of data, including encryption and from-the-ground-up engineering.

THREATS

Malicious software

A computer user can be tricked or forced into downloading software onto a computer that is of malicious intent. Such software comes in many forms, such as viruses, Trojan horses, spyware, and worms.

- Malware, short for malicious software, is any software used to disrupt computer operation, gather sensitive information, or gain access to private computer systems. Malware is defined by its malicious intent, acting against the requirements of the computer user, and does not include software that causes unintentional harm due to some deficiency. The term badware is sometimes used, and applied to both true (malicious) malware and unintentionally harmful software.
- A botnet is a network of zombie computers that have been taken over by a robot or bot that performs large-scale malicious acts for the creator of the botnet.
- Computer Viruses are programs that can replicate their structures or effects by infecting other files or structures on a computer. The common use of a virus is to take over a computer to steal data.

- Computer worms are programs that can replicate themselves throughout a computer network, performing malicious tasks throughout.
- Ransomware is a type of malware which restricts access to the computer system that it infects, and demands a ransom paid to the creator(s) of the malware in order for the restriction to be removed.
- Scareware is scam software with malicious payloads, usually of limited or no benefit, that are sold to consumers via certain unethical marketing practices. The selling approach uses social engineering to cause shock, anxiety, or the perception of a threat, generally directed at an unsuspecting user.
- Spyware refers to programs that surreptitiously monitor activity on a computer system and report that information to others without the user's consent.
- A Trojan horse, commonly known as a Trojan, is a general term for malicious software that pretends to be harmless, so that a user willingly allows it to be downloaded onto the computer.

Denial-of-service attacks

A denial-of-service attack (DoS attack) or distributed denial-of-service attack (DDoS attack) is an attempt to make a computer resource unavailable to its intended users. Although the means to carry out, motives for, and targets of a DoS attack may vary, it generally consists of the concerted efforts to prevent an Internet site or service from functioning efficiently or at all, temporarily or indefinitely. According to businesses who participated in an international business security survey, 25% of respondents experienced a DoS attack in 2007 and 16. 8% experienced one in 2010.

Phishing

Phishing occurs when the attacker pretends to be a trustworthy entity, either via email or web page. Victims are directed to fake web pages, which are dressed to look legitimate, via spoof emails, instant messenger/social media or other avenues. Often tactics such as email spoofing are used to make emails appear to be from legitimate senders, or long complex subdomains hide the real website host. Insurance group RSA said that phishing accounted for worldwide losses of $1. 5 billion in 2012.

Application vulnerabilities

Applications used to access Internet resources may contain security vulnerabilities such as memory safety bugs or flawed authentication checks. The most severe of these bugs can give network attackers full control over the computer. Most security applications and suites are incapable of adequate defense against these kinds of attacks.

REMEDIES

Network layer security

TCP/IP protocols may be secured with cryptographic methods and security protocols. These protocols include Secure Sockets Layer (SSL), succeeded by Transport Layer Security (TLS) for web traffic, Pretty Good Privacy (PGP) for email, and IPsec for the network layer security.

Internet Protocol Security (IPsec)

IPsec is designed to protect TCP/IP communication in a secure manner. It is a set of security extensions developed by the Internet Task Force (IETF). It provides security and authentication at the IP layer by transforming data using encryption. Two main types of transformation that form the basis of IPsec: the Authentication Header (AH) and ESP. These two protocols provide data integrity, data origin authentication, and anti-replay service. These protocols can be used alone or in combination to provide the desired set of security services for the Internet Protocol (IP) layer.

The basic components of the IPsec security architecture are described in terms of the following functionalities:

- Security protocols for AH and ESP
- Security association for policy management and traffic processing
- Manual and automatic key management for the Internet key exchange (IKE)
- Algorithms for authentication and encryption

The set of security services provided at the IP layer includes access control, data origin integrity, protection against replays, and confidentiality. The algorithm allows these sets to work independently without affecting other parts of the implementation. The IPsec implementation is operated in a host or security gateway environment giving protection to IP traffic.

Security token

Some online sites offer customers the ability to use a six-digit code which randomly changes every 30–60 seconds on a security token. The keys on the security token have built in mathematical computations and manipulate numbers based on the current time built into the device. This means that every thirty seconds there is only a certain array of numbers possible which would be correct to validate access to the online account. The website that the user is logging into would be made aware of that devices' serial number and would know the computation and correct time built into the device to verify that the number given is indeed one of the handful of six-digit numbers that works in that given

30-60 second cycle. After 30–60 seconds the device will present a new random six-digit number which can log into the website.

ELECTRONIC MAIL SECURITY

Background

Email messages are composed, delivered, and stored in a multiple step process, which starts with the message's composition. When the user finishes composing the message and sends it, the message is transformed into a standard format: an RFC 2822 formatted message. Afterwards, the message can be transmitted. Using a network connection, the mail client, referred to as a mail user agent (MUA), connects to a mail transfer agent (MTA) operating on the mail server. The mail client then provides the sender's identity to the server. Next, using the mail server commands, the client sends the recipient list to the mail server. The client then supplies the message. Once the mail server receives and processes the message, several events occur: recipient server identification, connection establishment, and message transmission. Using Domain Name System (DNS) services, the sender's mail server determines the mail server(s) for the recipient(s). Then, the server opens up a connection(s) to the recipient mail server(s) and sends the message employing a process similar to that used by the originating client, delivering the message to the recipient(s).

Pretty Good Privacy (PGP)

Pretty Good Privacy provides confidentiality by encrypting messages to be transmitted or data files to be stored using an encryption algorithm such as Triple DES or CAST-128. Email messages can be protected by using cryptography in various ways, such as the following:

- Signing an email message to ensure its integrity and confirm the identity of its sender.
- Encrypting the body of an email message to ensure its confidentiality.
- Encrypting the communications between mail servers to protect the confidentiality of both message body and message header.

The first two methods, message signing and message body encryption, are often used together; however, encrypting the transmissions between mail servers is typically used only when two organizations want to protect emails regularly sent between each other. For example, the organizations could establish a virtual private network (VPN) to encrypt the communications between their mail servers over the Internet. Unlike methods that can only encrypt a message body, a VPN can encrypt entire messages, including email header information such as senders, recipients, and subjects. In some cases, organizations may need to protect header information. However, a VPN solution alone cannot provide a message signing mechanism, nor can it provide protection for email messages along the entire route from sender to recipient.

Multipurpose Internet Mail Extensions (MIME)

MIME transforms non-ASCII data at the sender's site to Network Virtual Terminal (NVT) ASCII data and delivers it to client's Simple Mail Transfer Protocol (SMTP) to be sent through the Internet. The server SMTP at the receiver's side receives the NVT ASCII data and delivers it to MIME to be transformed back to the original non-ASCII data.

Message Authentication Code

A Message authentication code (MAC) is a cryptography method that uses a secret key to encrypt a message. This method outputs a MAC value that can be decrypted by the receiver, using the same secret key used by the sender. The Message Authentication Code protects both a message's data integrity as well as its authenticity.

Firewalls

A computer firewall controls access between networks. It generally consists of gateways and filters which vary from one firewall to another. Firewalls also screen network traffic and are able to block traffic that is dangerous. Firewalls act as the intermediate server between SMTP and Hypertext Transfer Protocol (HTTP) connections.

Role of firewalls in web security

Firewalls impose restrictions on incoming and outgoing Network packets to and from private networks. Incoming or outgoing traffic must pass through the firewall; only authorized traffic is allowed to pass through it. Firewalls create checkpoints between an internal private network and the public Internet, also known as choke points (borrowed from the identical military term of a combat limiting geographical feature). Firewalls can create choke points based on IP source and TCP port number. They can also serve as the platform for IPsec. Using tunnel mode capability, firewall can be used to implement VPNs. Firewalls can also limit network exposure by hiding the internal network system and information from the public Internet.

TYPES OF FIREWALL

Packet filter

A packet filter is a first generation firewall that processes network traffic on a packet-by-packet basis. Its main job is to filter traffic from a remote IP host, so a router is needed to connect the internal network to the Internet. The router is known as a screening router, which screens packets leaving and entering the network.

Stateful packet inspection

In a stateful firewall the circuit-level gateway is a proxy server that operates at the network level of an Open Systems Interconnection (OSI) model and statically defines what traffic will be allowed. Circuit proxies will forward Network packets (formatted unit of data) containing a given port number, if the port is permitted by the algorithm. The main advantage of a proxy server is its ability to provide Network Address Translation (NAT), which can hide the user's IP address from the Internet, effectively protecting all internal information from the Internet.

Application-level gateway

An application-level firewall is a third generation firewall where a proxy server operates at the very top of the OSI model, the IP suite application level. A network packet is forwarded only if a connection is established using a known protocol. Application-level gateways are notable for analyzing entire messages rather than individual packets of data when the data are being sent or received.

Browser choice

Web browser statistics tend to affect the amount a Web browser is exploited. For example, Internet Explorer 6, which used to own a majority of the Web browser market share, is considered extremely insecure because vulnerabilities were exploited due to its former popularity. Since browser choice is more evenly distributed (Internet Explorer at 28. 5%, Firefox at 18. 4%, Google Chrome at 40. 8%, and so on) and vulnerabilities are exploited in many different browsers.

INTERNET SECURITY PRODUCTS

Antivirus

Antivirus software and Internet security programs can protect a programmable device from attack by detecting and eliminating viruses; Antivirus software was mainly shareware in the early years of the Internet, but there are now several free security applications on the Internet to choose from for all platforms.

Password managers

A password manager is a software application that helps a user store and organize passwords. Password managers usually store passwords encrypted, requiring the user to create a master password; a single, ideally very strong password which grants the user access to their entire password database.

Security suites

So called security suites were first offered for sale in 2003 (McAfee) and contain a suite of firewalls, anti-virus, anti-spyware and more. They also offer theft protection, portable storage device safety check, private Internet browsing, cloud anti-spam, a file shredder or make security-related decisions (answering popup windows) and several were free of charge.

INFORMATION LITERACY CONCEPT

The United States National Forum on Information Literacy defines information literacy as "... the ability to know when there is a need for information, to be able to identify, locate, evaluate, and effectively use that information for the issue or problem at hand." The American Library Association defines "information literacy" as a set of abilities requiring individuals to "recognize when information is needed and have the ability to locate, evaluate, and use effectively the needed information. Other definitions incorporate aspects of "skepticism, judgement, free thinking, questioning, and understanding..." or incorporate competencies that an informed citizen of an information society ought to possess to participate intelligently and actively in that society.

A number of efforts have been made to better define the concept and its relationship to other skills and forms of literacy. Although other educational goals, including traditional literacy, computer literacy, library skills, and critical thinking skills, are related to information literacy and important foundations for its development, information literacy itself is emerging as a distinct skill set and a necessary key to one's social and economic well-being in an increasingly complex information society. According to McTavish (2009), in order to increase and maximize people's contributions to a healthy, democratic and pluralistic society and maintain a prosperous and sustainable economy, governments and industries around the world are challenging education systems to focus people's attention on literacy. In Canada, because of a great focus on a supposed literacy crisis, it has caused some alarm in some educational sectors. Brink (2006) researched government organization, such as Human Resources and Skill Development Canada, claims that almost half of working-age Canadians do not have the literacy skills they need to meet the ever-increasing demands of modern life.

History of the concept

The phrase information literacy first appeared in print in a 1974 report by Paul G. Zurkowski written on behalf of the National Commission on Libraries and Information Science. Zurkowski used the phrase to describe the "techniques and skills" learned by the information literate "for utilizing the wide range of information tools as well as primary sources in molding information solutions to their problems" and drew a relatively firm line between the "literates" and "information illiterates". The Presidential Committee on Information Literacy released a report on January 10, 1989, outlining the importance of information literacy, opportunities to develop information literacy, and an Information Age School. The report's final name is the Presidential Committee on Information Literacy: Final Report.

The recommendations of the Presidential Committee led to the creation later that year of the National Forum on Information Literacy, a coalition of more than 90 national and international organizations.

In 1998, the American Association of School Librarians and the Association for Educational Communications and Technology published Information Power: Building Partnerships for Learning, which further established specific goals for information literacy education, defining some nine standards in the categories of "information literacy", "independent learning", and "social responsibility".

Also in 1998, the Presidential Committee on Information Literacy produced an update on its Final Report. This update outlined the six main recommendations of the original report and examined areas where it made progress and areas that still needed work. The updated report supports further information literacy advocacy and reiterates its importance.

In 1999, the Society of College, National and University Libraries (SCONUL) in the UK, published "The Seven Pillars of Information Literacy" model to "facilitate further development of ideas amongst practitioners in the field... stimulate debate about the ideas and about how those ideas might be used by library and other staff in higher education concerned with the development of students' skills." A number of other countries have developed information literacy standards since then.

In 2003, the National Forum on Information Literacy, together with UNESCO and the National Commission on Libraries and Information Science, sponsored an international conference in Prague with representatives from some twenty-three countries to discuss the importance of information literacy within a global context. The resulting Prague Declaration described information literacy as a "key to social, cultural, and economic development of nations and communities, institutions and individuals in the 21st century" and declared its acquisition as "part of the basic human right of lifelong learning".

The Alexandria Proclamation linked Information literacy with lifelong learning. More than that, it sets Information Literacy as a basic Human right that it"promotes social inclusion of all nations".

On May 28, 2009, U. S. California Governor Arnold Schwarzenegger signed Executive Order S-06-09, establishing a California ICT Digital Literacy Leadership Council, which in turn, was directed to establish an ICT Digital Literacy Advisory Committee. "The

Leadership Council, in consultation with the Advisory Committee, shall develop an ICT Digital Literacy Policy, to ensure that California residents are digitally literate." The Executive Order states further: "ICT Digital Literacy is defined as using digital technology, communications tools and/or networks to access, manage, integrate, evaluate, create, and communicate information in order to function in a knowledge-based economy and society..." The Governor directs "... The Leadership Council, in consultation with the Advisory Committee... [to] develop a California Action Plan for ICT Digital Literacy (Action Plan)." He also directs "The California Workforce Investment Board (WIB)... [to] develop a technology literacy component for its five-year Strategic State Plan." His Executive Order ends with the following: "I FURTHER REQUEST that the Legislature and Superintendent of Public Instruction consider adopting similar goals, and that they join the Leadership Council in issuing a "Call to Action" to schools, higher education institutions, employers, workforce training agencies, local governments, community organizations, and civic leaders to advance California as a global leader in ICT Digital Literacy".

Information literacy rose to national consciousness in the U. S. with President Barack Obama's Proclamation designating October 2009 as National Information Literacy Awareness Month. President Obama's Proclamation stated that

"Rather than merely possessing data, we must also learn the skills necessary to acquire, collate, and evaluate information for any situation... Though we may know how to find the information we need, we must also know how to evaluate it. Over the past decade, we have seen a crisis of authenticity emerge. We now live in a world where anyone can publish an opinion or perspective, whether true or not, and have that opinion amplified within the information marketplace. At the same time, Americans have unprecedented access to the diverse and independent sources of information, as well as institutions such as libraries and universities, that can help separate truth from fiction and signal from noise."

Obama's proclamation ended with:

"Now, therefore, I, Barack Obama, President of the United States of America, by virtue of the authority vested in me by the Constitution and the laws of the United States, do hereby proclaim October 2009 as National Information Literacy Awareness Month. I call upon the people of the United States to recognize the important role information plays in our daily lives, and appreciate the need for a greater understanding of its impact."

Presidential Committee on Information Literacy

The Presidential Committee on Information Literacy was formed in 1987 by the American Library Association's president at the time Margaret Chisholm. The committee was formed with three specific purposes

1. to define Information Literacy within the higher literacies and its importance to student performance, lifelong learning, and active citizenship
2. to design one or more models for information literacy development appropriate to formal and informal learning environments throughout people's lifetimes
3. to determine implications for the continuing education and development for teachers

The American Library Association's Presidential Committee on Information Literacy defined information literacy as the ability "to recognize when information is needed and have the ability to locate, evaluate, and use effectively the needed information" and highlighted information literacy as a skill essential for lifelong learning and the production of an informed and prosperous citizenry. The committee outlined six principal recommendations: to "reconsider the ways we have organized information institutionally, structured information access, and defined information's role in our lives at home in the community, and in the work place"; to promote "public awareness of the problems created by information illiteracy"; to develop a national research agenda related to information and its use; to ensure the existence of "a climate conducive to students' becoming information literate"; to include information literacy concerns in teacher education; and to promote public awareness of the relationship between information literacy and the more general goals of "literacy, productivity, and democracy."

In March 1998 the Presidential Committee on Information Literacy re-evaluated its Final Report and published an update. The update looks at what the Final Report set out to accomplish, its six main goals, and how far it had come to that point in meeting those objectives. Before identifying what still needs to be done, the updated report recognizes what the previous report and the National Forum were able to accomplish. In realizing it still had not met all objectives, it set out further recommendations to ensure all were met. The updated report ends with an invitation, asking the National Forum and regular citizens to recognize that "the result of these combined efforts will be a citizenry which is made up of effective lifelong learners who can always find the information needed for the issue or decision at hand. This new generation of information literate citizens will truly be America's most valuable resource", and to continue working toward an information literate world.

One of the most important things to come out of the Presidential Committee on Information Literacy was the creation of the National Forum on Information Literacy.

NATIONAL FORUM ON INFORMATION LITERACY

Background

In 1983, the seminal report "A Nation at Risk: The Imperative for Educational Reform" declared that a "rising tide of mediocrity" was eroding the very foundations of the

American educational system. It was, in fact, the genesis of the current educational reform movement within the United States. Ironically, the report did not include in its set of reform recommendations the academic and/or the public library as one of the key architects in the redesign of our K-16 educational system. This report and several others that followed, in conjunction with the rapid emergence of the information society, led the American Library Association (ALA) to convene a blue ribbon panel of national educators and librarians in 1987. The ALA Presidential Committee on Information Literacy was charged with the following tasks:

(1) to define information literacy within the higher literacies and its importance to student performance, lifelong learning, and active citizenship;

(2) to design one or more models for information literacy development appropriate to formal and informal learning environments throughout people's lifetimes; and

(3) to determine implications for the continuing education and development of teachers.

In the release of its Final Report in 1989, the American Library Association Presidential Committee on Information Literacy summarized in its opening paragraphs the ultimate mission of the National Forum on Information Literacy:

"How our country deals with the realities of the Information Age will have enormous impact on our democratic way of life and on our nation's ability to compete internationally. Within America's information society, there also exists the potential of addressing many long-standing social and economic inequities. To reap such benefits, people—as individuals and as a nation—must be information literate. To be information literate, a person must be able to recognize when information is needed and have the ability to locate, evaluate, and use effectively the needed information. Producing such a citizenry will require that schools and colleges appreciate and integrate the concept of information literacy into their learning programs and that they play a leadership role in equipping individuals and institutions to take advantage of the opportunities inherent within the information society.

Ultimately, information literate people are those who have learned how to learn. They know how to learn because they know how knowledge is organized, how to find information, and how to use information in such a way that others can learn from them. They are people prepared for lifelong learning because they can always find the information needed for any task or decision at hand."

Acknowledging that the major obstacle to people becoming information literate citizens, who are prepared for lifelong learning, "is a lack of public awareness of the problems created by information illiteracy," the report recommended the formation of a coalition of national organizations to promote information literacy."

Thus, in 1989, the A. L. A. Presidential Committee established the National Forum on Information Literacy, a volunteer network of organizations committed to raising public awareness on the importance of information literacy to individuals, communities, the economy, and to engage citizenship participation.

The forum today

Since 1989, the National Forum on Information Literacy has evolved steadily under the leadership of its first chair, Dr. Patricia Senn Breivik. Today, the Forum represents over 90 national and international organizations, all dedicated to mainstreaming the philosophy of information literacy across national and international landscapes, and throughout every educational, domestic, and workplace venue.

Although the initial intent of the Forum was to raise public awareness and support on a national level, over the last several years, the National Forum on Information Literacy has made significant strides internationally in promoting the importance of integrating information literacy concepts and skills throughout all educational, governmental, and workforce development programs. For example, the National Forum co-sponsored with UNESCO and IFLA several "experts meetings", resulting in the Prague Declaration (2003) and the Alexandria Proclamation (2005) each underscoring the importance of information literacy as a basic fundamental human right and lifelong learning skill.

In the United States, however, information literacy skill development has been the exception and not the rule, particularly as it relates to the integration of information literacy practices within our educational and workforce development infrastructures. In a 2000 peer-reviewed publication, Nell K. Duke, found that students in first grade classrooms were exposed to an average of 3. 6 minutes of informational text in a school day. In October 2006, the first national Summit on Information Literacy brought together over 100 representatives from education, business, and government to address America's information literacy deficits as a nation currently competing in a global marketplace. This successful collaboration was sponsored by the National Forum on Information Literacy, Committee for Economic Development, Educational Testing Service, the Institute for a Competitive Workforce, and National Education Association (NEA). The Summit was held at NEA headquarters in Washington, D. C.

A major outcome of the Summit was the establishment of a national ICT literacy policy council to provide leadership in creating national standards for ICT literacy in the United States.

As stated on the Forum's Main Web page, it recognizes that achieving information literacy has been much easier for those with money and other advantages. For those who are poor, non-White, older, disabled, living in rural areas or otherwise disadvantaged, it has been much harder to overcome the digital divide. A number of the Forum's members address the specific challenges for those disadvantaged. For example, The Children's Partnership advocates for the nearly 70 million children and youth in the country, many of whom are disadvantaged. The Children's Partnership currently runs three programs, two of which specifically address the needs of those with low-incomes: Online content for Low-Income and Underserved Americans Initiative, and the California Initiative Program. Another example is the National Hispanic Council on Aging, which is:

Dedicated to improving the quality of life for Latino elderly, families, and communities through advocacy, capacity and institution building, development of educational materials, technical assistance, demonstration projects, policy analysis and research (National Hispanic Council on Aging, and, Mission Statement section).

The National Forum on Information Literacy will continue to work closely with educational, business, and non-profit organizations in the U. S. to promote information literacy skill development at every opportunity, particularly in light of the ever-growing social, economic, and political urgency of globalization, prompting citizens to re-energize our promotional and collaborative efforts.

Effects on education

The rapidly evolving information landscape has demonstrated a need for education methods and practices to evolve and adapt accordingly. Information literacy is a key focus of educational institutions at all levels and in order to uphold this standard, institutions are promoting a commitment to lifelong learning and an ability to seek out and identify innovations that will be needed to keep pace with or outpace changes.

Educational methods and practices, within our increasingly information-centric society, must facilitate and enhance a student's ability to harness the power of information. Key to harnessing the power of information is the ability to evaluate information, to ascertain among other things its relevance, authenticity and modernity. The information evaluation process is crucial life skill and a basis for lifelong learning. According to Lankshear and Knobel, what is needed in our education system is a new understanding of literacy, information literacy and on literacy teaching. Educators need to learn to account for the context of our culturally and linguistically diverse and increasingly globalized societies. We also need to take account for the burgeoning variety of text forms associated with information and multimedia technologies.

Evaluation consists of several component processes including metacognition, goals, personal disposition, cognitive development, deliberation, and decision-making. This is both a difficult and complex challenge and underscores the importance of being able to think critically.

Critical thinking is an important educational outcome for students. Education institutions have experimented with several strategies to help foster critical thinking, as a means to enhance information evaluation and information literacy among students. When evaluating evidence, students should be encouraged to practice formal argumentation. Debates and formal presentations must also be encouraged to analyze and critically evaluate information.

Education professionals must underscore the importance of high information quality. Students must be trained to distinguish between fact and opinion. They must be encouraged to use cue words such as "I think" and "I feel" to help distinguish between factual information and opinions. Information related skills that are complex or difficult to comprehend must be broken down into smaller parts. Another approach would be to train students in familiar contexts. Education professionals should encourage students to examine "causes" of behaviors, actions and events. Research shows that people evaluate more effectively if causes are revealed, where available.

Some call for increased critical analysis in Information Literacy instruction. Smith (2013) identifies this as beneficial "to individuals, particularly young people during their period of formal education. It could equip them with the skills they need to understand the political system and their place within it, and, where necessary, to challenge this" (p. 16).

National content standards, state standards, and information literacy skills terminology may vary, but all have common components relating to information literacy. Information literacy skills are critical to several of the National Education Goals outlined in the Goals 2000: Educate America Act, particularly in the act's aims to increase "school readiness", "student achievement and citizenship", and "adult literacy and lifelong learning". Of specific relevance are the "focus on lifelong learning, the ability to think critically, and on the use of new and existing information for problem solving", all of which are important components of information literacy.

In 1998, the American Association of School Librarians and the Association for Educational Communications and Technology published "Information Literacy Standards for Student Learning", which identified nine standards that librarians and teachers in K-12 schools could use to describe information literate students and define the relationship of information literacy to independent learning and social responsibility:

- Standard One: The student who is information literate accesses information efficiently and effectively.
- Standard Two: The student who is information literate evaluates information critically and competently.

- Standard Three: The student who is information literate uses information accurately and creatively.
- Standard Four: The student who is an independent learner is information literate and pursues information related to personal interests.
- Standard Five: The student who is an independent learner is information literate and appreciates literature and other creative expressions of information.
- Standard Six: The student who is an independent learner is information literate and strives for excellence in information seeking and knowledge generation.
- Standard Seven: The student who contributes positively to the learning community and to society is information literate and recognizes the importance of information to a democratic society.
- Standard Eight: The student who contributes positively to the learning community and to society is information literate and practices ethical behavior in regard to information and information technology.
- Standard Nine: The student who contributes positively to the learning community and to society is information literate and participates effectively in groups to pursue and generate information.

In 2007 AASL expanded and restructured the standards that school librarians should strive for in their teaching. These were published as "Standards for the 21st Century Learner" and address several literacies: information, technology, visual, textual, and digital. These aspects of literacy were organized within four key goals: that "learners use of skills, resources, & tools" to "inquire, think critically, and gain knowledge"; to "draw conclusions, make informed decisions, apply knowledge to new situations, and create new knowledge"; to "share knowledge and participate ethically and productively as members of our democratic society"; and to "pursue personal and aesthetic growth".

In 2000, the Association of College and Research Libraries (ACRL), a division of the American Library Association (ALA), released "Information Literacy Competency Standards for Higher Education", describing five standards and numerous performance indicators considered best practices for the implementation and assessment of postsecondary information literacy programs. The five standards are:

- Standard One: The information literate student determines the nature and extent of the information needed.
- Standard Two: The information literate student accesses needed information effectively and efficiently.

- Standard Three: The information literate student evaluates information and its sources critically and incorporates selected information into his or her knowledge base and value system.
- Standard Four: The information literate student, individually or as a member of a group, uses information effectively to accomplish a specific purpose.
- Standard Five: The information literate student understands many of the economic, legal, and social issues surrounding the use of information and accesses and uses information ethically and legally.

These standards are meant to span from the simple to more complicated, or in terms of Bloom's Taxonomy of Educational Objectives, from the "lower order" to the "higher order". Lower order skills would involve for instance being able to use an online catalog to find a book relevant to an information need in an academic library. Higher order skills would involve critically evaluating and synthesizing information from multiple sources into a coherent interpretation or argument.

In 2016, the Association of College and Research Librarians (ACRL) rescinded the Standards and replaced them with the Framework for Information Literacy for Higher Education, which offers the following set of core ideas:

- Authority is Constructed and Contextual
- Information Creation as a Process
- Information Has Value
- Research as Inquiry
- Scholarship as Conversation
- Searching as Strategic Exploration

The Framework is based on a cluster of interconnected core concepts, with flexible options for implementation, rather than on a set of standards or learning outcomes, or any prescriptive enumeration of skills. At the heart of this Framework are conceptual understandings that organize many other concepts and ideas about information, research, and scholarship into a coherent whole.

K-12 EDUCATION RESTRUCTURING

Today instruction methods have changed drastically from the mostly one-directional teacher-student model, to a more collaborative approach where the students themselves feel empowered. Much of this challenge is now being informed by the American Association of School Librarians that published new standards for student learning in 2007.

Within the K-12 environment, effective curriculum development is vital to imparting Information Literacy skills to students. Given the already heavy load on students, efforts must be made to avoid curriculum overload. Eisenberg strongly recommends adopting a collaborative approach to curriculum development among classroom teachers, librarians, technology teachers, and other educators. Staff must be encouraged to work together to analyze student curriculum needs, develop a broad instruction plan, set information literacy goals, and design specific unit and lesson plans that integrate the information skills and classroom content. These educators can also collaborate on teaching and assessment duties

Educators are selecting various forms of resource-based learning (authentic learning, problem-based learning and work-based learning) to help students focus on the process and to help students learn from the content. Information literacy skills are necessary components of each. Within a school setting, it is very important that a students' specific needs as well as the situational context be kept in mind when selecting topics for integrated information literacy skills instruction. The primary goal should be to provide frequent opportunities for students to learn and practice information problem solving. To this extent, it is also vital to facilitate repetition of information seeking actions and behavior. The importance of repetition in information literacy lesson plans cannot be underscored, since we tend to learn through repetition. A students' proficiency will improve over time if they are afforded regular opportunities to learn and to apply the skills they have learnt.

The process approach to education is requiring new forms of student assessment. Students demonstrate their skills, assess their own learning, and evaluate the processes by which this learning has been achieved by preparing portfolios, learning and research logs, and using rubrics.

EFFORTS IN K-12 EDUCATION

Many states have either fully adopted AASL information literacy standards or have adapted them to suit their needs. States such as Oregon (OSLIS, 2009) increasing rely on these guidelines for curriculum development and setting information literacy goals. Virginia, on the other hand, chose to undertake a comprehensive review, involving all relevant stakeholders and formulate its own guidelines and standards for information literacy. At an international level, two framework documents jointly produced by UNESCO and the IFLA (International Federation of Library Associations and Institutions) developed two framework documents that laid the foundations in helping define the educational role to be played by school libraries: the School library manifesto (1999),.

Another immensely popular approach to imparting information literacy is the Big6 set of skills. Eisenberg claims that the Big6 is the most widely used model in K-12 education. This set of skills seeks to articulate the entire information seeking life cycle. The Big6 is made up of six major stages and two sub-stages under each major stages. It defines the six steps as being: task definition, information seeking strategies, location and access, use of information, synthesis, and evaluation. Such approaches seek to cover the full range of information problem-solving actions that a person would normally undertake, when faced with an information problem or with making a decision based on available resources.

EFFORTS IN HIGHER EDUCATION

Information literacy instruction in higher education can take a variety of forms: stand-alone courses or classes, online tutorials, workbooks, course-related instruction, or course-integrated instruction. One attempt in the area of physics was published in 2009.

The six regional accreditation boards have added information literacy to their standards, Librarians often are required to teach the concepts of information literacy during "one shot" classroom lectures. There are also credit courses offered by academic librarians to prepare college students to become information literate.

In 2016, the Association of College & Research Libraries (ACRL, part of the American Library Association) adopted a new Framework for Information Literacy for Higher Education, replacing the ACRL's Information Literacy Standards for Higher Education that had been approved in 2000. The standards were largely criticized by proponents of critical information literacy, a concept deriving from critical pedagogy, for being too prescriptive. It's termed a "framework" because it consists of interconnected core concepts designed to be interpreted and implemented locally depending on the context and needs of the audience. The framework draws on recent research around threshold concepts, or the ideas that are gateways to broader understanding or skills in a given discipline. It also draws on newer research around meta-literacy, and assumes a more holistic view of information literacy that includes creation and collaboration in addition to consumption, so is appropriate for current practices around social media and Web 2. 0. The six concepts, or frames, are:

- Authority Is Constructed and Contextual
- Information Creation as a Process
- Information Has Value
- Research as Inquiry
- Scholarship as Conversation

7

RECORDS MANAGEMENT THEORY

The records life-cycle consists of discrete phases covering the life span of a record from its creation to its final disposition. In the creation phase, records growth is expounded by modern electronic systems. Records will continue to be created and captured by the organization at an explosive rate as it conducts the business of the organization. Correspondence regarding a product failure is written for internal leadership, financial statements and reports are generated for public and regulatory scrutiny, the old corporate logo is retired, and a new one - including color scheme and approved corporate font - takes its place in the organization's history.

Examples of records phases include those for creation of a record, modification of a record, movement of a record through its different states while in existence, and destruction of a record. Throughout the records life cycle, issues such as security, privacy, disaster recovery, emerging technologies, and mergers are addressed by the records and information management professional responsible for organizational programs. Records and information management professionals are instrumental in controlling and safeguarding the information assets of the entity. They understand how to manage the creation, access, distribution, storage, and disposition of records and information in an efficient and cost-effective manner using records and information management methodology, principles, and best practices in compliance with records and information laws and regulations.

An organization or organisation is an entity comprising multiple people, such as an institution or an association, that has a particular purpose.

The word is derived from the Greek word organon, which means tool or instrument, musical instrument, and organ.

TYPES

There are a variety of legal types of organisations, including corporations, governments, non-governmental organisations, political organisations, international organisations, armed forces, charities, not-for-profit corporations, partnerships, cooperatives, and educational institutions.

A hybrid organisation is a body that operates in both the public sector and the private sector simultaneously, fulfilling public duties and developing commercial market activities.

A voluntary association is an organisation consisting of volunteers. Such organisations may be able to operate without legal formalities, depending on jurisdiction, including informal clubs.

Organisations may also operate secretly or illegally in the case of secret societies, criminal organisations and resistance movements.

Compare the concept of social groups, which may include non-organizations.

Structures

The study of organisations includes a focus on optimising organisational structure. According to management science, most human organisations fall roughly into four types:

- Committees or juries
- Ecologies
- Matrix organisations
- Pyramids or hierarchies

Committees or juries

These consist of a group of peers who decide as a group, perhaps by voting. The difference between a jury and a committee is that the members of the committee are usually assigned to perform or lead further actions after the group comes to a decision, whereas members of a jury come to a decision. In common law countries, legal juries render decisions of guilt, liability and quantify damages; juries are also used in athletic contests, book awards and similar activities. Sometimes a selection committee functions like a jury. In the Middle Ages, juries in continental Europe were used to determine the law according to consensus among local notables.

Committees are often the most reliable way to make decisions. Condorcet's jury theorem proved that if the average member votes better than a roll of dice, then adding more members increases the number of majorities that can come to a correct vote (however correctness is defined). The problem is that if the average member is subsequently worse than a roll of dice, the committee's decisions grow worse, not better; therefore, staffing is crucial.

Parliamentary procedure, such as Robert's Rules of Order, helps prevent committees from engaging in lengthy discussions without reaching decisions.

Ecologies

This organisational structure promotes internal competition. Inefficient components of the organisation starve, while effective ones get more work. Everybody is paid for what they actually do, and so runs a tiny business that has to show a profit, or they are fired.

Companies who utilise this organisation type reflect a rather one-sided view of what goes on in ecology. It is also the case that a natural ecosystem has a natural border - ecoregions do not, in general, compete with one another in any way, but are very autonomous.

The pharmaceutical company GlaxoSmithKline talks about functioning as this type of organisation in this external article from The Guardian. By:Bastian Batac De Leon.

Matrix organisation

This organisational type assigns each worker two bosses in two different hierarchies. One hierarchy is "functional" and assures that each type of expert in the organisation is well-trained, and measured by a boss who is super-expert in the same field. The other direction is "executive" and tries to get projects completed using the experts. Projects might be organised by products, regions, customer types, or some other schemes.

As an example, a company might have an individual with overall responsibility for products X and Y, and another individual with overall responsibility for engineering, quality control, etc. Therefore, subordinates responsible for quality control of project X will have two reporting lines.

Pyramids or hierarchical

A hierarchy exemplifies an arrangement with a leader who leads other individual members of the organisation. This arrangement is often associated with basis that there are enough imagine a real pyramid, if there are not enough stone blocks to hold up the higher ones, gravity would irrevocably bring down the monumental structure. So one can imagine that if the leader does not have the support of his subordinates, the entire structure will collapse. Hierarchies were satirised in The Peter Principle (1969), a book that introduced hierarchiology and the saying that "in a hierarchy every employee tends to rise to his level of incompetence."

Theories

In the social sciences, organisations are the object of analysis for a number of disciplines, such as sociology, economics, political science, psychology, management, and organisational communication. The broader analysis of organisations is commonly referred to as organisational structure, organisational studies, organisational behaviour, or organisation analysis. A number of different perspectives exist, some of which are compatible:

- From a functional perspective, the focus is on how entities like businesses or state authorities are used.
- From an institutional perspective, an organisation is viewed as a purposeful structure within a social context.
- From a process-related perspective, an organisation is viewed as an entity is being (re-)organised, and the focus is on the organisation as a set of tasks or actions.

Sociology can be defined as the science of the institutions of modernity; specific institutions serve a function, akin to the individual organs of a coherent body. In the social and political sciences in general, an "organisation" may be more loosely understood as the planned, coordinated and purposeful action of human beings working through collective action to reach a common goal or construct a tangible product. This action is usually framed by formal membership and form (institutional rules). Sociology distinguishes the term organisation into planned formal and unplanned informal (i.e. spontaneously formed) organisations. Sociology analyses organisations in the first line from an institutional perspective. In this sense, organisation is an enduring arrangement of elements. These elements and their actions are determined by rules so that a certain task can be fulfilled through a system of coordinated division of labour.

Economic approaches to organisations also take the division of labour as a starting point. The division of labour allows for (economies of) specialisation. Increasing specialisation necessitates coordination. From an economic point of view, markets and organisations are alternative coordination mechanisms for the execution of transactions.

An organisation is defined by the elements that are part of it (who belongs to the organisation and who does not?), its communication (which elements communicate and how do they communicate?), its autonomy (which changes are executed autonomously by the organisation or its elements?), and its rules of action compared to outside events (what causes an organisation to act as a collective actor?).

By coordinated and planned cooperation of the elements, the organisation is able to solve tasks that lie beyond the abilities of the single elements. The price paid by the elements is the limitation of the degrees of freedom of the elements. Advantages of organisations are enhancement (more of the same), addition (combination of different features) and extension. Disadvantages can be inertness (through co-ordination) and loss of interaction.

Among the theories that are or have been influential are:

- Activity theory is the major theoretical influence, acknowledged by de Clodomir Santos de Morais in the development of Organisation Workshop method.
- Actor-network theory, an approach to social theory and research, originating in the field of science studies, which treats objects as part of social networks.
- Complexity theory and organisations, the use of complexity theory in the field of strategic management and organisational studies.
- Contingency theory, a class of behavioural theory that claims that there is no best way to organize a corporation, to lead a company, or to make decisions.
- Critical management studies, a loose but extensive grouping of theoretically informed critiques of management, business, and organisation, grounded originally in a critical theory perspective
- Economic sociology, studies both the social effects and the social causes of various economic phenomena.
- Enterprise architecture, the conceptual model that defines the coalescence of organisational structure and organisational behaviour.
- Garbage Can Model, describes a model which disconnects problems, solutions and decision makers from each other.
- Principal-agent problem, concerns the difficulties in motivating one party (the "agent"), to act in the best interests of another (the "principal") rather than in his or her own interests
- Scientific management (mainly following Frederick W. Taylor), a theory of management that analyses and synthesises workflows.
- Social entrepreneurship, the process of pursuing innovative solutions to social problems.
- Transaction cost theory, the idea that people begin to organise their production in firms when the transaction cost of coordinating production through the market exchange, given imperfect information, is greater than within the firm.
- Weber's Ideal of Bureaucracy (refer to Max Weber's chapter on "Bureaucracy" in his book Economy and Society)

Leadership

A leader in a formal, hierarchical organisation, is appointed to a managerial position and has the right to command and enforce obedience by virtue of the authority of his position. However, he must possess adequate personal attributes to match his authority, because authority is only potentially available to him. In the absence of sufficient personal competence, a manager may be confronted by an emergent leader who can challenge his role in the organisation and reduce it to that of a figurehead. However, only authority of position has the backing of formal sanctions. It follows that whoever wields personal influence and power can legitimise this only by gaining a formal position in the hierarchy, with commensurate authority.

FORMAL ORGANISATIONS

An organisation that is established as a means for achieving defined objectives has been referred to as a formal organisation. Its design specifies how goals are subdivided and reflected in subdivisions of the organisation. Divisions, departments, sections, positions, jobs, and tasks make up this work structure. Thus, the formal organisation is expected to behave impersonally in regard to relationships with clients or with its members. According to Weber's definition, entry and subsequent advancement is by merit or seniority. Each employee receives a salary and enjoys a degree of tenure that safeguards him from the arbitrary influence of superiors or of powerful clients. The higher his position in the hierarchy, the greater his presumed expertise in adjudicating problems that may arise in the course of the work carried out at lower levels of the organisation. It is this bureaucratic structure that forms the basis for the appointment of heads or chiefs of administrative subdivisions in the organisation and endows them with the authority attached to their position.

Informal organisations

In contrast to the appointed head or chief of an administrative unit, a leader emerges within the context of the informal organisation that underlies the formal structure. The informal organisation expresses the personal objectives and goals of the individual membership. Their objectives and goals may or may not coincide with those of the formal organisation. The informal organisation represents an extension of the social structures that generally characterise human life - the spontaneous emergence of groups and organisations as ends in themselves.

In prehistoric times, man was preoccupied with his personal security, maintenance, protection, and survival. Now man spends a major portion of his waking hours working for organisations. His need to identify with a community that provides security, protection, maintenance, and a feeling of belonging continues unchanged from prehistoric times. This need is met by the informal organisation and its emergent, or unofficial, leaders. Leaders emerge from within the structure of the informal organisation. Their personal qualities, the demands of the situation, or a combination of these and other factors attract followers who accept their leadership within one or several overlay structures. Instead of the authority of position held by an appointed head or chief, the emergent leader wields influence or power. Influence is the ability of a person to gain cooperation from others by means of persuasion or control over rewards. Power is a stronger form of influence because it reflects a person's ability to enforce action through the control of a means of punishment.

Records life-cycle

Records life-cycle consisting three stages: creation, maintenance, and disposition of the record.

Records life-cycle in records management refers to the following stages of a records "life span": from its creation to its preservation (in an archives) or disposal. While various models of the records life-cycle exist, they all feature creation or receipt, use, and disposition.

The records management phase of the records life-cycle consists of creation, classification, maintenance and disposition. Creation occurs during the receipt of information in the form of records. Records or their information is classified in some logical system. As records are used they require maintenance. Disposition encompasses the destruction or transfer to an archive for future reference.

This is then followed by a second, archival phase consisting of the selection or acquisition of the records by an archives, a description of the records in inventories, finding aids, and the like and the preservation of the records or, perhaps, the information in the records. Researchers and scholars may continue to reference and use of the information contained within the records.

Continuum model

Richard Berner of the University of Washington proposed a single records management-archives goal: "responsible records use and administration leading to either authorized destruction or archival preservation and administration."

The professions of records management and archives, while distinct, surely are working towards the same objective: the effective management of recorded information through all stages of the continuum, from creation to disposal. Effective management of recorded information (what Berner calls "responsible records use and administration") requires ongoing cooperative interaction between the records manager and the archivist in order to:

- ensure the creation of the right records, containing the right information, in the right format;

- organize the records and analyze their content and significance to facilitate their availability;
- make them available promptly to those (administrators and researchers alike) who have a right and a requirement to see them;
- systematically dispose of records that are no longer required; and
- protect and preserve the information for as long as it may be needed (if necessary, forever).

RECORDS CONTINUUM MODEL

The records continuum theory is an abstract conceptual model that helps to understand and explore recordkeeping activities in relation to multiple contexts over space and time.

Records management practices and concepts

A Records Manager is someone who is responsible for records management in an organizatioN

Section 4 of the ISO 15489-1:2001 states that records management includes:

- setting policies and standards
- assigning responsibilities and authorities
- establishing and promulgating procedures and guidelines
- providing a range of services relating to the management and use of records
- designing, implementing and administering specialized systems for managing records
- integrating records management into business systems and processes

Thus, the practice of records management may involve:

- planning the information needs of an organization
- identifying information requiring capture
- creating, approving, and enforcing policies and practices regarding records, including their organization and disposal
- developing a records storage plan, which includes the short and long-term housing of physical records and digital information
- identifying, classifying, and storing records
- coordinating access to records internally and outside of the organization, balancing the requirements of business confidentiality, data privacy, and public access.

- identification and maintenance of records per a specified retention period
- executing a retention policy on the disposal of records which are no longer required for operational reasons; according to organizational policies, statutory requirements, and other regulations this may involve either their destruction or permanent preservation in an archive.

Records-management principles and automated records-management systems aid in the capture, classification, and ongoing management of records throughout their lifecycle. Such a system may be paper-based (such as index cards as used in a library), or may involve a computer system, such as an electronic records-management application.

Records Continuum Model

The Records Continuum Model (RCM) was created in the 1990s by Monash University academic Frank Upward with input from colleagues Sue McKemmish and Livia Iacovino as a response to evolving discussions about the challenges of managing digital records and archives in the discipline of Archival Science. The RCM was first published in Upward's 1996 paper "Structuring the Records Continuum - Part One: Postcustodial principles and properties". Upward describes the RCM within the broad context of a continuum where activities and interactions transform documents into records, evidence and memory that are used for multiple purposes over time. Upward places the RCM within a post-custodial, postmodern and structuration conceptual framework. Australian academics and practitioners continue to explore, develop and extend the RCM and records continuum theory, along with international collaborators, via the Records Continuum Research Group (RCRG) at Monash University.

Description

The RCM is an abstract conceptual model that helps to understand and explore recordkeeping activities (as interaction) in relation to multiple contexts over space and time (spacetime). Recordkeeping activities take place from before the records are created by identifying recordkeeping requirements in policies, systems, organizations, processes, laws, social mandates that impact on what is created and how it is managed over spacetime. In a continuum, recordkeeping processes, such as adding metadata, fix documents so that they can be managed as evidence. Those records deemed as having continuing value are retained and managed as an archive. The implication of an RCM approach to records and archives is that systems and processes can be designed and put in place before records are even created. A continuum approach therefore highlights that records are both current and archival at the point of creation.

The RCM is represented as a series of concentric rings (dimensions of Create, Capture, Organize and Pluralize) and crossed axes (transactionality, evidentiality, recordkeeping and identity) with each axis labelled with a description of the activity or interaction that occurs at that intersection. Create, Capture, Organize and Pluralize represent recordkeeping activities that occur within spacetime. Activities that occur in these dimensions across the axes are explained in the table below:

The value of the RCM is that it can help to map where on a continuum recordkeeping activities are or can be placed. The RCM can then be used to explore the conceptual and practical assumptions that underpin the practice, in particular the dualisms inherent in the usage and practice of the terms "records" and "archives". This definition lends itself to a linear reading of the RCM - starting at Create as the initiating phase and working outwards towards Pluralization of recorded information. Another linear reading is to consider design first - the role that systems of Pluralization and Organization play in designing, planning and implementing recordkeeping and then considering the implications for Create and Capture. However, these are just two of many ways to interpret the model as the dimensions and axes represent multiple realities that occur within spacetime, any of which can occur simultaneously, concurrently and sequentially in electronic or digital environments, and/or physical spaces.

By representing multiple realities, the RCM articulates the numerous and diverse perspectives that contribute to records and archives including individual, group, community, organizational, institutional and societal. These contexts reveal the need to take into account various stakeholders and co-contributors in relation to use, access and appraisal of records and archives. Over the lifespan of a record multiple decisions are made by various stakeholders of the records that include, but are not limited to records managers and archivists. Other stakeholders can be identified at various dimensions of interaction, including those involved in providing information (not only the person or organization who produced or captured it), as well as their family and community. Records are therefore not simply physical or digital representations of physical objects held and managed in an archive or repository, but are evidence of multiple perspectives, narratives and contexts that contributed to their formation.

The RCM is often described as being in contrast or at odds with the lifecycle records model. While the RCM is inclusive of multiple ways of conceptualizing and performing recordkeeping, including a lifecycle approach, there are some significant differences. Firstly, where the lifecycle approach shows clearly demarcated phases in the management of records, a continuum approach conceptualizes elements as continuous with no discernable parts. Secondly, the lifecycle approach identifies clear conceptual and procedural boundaries between active or current records and inactive or historical records, but a continuum approach sees records processes as more integrated across spacetime. In the continuum it is recordkeeping processes that carry records forward through spacetime to enable their use for multiple purposes. What this means is that records are always "in a state of always becoming...", and able to contribute new contexts via the recordkeeping processes that occur with them. Archival records are therefore not just historical, but are able to be re-interpreted, re-created, and re-contextualized according to their place and use in spacetime. In this way, archival institutions are nodes in the network of recorded information and its contexts, rather than the end point in a lifecycle stage for records that are managed as "relics".

THEORY AND INFLUENCES

The RCM is a representation of what is commonly referred to as records continuum theory, as well as Australian continuum thinking and/or approaches. These ideas were evolved as part of an Australian approach to archival management espoused by Ian Maclean, Chief Archivist of the Commonwealth Archives Office in Australia in the 1950s and 1960s. Maclean, whose ideas and practices were the subject of the first RCRG publication in 1994, referred in a 1959 American Archivist article to a "continuum of (public) records administration" from administrative efficiency through recordkeeping to the safe keeping of a "cultural end-product". Maclean's vision challenged the divide between current recordkeeping and archival practice. Fellow contemporary at the Commonwealth Archives Office Peter Scott is also included as a core influence on Australian records continuum theory with his development of the Australian Series System, a registry system that helped identify and document the complex and multiple "social, functional, provenancial, and documentary relationships" involved in managing records and recordkeeping processes over spacetime.

Further influences on the RCRG group include archival professionals and researchers like David Bearman and his work on transactionality and systems thinking, and Terry Cook's ideas about postcustodialism and macroappraisal. Wider influencing ideas include those from philosophers and social theorists Jacques Lacan, Michel Foucault, Jacques Derrida, and Jean-François Lyotard, as well as sociologist Anthony Giddens, with structuration theory being a core component of understanding social interaction over spacetime. Canadian archivist Jay Atherton's critique of the division between records managers and archivists in the 1980s and use of the term "records continuum" re-commenced the conversation MacLean began during his career and helped to bring his ideas and this term to Australian records continuum thinking. Atherton's use of the term records continuum has several significant differences in conception, application and heritage when compared to Australian records continuum thinking.

Post-custodiality as an archival concept plays a major role in how the RCM was conceived. This term was born from an identified and urgent need to address the complexities of computer technologies on records creation and management over time and space. Post-custodiality is discussed by Frank Upward and Sue McKemmish in 1994 as part of an exploration of changes in archival discourse commencing in the 1980s by Gerald Ham and expanded on by Terry Cook as part of a "post-custodial paradigm shift". Post-custodiality in relation to the RCM is explored by Upward and McKemmish as an entry point into a wider conversation about records and recordkeeping being part of a process in which archival institutions have a part to play beyond that of the archival authority handling, appraisal, describing and arranging physical objects in their custody.

Drawing from the above theoretical foundations, the RCM as a framework acknowledges the central role that recordkeeping activities have on the creation, capture, organization and ongoing management of records over time and throughout spaces such as organizations and institutional archives. Recordkeeping is a practice and a concept clearly defined in the archival and records literature by continuum writers as "a broad and inclusive concept of integrated recordkeeping and archiving processes for current, regulatory, and historical recordkeeping purposes". Recordkeeping refers to the activities performed on records that add new contexts such as capturing a record into a system, adding metadata, or selecting it for an archive. In the RCM records are therefore not defined according to their status as objects. Rather, records are understood as being part of a continuum of activity related to known (as well as potentially unknown) contexts. A record (as well as records, collections and archives) are therefore part of larger social, cultural, political, legal and archival processes. It is these contexts that are vital to understanding the role, value and evidential qualities of records in and across spacetime (past, present and potential future).

Other information continuum models

The RCM is the most well-known of all the continuum models created, but does not exist in isolation. Several other complementary models have been created by RCM creator Frank Upward, and there are others created by continuum researchers that offer enhanced or alternative ways of understanding the continuum.

The series of continuum models created by Frank Upward include:

- Information Systems (Data) Continuum Model (data modeling and data flow)
- Cultural Herita
- ge Continuum Model (the stories the documents tell and the significance of those stories to others)
- Publication (Access) Continuum Model (the reach of accessibility and the way the document is issued)

Models created in collaboration:

- Information Continuum Model (Barbara Reed, Don Schauder, Frank Upward) (the technologies driving the system and classification methods)

Other models:

- Juridical contexts of the Records Continuum Model (Livia Iacovino)
- Mediated Recordkeeping: culture-as-evidence (Leisa Gibbons)

A defensible solution is one that can be supported with clearly documented policies, processes and procedures that drive how and why work is performed, as well as one that has clearly documented proof of behavior patterns, proving that an organization follows such documented constraints to the best of their ability.

While defensibility applies to all aspects of records life cycle, it is considered most important in the context of records destruction, where it is known as "defensible disposition" or "defensible destruction," and helps an organization explicitly justify and prove things like who destroys records, why they destroy them, how they destroy them, when they destroy them, and where they destroy them.

Classification

Records managers use classification or categorization of record types as a means of working with records. Such classifications assist in functions such as creation, organization, storage, retrieval, movement, and destruction of records.

At the highest level of classification are physical versus electronic records. (This is disputable; records are defined as such regardless of media. ISO 15489 and other best practices promulgate a functions based, rather than media based classification, because the law defines records as certain kinds of information regardless of media.)

Physical records are those records, such as paper, that can be touched and which take up physical space.

Electronic records, also often referred to as digital records, are those records that are generated with and used by information technology devices.

Classification of records is achieved through the design, maintenance, and application of taxonomies, which allow records managers to perform functions such as the categorization, tagging, segmenting, or grouping of records according to various traits.

Enterprise records

Enterprise records represent those records that are common to most enterprises, regardless of their function, purpose, or sector. Such records often revolve around the day-to-day operations of an enterprise and cover areas such as but not limited litigation, employee management, consultant or contractor management, customer engagements, purchases, sales, and contracts.

The types of enterprises that produce and work with such records include but are not limited to for-profit companies, non-profit companies, and government agencies.

Industry records

Industry records represent those records that are common and apply only to a specific industry or set of industries. Examples include but are not limited to medical industry records (e.g., the Health Insurance Portability and Accountability Act), pharmaceutical industry records, and food industry records.

Health Insurance Portability and Accountability Act

The Health Insurance Portability and Accountability Act of 1996 (HIPAA; Pub.L. 104-191, 110 Stat. 1936, enacted August 21, 1996) was enacted by the United States Congress and signed by President Bill Clinton in 1996. It was created primarily to modernize the flow of healthcare information, stipulate how Personally Identifiable Information maintained by the healthcare and healthcare insurance industries should be protected from fraud and theft, and address limitations on healthcare insurance coverage. It has been known as the Kennedy-Kassebaum Act or Kassebaum-Kennedy Act after two of its leading sponsors. The Act consists of five Titles. Title I of HIPAA protects health insurance coverage for workers and their families when they change or lose their jobs. Title II of HIPAA, known as the Administrative Simplification (AS) provisions, requires the establishment of national standards for electronic health care transactions and national identifiers for providers, health insurance plans, and employers. Title III sets guidelines for pre-tax medical spending accounts, Title IV sets guidelines for group health plans, and Title V governs company-owned life insurance policies.

TITLES

There are five sections to the act, known as titles.

Title I: Health Care Access, Portability, and Renewability

Title I of HIPAA regulates the availability and breadth of group health plans and certain individual health insurance policies. It amended the Employee Retirement Income Security Act, the Public Health Service Act, and the Internal Revenue Code.

Title I requires the coverage of and also limits restrictions that a group health plan can place on benefits for preexisting conditions. Group health plans may refuse to provide benefits in relation to preexisting conditions for either 12 months following enrollment in the plan or 18 months in the case of late enrollment. Title I allows individuals to reduce the exclusion period by the amount of time that they have had "creditable coverage" before enrolling in the plan and after any "significant breaks" in coverage. "Creditable coverage" is defined quite broadly and includes nearly all group and individual health plans, Medicare, and Medicaid. A "significant break" in coverage is defined as any 63-day period without any creditable coverage. Along with an exception, allowing employers to tie premiums or co-payments to tobacco use, or body mass index.

Title I also requires insurers to issue policies without exclusion to those leaving group health plans with creditable coverage (see above) exceeding 18 months, and renew individual policies for as long as they are offered or provide alternatives to discontinued plans for as long as the insurer stays in the market without exclusion regardless of health condition.

Some health care plans are exempted from Title I requirements, such as long-term health plans and limited-scope plans like dental or vision plans offered separately from the general health plan. However, if such benefits are part of the general health plan, then HIPAA still applies to such benefits. For example, if the new plan offers dental benefits, then it must count creditable continuous coverage under the old health plan towards any of its exclusion periods for dental benefits.

An alternate method of calculating creditable continuous coverage is available to the health plan under Title I. That is, 5 categories of health coverage can be considered separately, including dental and vision coverage. Anything not under those 5 categories must use the general calculation (e.g., the beneficiary may be counted with 18 months of general coverage, but only 6 months of dental coverage, because the beneficiary did not have a general health plan that covered dental until 6 months prior to the application date). Since limited-coverage plans are exempt from HIPAA requirements, the odd case exists in which the applicant to a general group health plan cannot obtain certificates of creditable continuous coverage for independent limited-scope plans, such as dental to apply towards exclusion periods of the new plan that does include those coverages.

Hidden exclusion periods are not valid under Title I (e.g., "The accident, to be covered, must have occurred while the beneficiary was covered under this exact same health insurance contract"). Such clauses must not be acted upon by the health plan. Also, they must be re-written so they can comply with HIPAA. Title II: Preventing Health Care Fraud and Abuse; Administrative Simplification; Medical Liability Reform

Title II of HIPAA establishes policies and procedures for maintaining the privacy and the security of individually identifiable health information, outlines numerous offenses relating to health care, and establishes civil and criminal penalties for violations. It also creates several programs to control fraud and abuse within the health-care system. However, the most significant provisions of Title II are its Administrative Simplification rules. Title II requires the Department of Health and Human Services (HHS) to increase the efficiency of the health-care system by creating standards for the use and dissemination of health-care information.

These rules apply to "covered entities", as defined by HIPAA and the HHS. Covered entities include health plans, health care clearinghouses (such as billing services and community health information systems), and health care providers that transmit health care data in a way regulated by HIPAA.

Per the requirements of Title II, the HHS has promulgated five rules regarding Administrative Simplification: the Privacy Rule, the Transactions and Code Sets Rule, the Security Rule, the Unique Identifiers Rule, and the Enforcement Rule.

Privacy Rule

The HIPAA Privacy Rule is composed of national regulations for the use and disclosure of Protected Health Information (PHI) in healthcare treatment, payment and operations by covered entities.

The effective compliance date of the Privacy Rule was April 14, 2003, with a one-year extension for certain "small plans". The HIPAA Privacy Rule regulates the use and disclosure of protected health information (PHI) held by "covered entities" (generally, health care clearinghouses, employer-sponsored health plans, health insurers, and medical service providers that engage in certain transactions). By regulation, the HHS extended the HIPAA privacy rule to independent contractors of covered entities who fit within the definition of "business associates". PHI is any information that is held by a covered entity regarding health status, provision of health care, or health care payment that can be linked to any individual. This is interpreted rather broadly and includes any part of an individual's medical record or payment history. Covered entities must disclose PHI to the individual within 30 days upon request. Also, they must disclose PHI when required to do so by law such as reporting suspected child abuse to state child welfare agencies.

Covered entities may disclose protected health information to law enforcement officials for law enforcement purposes as required by law (including court orders, court-ordered warrants, subpoenas) and administrative requests; or to identify or locate a suspect, a fugitive, a material witness, or a missing person.

A covered entity may disclose PHI to certain parties to facilitate treatment, payment, or health care operations without a patient's express written authorization. Any other disclosures of PHI require the covered entity to obtain written authorization from the individual for the disclosure. In any case, when a covered entity discloses any PHI, it must make a reasonable effort to disclose only the minimum necessary information required to achieve its purpose.

The Privacy Rule gives individuals the right to request a covered entity to correct any inaccurate PHI. Also, it requires covered entities to take some reasonable steps on ensuring the confidentiality of communications with individuals. For example, an individual can ask to be called at his or her work number instead of home or cell phone numbers. The Privacy Rule requires covered entities to notify individuals of uses of their PHI. Covered entities must also keep track of disclosures of PHI and document privacy policies and procedures. They must appoint a Privacy Official and a contact person responsible for receiving complaints and train all members of their workforce in procedures regarding PHI.

An individual who believes that the Privacy Rule is not being upheld can file a complaint with the Department of Health and Human Services Office for Civil Rights (OCR). However, according to the Wall Street Journal, the OCR has a long backlog and ignores most complaints. "Complaints of privacy violations have been piling up at the Department of Health and Human Services. Between April of 2003 and November 2006, the agency fielded 23,886 complaints related to medical-privacy rules, but it has not yet taken any enforcement actions against hospitals, doctors, insurers or anyone else for rule violations. A spokesman for the agency says it has closed three-quarters of the complaints, typically because it found no violation or after it provided informal guidance to the parties involved." However, in July 2011, UCLA agreed to pay $865,500 in a settlement regarding potential HIPAA violations. An HHS Office for Civil Rights investigation showed that from 2005 to 2008, unauthorized employees repeatedly and without legitimate cause looked at the electronic protected health information of numerous UCLAHS patients.

2013 Final Omnibus Rule Update

In January 2013, HIPAA was updated via the Final Omnibus Rule. The updates included changes to the Security Rule and Breach Notification portions of the HITECH Act. The most significant changes related to the expansion of requirements to include business associates, where only covered entities had originally been held to uphold these sections of the law.

In addition, the definition of "significant harm" to an individual in the analysis of a breach was updated to provide more scrutiny to covered entities with the intent of disclosing breaches that previously were unreported. Previously, an organization needed proof that harm had occurred whereas now organizations must prove that harm had not occurred. Protection of PHI was changed from indefinite to 50 years after death. More severe penalties for violation of PHI privacy requirements were also approved. The HIPAA Privacy rule may be waived during natural disaster. This was the case with Hurricane Harvey in 2017.

Right to access your PHI

The Privacy Rule requires medical providers to give individuals access to their PHI. After an individual requests information in writing (typically using the provider's form for this purpose), a provider has up to 30 days to provide a copy of the information to the individual. An individual may request the information in electronic form or hard-copy, and the provider is obligated to attempt to conform to the requested format. For providers using an electronic health record (EHR) system that is certified using CEHRT (Certified Electronic Health Record Technology) criteria, individuals must be allowed to obtain the PHI in electronic form. Providers are encouraged to provide the information expediently, especially in the case of electronic record requests.

Individuals have the right to access all health-related information, including health condition, treatment plan, notes, images, lab results, and billing information. Explicitly excluded are the private psychotherapy notes of a provider, and information gathered by a provider to defend against a lawsuit.

Providers can charge a reasonable amount that relates to their cost of providing the copy, however, no charge is allowable when providing data electronically from a certified EHR using the "view, download, and transfer" feature which is required for certification. When delivered to the individual in electronic form, the individual may authorize delivery using either encrypted or un-encrypted email, delivery using media (USB drive, CD, etc., which may involve a charge), direct messaging (a secure email technology in common use in the healthcare industry), or possibly other methods. When using un-encrypted email, the individual must understand and accept the risks to privacy using this technology (the information may be intercepted and examined by others). Regardless of delivery technology, a provider must continue to fully secure the PHI while in their system and can deny the delivery method if it poses additional risk to PHI while in their system.

An individual may also request (in writing) that their PHI is delivered to a designated third party such as a family care provider.

An individual may also request (in writing) that the provider send PHI to a designated service used to collect or manage their records, such as a Personal Health Record application. For example, a patient can request in writing that her ob-gyn provider digitally transmit records of her latest pre-natal visit to a pregnancy self-care app that she has on her mobile phone.

Disclosure to relatives

According to their interpretations of HIPAA, hospitals will not reveal information over the phone to relatives of admitted patients. This has in some instances impeded the location of missing persons. After the Asiana Airlines Flight 214 San Francisco crash, some hospitals were reluctant to disclose the identities of passengers that they were treating, making it difficult for Asiana and the relatives to locate them. In one instance, a man in Washington state was unable to obtain information about his injured mother.

Janlori Goldman, director of the advocacy group Health Privacy Project, said that some hospitals are being "overcautious" and misapplying the law, the Times reports. Suburban Hospital in Bethesda, Md., has interpreted a federal regulation that requires hospitals to allow patients to opt out of being included in the hospital directory as meaning that patients want to be kept out of the directory unless they specifically say otherwise. As a result, if a patient is unconscious or otherwise unable to choose to be included in the directory, relatives and friends might not be able to find them, Goldman said.

Transactions and Code Sets Rule

HIPAA was intended to make the health care system in the United States more efficient by standardizing health care transactions. HIPAA added a new Part C titled "Administrative Simplification" to Title XI of the Social Security Act. This is supposed to simplify healthcare transactions by requiring all health plans to engage in health care transactions in a standardized way.

The HIPAA/EDI provision was scheduled to take effect from October 16, 2003, with a one-year extension for certain "small plans". However, due to widespread confusion and difficulty in implementing the rule, CMS granted a one-year extension to all parties. On January 1, 2012 newer versions, ASC X12 005010 and NCPDP D.0 become effective, replacing the previous ASC X12 004010 and NCPDP 5.1 mandate. The ASC X12 005010 version provides a mechanism allowing the use of ICD-10-CM as well as other improvements.

After July 1, 2005 most medical providers that file electronically had to file their electronic claims using the HIPAA standards in order to be paid.

Under HIPAA, HIPAA-covered health plans are now required to use standardized HIPAA electronic transactions. See, 42 USC § 1320d-2 and 45 CFR Part 162. Information about this can be found in the final rule for HIPAA electronic transaction standards (74 Fed. Reg. 3296, published in the Federal Register on January 16, 2009), and on the CMS website.

Key EDI (X12) transactions used for HIPAA compliance are:

EDI Health Care Claim Transaction set (837) is used to submit health care claim billing information, encounter information, or both, except for retail pharmacy claims (see EDI Retail Pharmacy Claim Transaction). It can be sent from providers of health care services to payers, either directly or via intermediary billers and claims clearinghouses. It can also be used to transmit health care claims and billing payment information between payers with different payment responsibilities where coordination of benefits is required or between payers and regulatory agencies to monitor the rendering, billing, and/or payment of health care services within a specific health care/insurance industry segment. For example, a state mental health agency may mandate all healthcare claims, Providers and health plans who trade professional (medical) health care claims electronically must use the 837 Health Care Claim: Professional standard to send in claims. As there are many different business applications for the Health Care claim, there can be slight derivations to cover off claims involving unique claims such as for institutions, professionals, chiropractors, and dentists etc.

EDI Retail Pharmacy Claim Transaction (NCPDP Telecommunications Standard version 5.1) is used to submit retail pharmacy claims to payers by health care professionals who dispense medications, either directly or via intermediary billers and claims clearinghouses. It can also be used to transmit claims for retail pharmacy services and billing payment information between payers with different payment responsibilities where coordination of benefits is required or between payers and regulatory agencies to monitor the rendering, billing, and/or payment of retail pharmacy services within the pharmacy health care/insurance industry segment.

EDI Health Care Claim Payment/Advice Transaction Set (835) can be used to make a payment, send an Explanation of Benefits (EOB), send an Explanation of Payments (EOP) remittance advice, or make a payment and send an EOP remittance advice only from a health insurer to a health care provider either directly or via a financial institution.

EDI Benefit Enrollment and Maintenance Set (834) can be used by employers, unions, government agencies, associations or insurance agencies to enroll members to a payer. The payer is a healthcare organization that pays claims, administers insurance or benefit or product. Examples of payers include an insurance company, healthcare professional (HMO), preferred provider organization (PPO), government agency (Medicaid, Medicare etc.) or any organization that may be contracted by one of these former groups.

EDI Payroll Deducted and another group Premium Payment for Insurance Products (820) is a transaction set for making a premium payment for insurance products. It can be used to order a financial institution to make a payment to a payee.

EDI Health Care Eligibility/Benefit Inquiry (270) is used to inquire about the health care benefits and eligibility associated with a subscriber or dependent.

EDI Health Care Eligibility/Benefit Response (271) is used to respond to a request inquiry about the health care benefits and eligibility associated with a subscriber or dependent. EDI Health Care Claim Status Request (276) This transaction set can be used by a provider, recipient of health care products or services or their authorized agent to request the status of a health care claim.

EDI Health Care Claim Status Notification (277) This transaction set can be used by a healthcare payer or authorized agent to notify a provider, recipient or authorized agent regarding the status of a health care claim or encounter, or to request additional information from the provider regarding a health care claim or encounter. This transaction set is not intended to replace the Health Care Claim Payment/Advice Transaction Set (835) and therefore, is not used for account payment posting. The notification is at a summary or service line detail level. The notification may be solicited or unsolicited.

EDI Health Care Service Review Information (278) This transaction set can be used to transmit health care service information, such as subscriber, patient, demographic, diagnosis or treatment data for the purpose of the request for review, certification, notification or reporting the outcome of a health care services review.

EDI Functional Acknowledgement Transaction Set (997) this transaction set can be used to define the control structures for a set of acknowledgments to indicate the results of the syntactical analysis of the electronically encoded documents. Although it is not specifically named in the HIPAA Legislation or Final Rule, it is necessary for X12 transaction set processing. The encoded documents are the transaction sets, which are grouped in functional groups, used in defining transactions for business data interchange. This standard does not cover the semantic meaning of the information encoded in the transaction sets.

Brief 5010 Transactions and Code Sets Rules Update Summary

1. Transaction Set (997) will be replaced by Transaction Set (999) "acknowledgment report".
2. The size of many fields {segment elements} will be expanded, causing a need for all IT providers to expand corresponding fields, element, files, GUI, paper media, and databases.
3. Some segments have been removed from existing Transaction Sets.
4. Many segments have been added to existing Transaction Sets allowing greater tracking and reporting of cost and patient encounters.
5. Capacity to use both "International Classification of Diseases" versions 9 (ICD-9) and 10 (ICD-10-CM) has been added.

Security Rule

The Final Rule on Security Standards was issued on February 20, 2003. It took effect on April 21, 2003, with a compliance date of April 21, 2005, for most covered entities and April 21, 2006, for "small plans".The Security Rule complements the Privacy Rule. While the Privacy Rule pertains to all Protected Health Information (PHI) including paper and electronic, the Security Rule deals specifically with Electronic Protected Health Information (EPHI). It lays out three types of security safeguards required for compliance: administrative, physical, and technical. For each of these types, the Rule identifies various security standards, and for each standard, it names both required and addressable implementation specifications. Required specifications must be adopted and administered as dictated by the Rule. Addressable specifications are more flexible. Individual covered entities can evaluate their own situation and determine the best way to implement addressable specifications. Some privacy advocates have argued that this "flexibility" may provide too much latitude to covered entities. The standards and specifications are as follows:

- Administrative Safeguards - policies and procedures designed to clearly show how the entity will comply with the act
- Covered entities (entities that must comply with HIPAA requirements) must adopt a written set of privacy procedures and designate a privacy officer to be responsible for developing and implementing all required policies and procedures.
- The policies and procedures must reference management oversight and organizational buy-in to compliance with the documented security controls.
- Procedures should clearly identify employees or classes of employees who have access to electronic protected health information (EPHI). Access to EPHI must be restricted to only those employees who have a need for it to complete their job function.
- The procedures must address access authorization, establishment, modification, and termination.
- Entities must show that an appropriate ongoing training program regarding the handling of PHI is provided to employees performing health plan administrative functions.
- Covered entities that out-source some of their business processes to a third party must ensure that their vendors also have a framework in place to comply with HIPAA requirements. Companies typically gain this assurance through clauses in the contracts stating that the vendor will meet the same data protection requirements that apply to the covered entity. Care must be taken to determine if the vendor further out-sources any data handling functions to other vendors and monitor whether appropriate contracts and controls are in place.
- A contingency plan should be in place for responding to emergencies. Covered entities are responsible for backing up their data and having disaster recovery procedures in place. The plan should document data priority and failure analysis, testing activities, and change control procedures.
- Internal audits play a key role in HIPAA compliance by reviewing operations with the goal of identifying potential security violations. Policies and procedures

should specifically document the scope, frequency, and procedures of audits. Audits should be both routine and event-based.

- Procedures should document instructions for addressing and responding to security breaches that are identified either during the audit or the normal course of operations.
- Physical Safeguards - controlling physical access to protect against inappropriate access to protected data
- Controls must govern the introduction and removal of hardware and software from the network. (When equipment is retired it must be disposed of properly to ensure that PHI is not compromised.)
- Access to equipment containing health information should be carefully controlled and monitored.
- Access to hardware and software must be limited to properly authorized individuals.
- Required access controls consist of facility security plans, maintenance records, and visitor sign-in and escorts.
- Policies are required to address proper workstation use. Workstations should be removed from high traffic areas and monitor screens should not be in direct view of the public.
- If the covered entities utilize contractors or agents, they too must be fully trained on their physical access responsibilities.
- Technical Safeguards - controlling access to computer systems and enabling covered entities to protect communications containing PHI transmitted electronically over open networks from being intercepted by anyone other than the intended recipient.
- Information systems housing PHI must be protected from intrusion. When information flows over open networks, some form of encryption must be utilized. If closed systems/networks are utilized, existing access controls are considered sufficient and encryption is optional.
- Each covered entity is responsible for ensuring that the data within its systems has not been changed or erased in an unauthorized manner.
- Data corroboration, including the use of a checksum, double-keying, message authentication, and digital signature may be used to ensure data integrity.
- Covered entities must also authenticate entities with which they communicate.

Authentication consists of corroborating that an entity is who it claims to be. Examples of corroboration include password systems, two or three-way handshakes, telephone callback, and token systems.

- Covered entities must make documentation of their HIPAA practices available to the government to determine compliance.
- In addition to policies and procedures and access records, information technology documentation should also include a written record of all configuration settings on the components of the network because these components are complex, configurable, and always changing.
- Documented risk analysis and risk management programs are required. Covered entities must carefully consider the risks of their operations as they implement systems to comply with the act. (The requirement of risk analysis and risk management implies that the act's security requirements are a minimum standard and places responsibility on covered entities to take all reasonable precautions necessary to prevent PHI from being used for non-health purposes.)

Unique Identifiers Rule (National Provider Identifier)

HIPAA covered entities such as providers completing electronic transactions, healthcare clearinghouses, and large health plans must use only the National Provider Identifier (NPI) to identify covered healthcare providers in standard transactions by May 23, 2007. Small health plans must use only the NPI by May 23, 2008. Effective from May 2006 (May 2007 for small health plans), all covered entities using electronic communications (e.g., physicians, hospitals, health insurance companies, and so forth) must use a single new NPI. The NPI replaces all other identifiers used by health plans, Medicare, Medicaid, and other government programs. However, the NPI does not replace a provider's DEA number, state license number, or tax identification number. The NPI is 10 digits (may be alphanumeric), with the last digit being a checksum. The NPI cannot contain any embedded intelligence; in other words, the NPI is simply a number that does not itself have any additional meaning. The NPI is unique and national, never re-used, and except for institutions, a provider usually can have only one. An institution may obtain multiple NPIs for different "sub-parts" such as a free-standing cancer center or rehab facility.

Enforcement Rule

On February 16, 2006, HHS issued the Final Rule regarding HIPAA enforcement. It became effective on March 16, 2006. The Enforcement Rule sets civil money penalties for violating HIPAA rules and establishes procedures for investigations and hearings for HIPAA violations. For many years there were few prosecutions for violations.

This may have changed with the fining of $50,000 to the Hospice of North Idaho (HONI) as the first entity to be fined for a potential HIPAA Security Rule breach affecting fewer than 500 people. Rachel Seeger, a spokeswoman for HHS, stated, "HONI did not conduct an accurate and thorough risk analysis to the confidentiality of ePHI as part of its security management process from 2005 through Jan. 17, 2012." This investigation was initiated with the theft from an employees vehicle of an unencrypted laptop containing 441 patient records. As of March 2013, the U.S. Dept. of Health and Human Services (HHS) has investigated over 19,306 cases that have been resolved by requiring changes in privacy practice or by corrective action. If noncompliance is determined by HHS, entities must apply corrective measures. Complaints have been investigated against many different types of businesses such as national pharmacy chains, major health care centers, insurance groups, hospital chains and other small providers. There were 9,146 cases where the HHS investigation found that HIPAA was followed correctly. There were 44,118 cases that HHS did not find eligible cause for enforcement; for example, a violation that started before HIPAA started; cases withdrawn by the pursuer; or an activity that does not actually violate the Rules. According to the HHS website, the following lists the issues that have been reported according to frequency:

1. Misuse and disclosures of PHI
2. No protection in place of health information
3. Patient unable to access their health information
4. Using or disclosing more than the minimum necessary protected health information
5. No safeguards of electronic protected health information.

The most common entities required to take corrective action to be in voluntary compliance according to HHS are listed by frequency:

1. Private Practices
2. Hospitals
3. Outpatient Facilities
4. Group plans such as insurance groups
5. Pharmacies

Title III: Tax-related health provisions governing medical savings accounts

Title III standardizes the amount that may be saved per person in a pre-tax medical savings account. Beginning in 1997, medical savings account ("MSA") are available to employees covered under an employer-sponsored high deductible plan of a small employer and self-employed individuals.

Title IV: Application and enforcement of group health insurance requirements

Title IV specifies conditions for group health plans regarding coverage of persons with pre-existing conditions, and modifies continuation of coverage requirements. It also clarifies continuation coverage requirements and includes COBRA clarification.

Title V: Revenue offset governing tax deductions for employers

Title V includes provisions related to company-owned life insurance for employers providing company-owned life insurance premiums, prohibiting the tax-deduction of interest on life insurance loans, company endowments, or contracts related to the company. It also repeals the financial institution rule to interest allocation rules. Finally, it amends provisions of law relating to people who give up United States citizenship or permanent residence, expanding the expatriation tax to be assessed against those deemed to be giving up their U.S. status for tax reasons, and making ex-citizens' names part of the public record through the creation of the Quarterly Publication of Individuals Who Have Chosen to Expatriate.

EFFECTS ON RESEARCH AND CLINICAL CARE

The enactment of the Privacy and Security Rules has caused major changes in the way physicians and medical centers operate. The complex legalities and potentially stiff penalties associated with HIPAA, as well as the increase in paperwork and the cost of its implementation, were causes for concern among physicians and medical centers. An August 2006 article in the journal Annals of Internal Medicine detailed some such concerns over the implementation and effects of HIPAA.

Effects on research

HIPAA restrictions on researchers have affected their ability to perform retrospective, chart-based research as well as their ability to prospectively evaluate patients by contacting them for follow-up. A study from the University of Michigan demonstrated that implementation of the HIPAA Privacy rule resulted in a drop from 96% to 34% in the proportion of follow-up surveys completed by study patients being followed after a heart attack. Another study, detailing the effects of HIPAA on recruitment for a study on cancer prevention, demonstrated that HIPAA-mandated changes led to a 73% decrease in patient accrual, a tripling of time spent recruiting patients, and a tripling of mean recruitment costs.

In addition, informed consent forms for research studies now are required to include extensive detail on how the participant's protected health information will be kept private. While such information is important, the addition of a lengthy, legalistic section on privacy may make these already complex documents even less user-friendly for patients who are asked to read and sign them. These data suggest that the HIPAA privacy rule, as currently implemented, may be having negative impacts on the cost and quality of medical research. Dr. Kim Eagle, professor of internal medicine at the University of Michigan, was quoted in the Annals article as saying, "Privacy is important, but research is also important for improving care. We hope that we will figure this out and do it right."

Effects on clinical care

The complexity of HIPAA, combined with potentially stiff penalties for violators, can lead physicians and medical centers to withhold information from those who may have a right to it. A review of the implementation of the HIPAA Privacy Rule by the U.S. Government Accountability Office found that health care providers were "uncertain about their legal privacy responsibilities and often responded with an overly guarded approach to disclosing information ... than necessary to ensure compliance with the Privacy rule". Reports of this uncertainty continue.

Costs of implementation

In the period immediately prior to the enactment of the HIPAA Privacy and Security Acts, medical centers and medical practices were charged with getting "into compliance". With an early emphasis on the potentially severe penalties associated with violation, many practices and centers turned to private, for-profit "HIPAA consultants" who were intimately familiar with the details of the legislation and offered their services to ensure that physicians and medical centers were fully "in compliance". In addition to the costs of developing and revamping systems and practices, the increase in paperwork and staff time necessary to meet the legal requirements of HIPAA may impact the finances of medical centers and practices at a time when insurance companies' and Medicare reimbursement is also declining.

Education and training

Education and training of healthcare providers is paramount to correct implementation of the HIPAA Privacy and Security Acts. Effective training must describe the statutory and regulatory background and purpose of HIPAA and a general summary of the principles and key provisions of the Privacy Rule.Although each HIPAA training course should be tailored towards the roles of employees attending the course, there are some vital elements that should be included:

- What is HIPAA?
- Why HIPAA is important?
- HIPAA Definitions
- Patient's rights

- HIPAA Privacy Rule
- Disclosures of PHI
- Breach Notifications
- BA Agreements
- HIPAA Security Rule
- Safeguarding ePHI
- Potential Violations
- Employee Sanctions

HIPAA acronym

Although HIPAA fits 1996 Public Law 104-191, Health Insurance Portability and Accountability Act, references to Title II's Privacy Rule are often stated as "Health Information Privacy and Portability Act (HIPPA)" by USA federal, state, county and other government sectors. Some governmental agencies have issued corrective followups regarding HIPPA and HIPAA.

Violations

According to the US Department of Health and Human Services Office for Civil Rights, between April 2003 and January 2013, it received 91,000 complaints of HIPAA violations, in which 22,000 led to enforcement actions of varying kinds (from settlements to fines) and 521 led to referrals to the US Department of Justice as criminal actions. Examples of significant breaches of protected information and other HIPAA violations include:

- The largest loss of data that affected 4.9 million people by Tricare Management of Virginia in 2011
- The largest fines of $5.5 million levied against Memorial Healthcare Systems in 2017 for accessing confidential information of 115,143 patients and of $4.3 million levied against Cignet Health of Maryland in 2010 for ignoring patients' requests to obtain copies of their own records and repeated ignoring of federal officials' inquiries
- The first criminal indictment was lodged in 2011 against a Virginia physician who shared information with a patient's employer "under the false pretenses that the patient was a serious and imminent threat to the safety of the public, when in fact he knew that the patient was not such a threat."

According to Koczkodaj et al., 2018, the total number of individuals affected since October 2009 is 173,398,820.

The differences between civil and criminal penalties are summarized in the following table:

LEGISLATIVE INFORMATION

Legal hold records are those records that are mandated, usually by legal counsel or compliance personnel, to be held for a period of time, either by a government or by an enterprise, and for the purposes of addressing potential issues associated with compliance audits and litigation. Such records are assigned Legal Hold traits that are in addition to classifications which are as a result of enterprise or industry classifications.

Legal hold data traits may include but are not limited to things such as legal hold flags (e.g. Legal Hold = True or False), the organization driving the legal hold, descriptions of why records must be legally held, what period of time records must be held for, and the hold location.

A legal hold is a process that an organization uses to preserve all forms of relevant information when litigation is reasonably anticipated.

The legal hold is initiated by a notice or communication from legal counsel to an organization that suspends the normal disposition or processing of records, such as backup tape recycling, archived media and other storage and management of documents and information. A legal hold will be issued as a result of current or anticipated litigation, audit, government investigation or other such matter to avoid evidence spoliation. Legal holds can encompass business procedures affecting active data, including backup tape recycling. Recent amendments to the United States Federal Rules of Civil Procedure (FRCP) address the discovery of electronically stored information (ESI) (aka e-discovery), expanding the use of a "legal hold" beyond preservation of paper documents. The amendments were written in anticipation of legal arguments and tactics related to the production of ESI, such as the cost and difficulty of producing such ESI and claims that such ESI was missing, deleted, or otherwise inaccessible when it really wasn't the case. These changes took effect December 1, 2006 and require organizations to hold all electronic records until each legal matter is formally settled, even if an organization only reasonably anticipates litigation.

8

LEGAL HOLD PROCESS

An organization has a duty to preserve relevant information when it learns, or reasonably should have learned of pending or threatened litigation, or of a regulatory investigation. In order to comply with its preservation obligations, the organization should inform records custodians of the respective custodian's duty to preserve relevant information. The organization should provide instructions for doing so.

This notification and subsequent related reminders should be created and distributed to specific custodians and should require the custodian to confirm receipt of such notification. This is far superior to the traditional use of read receipts reconciliation and follow-up because it allows for an unambiguous custodian response and provides real-time tracking and reporting on custodian responses. Further, automatic logging of all related audit trail information related to the legal hold notification process is also highly recommended.

Organizations that face multiple litigation and regulatory matters at once often struggle to handle the complex moving parts associated with the preservation process. To preserve evidence, organizations must-at a minimum-issue a proper litigation hold at the right time, send it to the right people, and include the appropriate set of data. In addition, the hold must include precise, clear language that informs all custodians of their responsibilities to preserve evidence. Once the organization issues the litigation hold, the lawyer's responsibilities toward this data do not end; rather, they must regularly prompt custodians to continue preserving evidence by sending out reminder notices.

To maximize defensibility, a litigation hold program must be grounded in sound, repeatable methodology. The easiest way to ensure consistency in this process is to use templates. Organizations can create litigation hold templates that include, among other things, standard hold language, hold notification text, interview questions, reminder instructions, tags, and release notification text. In short, the litigation hold itself is the foundation of preservation, and organizations that do not get this process correct endanger their entire litigation portfolio.

Segregated repository for ESI

The process of identifying and eliminating non-relevant documents while identifying and preserving the needed documents out of a set of potentially relevant documents is "culling". The relevant documents for the case are identified and preserved in a physical repository of relevant or potentially relevant documents subject to the legal hold.

The system must make use of a highly accurate policy-based approach that enables archived and current electronic communications - including e-mail, instant messages, web transactions and communications sent from handheld devices - to be categorized and tagged according to their relevance to specific corporate policy.

Due to the substantial risks associated with deleting, losing, or not having access to such data, this should be a segregated repository to better deal with the unique retention requirements and access needs of this subset of an organization's stored documents.

Ongoing preservation obligation

Once an organization is served with a litigation notice, all future relevant electronic communication is also subject to the legal hold.

Handling terminated employees on legal hold

When employees leave a company, the fact that their information may be subject to a litigation hold is likely the last thing on their minds. Likewise, IT is probably focused more on redeploying the employees' technology assets rather than preserving information. Therefore, organizations need a process to ensure that departing employees' data remains protected. Otherwise, they may be unable to comply with their discovery obligations and could face spoliation sanctions.

Creating a defensible legal hold audit trail

The risks organizations face in e-discovery often correlate directly with their litigation hold practices. Today, most sanctions result from flawed preservation processes that are rooted in the failure to identify all custodians, locate all data sources, or monitor compliance with a litigation hold. Some of the most critical yet most challenging steps in these processes are tracking custodians, the litigation hold notices issued, and the responses received from custodians. When custodians number into the hundreds or thousands, it can be difficult to determine whether they have responded to the initial hold, completed required questionnaires, or reconfirmed their compliance with subsequent hold reminders. Moreover, when companies still rely on manual methods, they may not follow up with custodians once sending out an initial notice, opening their preservation strategy to scrutiny from opposing counsel or the court.

Records retention schedule

A records retention schedule is a document, often developed using Archival appraisal concepts and analysis of business and legal contexts within the intended jurisdictions, that outlines how long certain types of records need to be retained for before they can be destroyed.

A retention schedule is a listing of organizational information types, or series of information in a manner which facilitates the understanding and application of the identified and approved retention period, and other information retention aspects.

Purpose

Retention schedules are an important aspect of records management. Many organizations are subject to rules and regulations (at the local, state or federal level) that govern for how long they are required to keep records before they can safely dispose of them. Holding onto records for longer than required can expose the organization to unnecessary liability, since such records are discoverable during lawsuits.

Basic information

- Record/series title (name)
- Description of information within record/series
- Approved retention period
- Appropriate security requirements
- Appropriate destruction method

Further items for schedule consideration

- Location of retention
- Date record type/series approved
- Responsible group/office/person(s) of record
- Remarks related to record/series
- Series number applied to a specific record/series

Managing physical records

Managing physical records involves different disciplines or capabilities and may draw on a variety of forms of expertise.

Identifying records

If an item is presented as a legal record, it needs to be authenticated. Forensic experts may need to examine a document or artifact to determine that it is not a forgery, and that any damage, alteration, or missing content is documented. In extreme cases, items may be subjected to a microscope, x-ray, radiocarbon dating or chemical analysis. This level of authentication is rare, but requires that special care be taken in the creation and retention of the records of an organization.

Storing records

Records must be stored in such a way that they are accessible and safeguarded against environmental damage. A typical paper document may be stored in a filing cabinet in an office. However, some organisations employ file rooms with specialized environmental controls including temperature and humidity. Vital records may need to be stored in a disaster-resistant safe or vault to protect against fire, flood, earthquakes and conflict. In extreme cases, the item may require both disaster-proofing and public access, such as the original, signed US Constitution. Civil engineers may need to be consulted to determine that the file room can effectively withstand the weight of shelves and file cabinets filled with paper; historically, some military vessels were designed to take into account the weight of their operating procedures on paper as part of their ballast equation (modern record-keeping technologies have transferred much of that information to electronic storage). In addition to on-site storage of records, many organizations operate their own off-site records centers or contract with commercial records centres.

Retrieval of records

In addition to being able to store records, enterprises must also establish the proper capabilities for retrieval of records, in the event they are needed for a purpose such as an audit or litigation, or for the case of destruction. Record retrieval capabilities become complex when dealing with electronic records, especially when they have not been adequately tagged or classified for discovery.

Circulating records

Tracking the record while it is away from the normal storage area is referred to as circulation. Often this is handled by simple written recording procedures. However, many modern records environments use a computerized system involving bar code scanners, or radio-frequency identification technology (RFID) to track movement of the records. These can also be used for periodic auditing to identify unauthorized movement of the record.

Disposal of records

Disposal of records does not always mean destruction. It can also include transfer to a historical archive, museum, or private individual. Destruction of records ought to be authorized by law, statute, regulation, or operating procedure, and the records should be disposed of with care to avoid inadvertent disclosure of information. The process needs to be well-documented, starting with a records retention schedule and policies and procedures that have been approved at the highest level. An inventory of the records disposed of should be maintained, including certification that they have been destroyed. Records should never simply be discarded as refuse. Most organizations use processes including pulverization, paper shredding or incineration. Commercially available products can manage records through all processes active, inactive, archival, retention scheduling and disposal. Some also utilize RFID technology for the tracking of the physical file.

Archival appraisal

Appraisal, in the context of archival science and archive administration, is a process usually conducted by a member of the record-holding institution (often a professional archivist) in which a body of records is examined to determine its value for that institution. When it occurs prior to acquisition, the appraisal process involves assessing records for inclusion in the archives. In connection with an institution's collecting policy, appraisal "represents a doorway into the archives through which all records must pass". Some considerations when conducting appraisal include how to meet the record-granting body's organizational needs, how to uphold requirements of organizational accountability (be they legal, institutional, or determined by archival ethics), and how to meet the expectations of the record-using community. While sometimes archival collecting is equated with appraisal, appraisal is still seen as a critical function of modern archival profession even though historical societies have been argued to contribute to the "general randomness of collecting", which stands against rigorous appraisal standards even as many collecting programs still "acquire the collections of private collectors" and some aspects require partnerships between varied institutions.

Overview

Appraisal is considered a core archival function, along with acquisition, arrangement and description, preservation and access. The official definition from the Society of American Archivists (SAA) is as follows:

In an archival context, appraisal is the process of determining whether records and other materials have permanent (archival) value. Appraisal may be done at the collection, creator, series, file, or item level. Appraisal can take place prior to donation and prior to physical transfer, at or after accessioning. The basis of appraisal decisions may include a number of factors, including the records' provenance and content, their authenticity and reliability, their order and completeness, their condition and costs to preserve them, and their intrinsic value. Appraisal often takes place within a larger institutional collecting policy and mission statement.

The SAA also says, in their "Guidelines for College and University Archives", that appraisal should be based on mission statement of archives and that archivists, using appraisal, will determine what records belong in the archives, based on the "long-term administrative, legal, fiscal, and research value" of the records themselves. They also note that archives will obtain the appropriate records that meet appraisal criteria, and that using the appraisal criteria, archives will develop a regularly updated, written acquisitions policy. Others have described appraisal as a unique skill that archivists bring to the table, especially when it comes to maintaining records and data, with problems when organizations have engaged in appraisal when they didn't have trained archivists on staff. Appraisal can be viewed as a balancing act between the demands of administrative and heritage objectives; between the context of creation and the use of records. Depending on the degree of her or his autonomy to make appraisal decisions, an archivist's role is more or less central to the memory of an institution or society. Jacques Grimard sees archivists as participating in the "management of the world's memory" in three ways, by developing, preserving and communicating memory. In Luciana Duranti's view, appraisal is an analogue for the archival profession as a whole. It is the duty of the profession to "act as a mediator between those who produce archives and those who use them, as a facilitator of public memory making and keeping". She is cautious in her use of the term value in the context of archives, if establishing value means compromising the relationships between documents and the "impartial societal evidence" they might convey to future generations. Other archivists have argued that appraisal is not only one of the acts of record creation, but it requires the impossible in that the archivist is looking into the future, making judgements "as to what information will be of value to researchers". Furthermore, other scholars have argued that appraisal allows for the real or perceived value of records to be determined, that value judgments are made by archivists, based on historical context and their personal beliefs, when they engage in appraisal, although the latter has been contested, and that seeing "naturalness" and "utility" in records upsets existing archival appraisal theory.

History of appraisal theory

Mostly concerned with the records of government bodies, the Manual for the Arrangement and Description of Archives: Drawn up by the Netherlands Association of Archivists (1898), commonly referred to as the "Dutch Manual", assumed, generally, that the archives would keep each record it acquired. The authors articulated concepts of provenance and original order that privileged an "organic bond" in a collection that precedes its transfer to an archival repository. Appraisal decisions that involve selecting individual records or groups of records for exclusion would consequently lie outside the responsibilities of the archivist, in their view.

Sir Hilary Jenkinson, 1922

Sir Hilary Jenkinson was a British archivist and Deputy Keeper of the Public Record Office upon his retirement. His great contribution to appraisal theory is his Manual of Archive Administration (1922; revised 1937; reissued 1965) in which he argued that archives are "documents which formed part of an official transaction and were preserved for official reference". For Jenkinson, the records creator is responsible for determining which records should be transferred to the archives for preservation. Since in his view records are "impartial", the task of selection is merely a matter of choosing documents that best describe "what happened". Jenkinson staked out a limited role for the archivist, positioned between the administrative body transferring the records and the researcher who might seek to access them. The archivist, according to Jenkinson, is to act as a steward of the records in his or her custody. Neither the archivist nor the historian is competent to make appraisal decisions. That process should be left to the donor. Jenkinson deals directly with destruction of records, which he sees as solely the purview of the creator of those records. As long as destruction is done in accordance with the needs of its "practical business" and the agency of origin refrains "from thinking of itself as a body producing historical evidence", its actions should not, in Jenkinson's view, be considered illegitimate, even by succeeding generations.

In 2010, scholar Richard J. Cox noted that many archivists still cling to Jenkinson's ideas on appraisal, which claims objectivity in appraisal because record creators engaged in "selection decisions" rather than archivists.

T. R. Schellenberg, 1956

T. R. Schellenberg's work in Modern Archives (1956) represents a departure from Jenkinson's approach, necessitated by the advent of mass duplication and an overwhelming influx of documents into archives. In his work, he divides the value of records into primary values (the original value for the creator; for their administrative, fiscal, and operating uses) and secondary values (their lasting value after they are no longer in current use; for those other than the original creator). He defines evidential value as deriving from the "evidence records contain of the organization and functioning of the Government body that produced them", and informational value as related to the "information records contain on persons, corporate bodies, things, problems, conditions, and the like, with which the Government body dealt". After defining the terms, Schellenberg details the manner in which an archivist could perform appraisal based on these criteria, placing a stress in every case on the importance of research and analysis on the part of the archivist.

According to Schellenberg, informational value is based on three criteria:

- Uniqueness: The information in the record cannot be found anywhere else and must also be unique in form (i.e., not duplicated elsewhere).
- Form: An archivist must, according to Schellenberg, consider the form of the information (the degree to which the information is concentrated) as well as the form of the records itself (whether or not they can easily be read by others, e.g., punchcards and tape recordings would involve the use of expensive machinery to decipher).
- Importance: When appraising records, one must judge records first based on the needs of the government itself, then on the needs of historians/social scientists, as well as local historians and genealogists; he encourages archivists to be wary of records with sentimental value.

Other scholars have added that evidence and information are among the goods that records provide underlines his appraisal model, since it emphasizes evidential and informational values, and that effective records management necessitates an appraisal process. Some have even said that new thinking on appraisal led some to see distinctions between Schellenberg's "evidential" and "informational" values as artificial, while others see the degree of use of records as the only means that acquisition or appraisal can be evaluated.

The archival appraisal theory of Schellenberg was a major factor in the American Friends Service Committee, et al. v. William H. Webster, et.al (1983) case, which began in June 1979 as social action organizations, historians, journalists, and others, sued the U.S. government to stop destruction of FBI files challenging an existing "archival appraisal decision" of the National Archives and Records Administration (then called NARS). In 1986, Susan D. Steinwall, then at the Area Research Center at University of Wisconsin-River Falls, wrote that this case not only warns archivists to not rely too much "on the opinions of nonarchivists", like FBI agents, regarding the usefulness of the records of a specific agency, but it calls into question commonly-held archival assumptions. In her article, she describes how the archivist whom appraised the FBI records not only relied on Schellenberg's manual, The Appraisal of Modern Public Records, but on FBI reference material and his own experience. Not only did NARS approving disposal requests for the FBI in 1945 and 1946, but it wasn't until 1978 that they reviewed their appraisal decisions of FBI files under "mounting public pressure", and in appraising these records they had relied on the FBI descriptions of their own files, discussing the records they were to dispose with FBI officials before "approving records disposition requests". After bringing in the writings of others in the field of archival appraisal, which was purportedly embryonic in the late 1970s, like Philip C. Brooks, JoAnne Yates, and Maynard Brichford she notes that often Schellenberg is evoked in discussion of appraisal because he provided archivists with vocab to describe documentation's "potential research values." She adds that in his book, The Appraisal of Modern Records, Schellenberg described how "modern public records" have two types of values, one for "immediate use of the originating agency and secondary for later use by other agencies and users", with secondary values considered "evidential or informational", with many larger series of records in the National Archives accessioned for information they "contained regarding matters other than government actions". She ends her article by arguing that this case, often called the "FBI files case", shows that government archivists should reconsider Schellenberg's appraisal philosophy, and notes how some archivists, like Frank Boles and Julia Marks Young, have advocates for not interpreting what Schellenberg says literally, noting that at times, records that have minimal administrative value may have not have, conversely, "minimal value to research."

SOME CURRENT APPROACHES TO APPRAISAL

With social movements in the United States in the 1960s and 1970s, existing Jenkinsonian and Schellenbergian ideas held by archivists began to be shaken, with efforts to broaden historical records beyond "elites and socially dominant groups", leading some to say that social justice was a call for justice for archives and tying it to appraisal itself. Some of these changes involved borrowing from experiences of librarians! In 1977, Howard Zinn argued that institutions has ignored "experiences of marginalized peoples", saying they had gaps in their collections which are often "presented as comprehensive representations of social history", following his speech to the Society of American Archivists in 1970 when he openly questioned the "notion of archival neutrality". Apart from Zinn, Hans Blooms also discussed, as did others, the societal role of archivists and how they influence appraisal, with some even posing feminist analysis of appraisal which bolstered social inclusion, placing archivists within ever-changing community dynamics. There have also been scholars whom have emphasized the importance of appraising personal archives because they show an individual's character and attitude that theories like macro-appraisal do not account for, necessitating more of an "archives of character than of achievement", with efforts to document our "complex inner humanity" rather than what is on the surface. One of the outgrowths of social change during that period and "rethinking" of archival principles, including of business records, was macro-appraisal in Canada and documentation strategy in the U.S., along with archives that reflect specific social issues and communities, reflecting a changing interest by archivists in "documenting the wider society" and a need to properly document not only society but "public interaction with state institutions".

Macro-appraisal

According to Terry Cook, North American appraisal theory is unplanned, taxonomic, random and fragmented, and has rarely embodied the concepts of institutional and societal dynamics which would lead archivists to a working model that would allow them to appraise the broad spectrum of human experience. His model is a top-down approach, which focuses on key processes through which a particular function is expressed by intersecting with structures and individuals.

Macro-appraisal is distinguished from micro-appraisal in that the former seeks to appraise the institution by understanding the context of creation and the interrelationships between, for instance, the different ministries or agencies within a government. In Cook's view, this institutional understanding should precede and inform the latter, micro-appraisal; the appraisal of documents. His approach to macro-appraisal does not just derive from the position of the creating body within an established hierarchy. It is not top-down in a conventional, bureaucratic sense. It is top-down in that it moves from macro to micro-appraisal.

This requires a planned, logical approach-archivists embarking upon appraisals are equipped with an understanding of the record creator, its mandate and functions, its structure and decision-making processes, the way it creates records, and changes to these processes over time. Macroappraisal assesses the societal value of both the functional-structural context and the work-place culture in which the records are created and used by the creator(s), and the interrelationship of citizens, groups, organizations - the "public" - with that functional-structural context. If appraisal designates the long-term value of the context of records, or series of records, for their potential research values, macroappraisal assesses the significance of the context of their creation and contemporary use.

Terry Cook, "Macroappraisal in Theory and Practice: Origins, Characteristics, and Implementation in Canada, 1950-2000

The benefits of this process are theoretical (identifying the important functions in society which should be documented) and practical (the ability to focus appraisal activities on records of the highest potential archival value).

Cook has also argued that in any appraisal model archivists need to remember the people who slip through the cracks of society, with the voice of marginalized groups often only heard and documented through "their interaction with such [white, male, and capitalist] institutions and hence the archivist must listen carefully to make sure these voices are heard". Julie Herrada, an archivist, added to this by noting there is value in collecting contemporary material and noted that sorting and weeding of records is best "left up to the archivist during the appraisal process".

Documentation strategy

Connected with the writings of Helen Willa Samuels, documentation strategy aims to reach beyond institutional frameworks when appraising collections. In the past, she says, archivists have been passive, concentrating on researchers' needs rather than understanding a document in context. This has led to a circular problem, as researchers state their needs based on the context that they deduce from the archives, and as the archives create an artificial context based on researchers' stated needs. "Archivists are challenged to select a lasting record", Samuels says, "but they lack techniques to support this decision making" (1992). Samuels argues that while archivists once needed to know and understand the complex bureaucratic structures of organizations, they must now understand the structures between organizations and ignore institutional boundaries.

However, this is increasingly impossible; archivists need to examine documentation in a comprehensive manner. A documentation strategy is, then, "a plan formulated to assure the documentation of an ongoing issue, activity or geographic area". Its development includes records creators, archivists, and users, and it is carried out through a system-wide understanding of the intended life-cycle of the record.

Appraisal and the digital world

Within the archival field, there has been some debate about how to engage in appraisal in the digital realm. Some have argued that effective appraisal, which prioritizes acquisitions by archival institutions, is part of a coordinated approach to data, but that criteria for appraisal should incorporate accepted "archival practice", assessing not only significance of data to the research community, but significance of data source and context, how materials would complement existing collections, uniqueness of data, potential usability of data, and "anticipated cost of processing". Additionally, others have described appraisal and selection by web archives as including selection of materials to be digitally "captured" and URLS where a "web crawler will start", which fits with those whom argue that the capacity to make appraisals in the "context of online representation and interpretation" is becoming possible. At the same time, some scholars have said that digitization of records may influence decision-making of appraisal since the greatest proportion of users for archives are generally family historians, often called genealogists, leading to implications for future record-keeping and entailing that digitization be clearly defined as just one component of appraisal which is "appropriately weighed against other considerations". Other informational professionals have also connected appraisal to digital curation of data, saying that one of the key areas of digital curation and digital preservation is selection and appraisal of materials.

Appraisal and the question of community archives

Apart from macro-appraisal, documentation strategy, and debate about the place of appraisal in the digital world, there has been questions of how appraisal relates to the phenomenon of community archives, or archival institutions which are run by and for the communities they serve, rather than a government or other external entity. Scholars are divided on approaches archivists should take, some saying that appraisal not only needs to be reframed when looking at community archives, while others say that communities should directly be enabled to participate in the appraisal process, defining what they see as valuable records, rather than having the archival profession take up this mantle. The latter was the case with a community archive documenting police brutality in Cleveland, Ohio, with scholars noting that citizen archivists maintain responsibility over management and direction of this people's archive, specifically as it pertains to outreach and appraisal of the archive itself, describing not only the archives' purpose but its construction. Even though, two archivists, Katie Shilton and Ramesh Srinivasan, proposed a "participatory archiving model" in 2007 in an effort to re-orient archival concepts such as provenance, ordering of records, and appraisal, hoping that it would help alleviate some representation by multicultural communities, this model would occur with a "traditional archives" rather than a community archives. They also acknowledged, when proposing this model, that it was labor-intensive and outside scope of most archival institutions.

Bias of archivists and appraisal

In the archival field, more, like Christian James and Ricardo L. Punzalan, have said that the core archival functions of provenance, original order, appraisal, and arrangement to be inadequate. Part of this change is a focus on bias and value judgments by archivists. Randall C. Jimmerson wrote about this in 2007, archivists need to be conscious of their "potential bias" by not only working to preserve records which are often overlooked but by documenting their appraisal decisions, while recognizing it is impossible to be "neutral or invisible" in archival appraisal. This was in line with what Elizabeth Yakel noted in 2003: the need to re-examine old appraisal decisions, and the suggestion of scholar Richard Cox to attribute appraisal decisions to specific individuals. Despite Jimmerson's suggestions, ten years later scholars were still lamenting that archivists seemed to not document "transformative effects" of their appraisal decisions and recommended that archivists should not only acknowledge their own role in appraisal, but not the appraisal criteria they applied and the assumptions they made in processing and describing records, along with the records they decided to not keep.

Archival appraisal and preservation selection in archives

Tyler O. Walters (1996) wrote about how challenging it is for writers in the archival and library field to create preservation priorities and appraisal methods. This is because archival managers understand the appraisal methods in setting preservation priorities in their archive, which is the first responsibility. To answer some questions in selection-for-preservation, he argues, archivists may want to evaluate the appraisal's value for preservation selection. This connects to a plan the Society of American Archivists has in place to promote preservation in archives and the need for selection within existing preservation models. This is due to the fact that, as scholar Paul Conway put it, archivists have long recognized that "their first professional responsibility is to identify and protect the small portion of the overall record that has long-term value." Specifically referring to the SAA report, he argues that the document "implies that systematic judgement is required...to select specific materials for preservation."

Managing digital records

The general principles of records management apply to records in any format. Digital records, however, raise specific issues. It is more difficult to ensure that the content, context and structure of records is preserved and protected when the records do not have a physical existence. This has important implications for the authenticity, reliability, and trustworthiness of records.

Much research is being conducted on the management of digital records. The International Research on Permanent Authentic Records in Electronic Systems (InterPARES) Project is one example of such an initiative. Based at the School of Library, Archival and Information Studies at the University of British Columbia, in Vancouver, British Columbia, Canada, the InterPARES Project is a collaborative project between researchers all across the world committed to developing theories and methodologies to ensure the reliability, accuracy, and authenticity of digital records.

Functional requirements for computer systems to manage digital records have been produced by the US Department of Defense, The United Kingdom's National Archives and the European Commission, whose MoReq (Model Requirements for the Management of Electronic Records) specification has been translated into at least twelve languages funded by the European Commission.

Particular concerns exist about the ability to access and read digital records over time, since the rapid pace of change in technology can make the software used to create the records obsolete, leaving the records unreadable. A considerable amount of research is being undertaken to address this, under the heading of digital preservation. The Public Record Office Victoria (PROV) located in Melbourne, Australia published the Victorian Electronic Records Strategy (VERS) which includes a standard for the preservation, long-term storage and access to permanent electronic records. The VERS standard has been adopted by all Victorian Government departments. A digital archive has been established by PROV to enable the general public to access permanent records. Archives New Zealand is also setting up a digital archive.

Electronic tax records

Electronic Tax Records are computer-based/non-paper versions of records required by tax agencies like the Internal Revenue Service. There is substantial confusion about what constitutes acceptable digital records for the IRS, as the concept is relatively new. The subject is discussed in Publication 583 and Bulletin 1997-13, but not in specific detail.

Businesses and individuals wishing to convert their paper records into scanned copies may be at risk if they do so. For example, it is unclear if an IRS auditor would accept a JPEG, PNG, or PDF format scanned copy of a purchase receipt for a deducted expense item.

Vital record

Vital records are records of life events kept under governmental authority, including birth certificates, marriage licenses (or marriage certificates), and death certificates. In some jurisdictions, vital records may also include records of civil unions or domestic partnerships.

In the United States, vital records are typically maintained at both the county and state levels. In the United Kingdom and numerous other countries vital records are recorded in the civil registry.

Various European countries are members of an International Commission on Civil Status which provides a mutually recognized convention on the coding of entries appearing in civil status documents, with common codes and translation tables between the language of the member states. They also provide an English unofficial translation.

In the fields of Records Management and Archival Science the term vital record is used to mean "records, regardless of medium, which are essential to the organization in order to continue with its business-crucial functions both during and after a disaster. They need not be permanent, might be active or inactive, originals or copies."

Note that only the life events meaning is restricted to government; the records management meaning in this article applies to both government and non-government organizations. In the past 10 years, there has been an overall increase in global birth registration rates of children under five from 58 percent to 65 percent. However, more than 100 developing countries still do not have functioning systems that can support efficient registration of births and other life events like marriages and death. Around the world, almost 230 million children under the age of five are not registered. Sub-Saharan Africa is home to 85 million of these children, while 135 million live in Asia and the Pacific. Progress with death registration has been much slower globally. In countries in most need of CRVS, up to 80 percent of deaths that occur outside health facilities and two-thirds of all deaths globally are not counted.

The governmental authority is tasked with the safekeeping of the vital records, effectively providing the government with another source of income through fees. The original copy of the vital record is always kept by the government authority. In the United States vital records are public and in most cases can be viewed by anyone in person at the governmental authority. Copies can also be requested for a fee. There are two types of copies: certified and uncertified. Certified copies are official copies that can be used as identification whereas uncertified copies do not contain the governmental authority's seal and often are marked that they should not be used for identification. There may be additional restrictions in place on who can actually request a certified copy, such as immediate family or someone with written authorization. Certified copies are usually much more expensive than uncertified copies. Some states have started making vital records available online for free. Vital records that are online typically are 90 or more years old and assume the person listed in the record is no longer alive.

A family register (also known in several variations, such as household register and family album, and, when discussing non-anglophone countries, the native-language names of the registers such as koseki in Japan, Familienbuch in Germany, and hukou in China) is a civil registry used in many countries to track information of a genealogical or family-centric legal interest.

Often, official recognition of certain events or status may only be granted when such event or status is registered in the family registry-for example, in Japan, a marriage is legally effective when and only when such filing is recorded into the household register (known as a koseki). In other cases, the family register serves as a centralized repository for family legal events, such as births, deaths, marriages, and expatriations, as with the familienbuch in use in Germany and the livret de famille [fr] in France, although it is not the sole source of official recognition for such events.

Use of government-sanctioned or administered family registers, while common in many European nations and in countries which use continental-style civil law (where the family or household is legally viewed as the fundamental unit of a nation), is nonetheless rare in English-speaking countries (for example, the closest equivalent in the United Kingdom is the electoral roll, which is also organised by household, but it is limited in the amount of information recorded).

Although the United States for example assigns most citizens and residents a social security number intended to be unique to the recipient and information regarding birth, death and work history (in the form of contributions to the social security system) is collected, the U.S. social security system has long been intentionally restricted in the scope of information collected and maintained regarding individuals where not directly related to social security benefits-as such, no information is centrally collected regarding marriage, citizenship status, parentage, or the like, in contrast to the German and Japanese family register systems.

Establishment of a more comprehensive personal information repository (along the lines of the Japanese or former German systems) has been criticized by civil liberties advocates as subject to governmental or criminal abuse, while proponents cite the benefits of simplified access to vital information.

In South Korea, use of the hojeok (similar to the Japanese household registry, written using identical Chinese characters) was repealed in 2005, in favor of a personal registry system.

The systems of household registers in China, Korea and Japan date back to the Tang Dynasty or Heian Period or earlier, both since the seventh century.

LIST OF HOUSEHOLD REGISTER SYSTEMS

East Asia

- The Hoju scheme is a family register system in North Korea. Hoju (Hangul: ??; Hanja: ??) means the 'head of the family', Hojuje is the 'head of the family' system, and Hojeok is the 'family register'.
- The former Hoju system in South Korea attracted controversy for being innately patriarchal and hence representing a 'violation of the right to gender equality'. It was abolished on 1 January 2008.
- The Koseki system in Japan.
- The Hukou system also known as Huji system, in China and in Taiwan.

Thailand

The Tabien Baan, or document proving House Registration, is distributed by a village, city, or other municipal authority. The Tabien Baan (sometimes spelled Tambien Baan) reflects the residents who live at a specific property (this document is not used as proof of Real Estate ownership, for that one must have a Thai Chanote or Title Deed). The Tabien Baan (House Registration) is issued to Thai Citizens and is used as a permanent address for service of process and other official mailings.

A Tabien Baan is an extremely important document for Thai nationals because it acts as proof of a Thai person's residence. Therefore, it is used to determine a Thai person's voting district and in the case of Thai men of military age, the Tabien Baan is used to ascertain what district the Thai man will be placed in when drawing for the military draft. This can be critical because if one district reaches a certain level of volunteers then it is not necessary to further draft any inhabitants of that district. As a result, a Thai man's House Registration

(Tabien Baan) can have a massive impact upon their life and career depending upon the district in which they live.

Indonesia

Kartu Keluarga (literally, Family Card) is a document in Indonesia that proves residency and which records relationships and family members. Every family in Indonesia is required to own one of these documents. This document records the identity of the family's head and the individual members. The document is kept by the family's head, 'ketua RT' (head of neighborhood association) and 'desa' or 'kelurahan' office. The document is a provincial government document, thus, it is not permitted to strike out, change, replace or make additions in the document. Every data change has to be reported to the village or 'kelurahan' office which will replace the old one with the updated one. Newcomers are not recorded in the document until they have been reported or have been deemed not to have a local residency status.

Changes in data have to be reported within 14 (fourteen) working days by the family's head to 'desa' or 'kelurahan' office. Each report of changes must be submitted with the copy that is held by the family's head and 'ketua RT'. Changes in data include: birth, death or migration (of a member).

However, if a family moves to different 'desa' or 'kelurahan', the document must be revoked by 'desa' or 'kelurahan' office, which must be submitted with the copy that held by family's head and 'ketua RT'. The official in the prior location will produce Surat Keterangan Pindah (Note of Migration) which will be used to make the new Kartu Keluarga in the arrival by 'desa' or 'kelurahan' office.

Continental Europe

- The former familienbuch system in Germany.
- The livret de famille [fr] system in France.
- The libro de familia [es] system in Spain.
- The former Propiska system in Russia.

Vital statistics (government records)

This article is about vital statistics in relation to government records. For other uses, see vital statistics (disambiguation). Vital statistics is accumulated data gathered on live births, deaths, fetal deaths, marriages and divorces. The most common way of collecting information on these events is through civil registration, an administrative system used by governments to record vital events which occur in their populations. Efforts to improve the quality of vital statistics will therefore be closely related to the development of civil registration systems in countries.

Overview

A vital statistics system is defined by the United Nations "as the total process of (a) collecting information by civil registration or enumeration on the frequency or occurrence of specified and defined vital events, as well as relevant characteristics of the events themselves and the person or persons concerned, and (b) compiling, processing, analyzing, evaluating, presenting, and disseminating these data in statistical form" (UN, 2001). Civil registration, as defined by the United Nations, is the" continuous, permanent, compulsory, and universal recording of the occurrence and characteristics of vital events (livebirths, deaths, fetal deaths, marriages, and divorces) and other civil status events pertaining to the population as provided by decree, law or regulation, in accordance with the legal requirements in each country."

The origin of vital statistics begins as early as 1854 with James Stark in Register House in Edinburgh in reaction to the Scottish Registration Act and death by social class was recorded in England beginning in 1921.

While the number of births and deaths can be obtained by enumeration at certain points in time (e.g. censuses and surveys), civil registration collects this information on a continuous basis and is the only source that provides individuals with a legal document. For instance, the importance of birth registration as the first legal recognition of the child is emphasized in Article 7 of the Convention on the Rights of the Child which states that "the child shall be registered immediately after birth and shall have the right from birth to a name, the right to acquire a nationality and, as far as possible, the right to know and be cared for by his or her parents". United Nations Children's Fund (UNICEF) and a number of non-governmental organizations (Plan International, Save the Children Fund, World Vision, etc.) have particularly promoted the human rights aspects of registration, while the United Nations Statistics Division (UNSD), United Nations Population Fund (UNFPA) and World Health Organization (WHO) have focused more on the statistical aspects of civil registration.

Countries which are signatories to the Convention on the Rights of the Child are therefore expected to set up systems to register the births of all children. Non-registration of a child can have negative consequences on the wider enjoyment of a child's fundamental rights to benefits such as identity, inheritance, education, health and other social services. Birth registration is also part of a broader strategy to ensure that children are less vulnerable to abuse and exploitation, especially if separated from their parents. In the absence of a functioning birth registration system, it is difficult to see how a country can enforce age-related legal concerns such as schooling, child labour, juvenile justice, early marriage, sexual exploitation and military recruitment. Recent natural disasters and calamities have also demonstrated the utility of a birth certificate for reuniting lost children with their families.

Many civil registration systems also collect information on causes of death. Statistics based on these death records are of particular importance in public health for identifying the magnitude and distribution of major disease problems, and are essential for the design, implementation, monitoring, and assessment of health programmes and policies.

Toronto scientist, professor Prabhat Jha argues that inexpensive recording of vital statistics in developing countries is the most effective means to improve global health and has outlined 5 options for expanding Cause of Death reporting.

"Despite the importance of tracking causes of death and the tradition since 1893 of standardisation of definitions and coding for causes of death in the International Classification of Diseases and Injuries (ICD), global assessments of causes of death are a major analytical challenge. Vital registration systems that include medical certification of the cause of death captured about 18.8 million deaths of an estimated annual total of 51.7 million deaths in 2005, which is the latest year for which the largest number of countries reported deaths from a vital registration system. Even for these deaths, the comparability of findings on the leading causes of death is affected by variation in certification skills among physicians, the diagnostic and pathological data available at the time of completing a death certificate, variations in medical culture in choosing the underlying cause, and legal and institutional frameworks for governing mortality reporting. For the remaining deaths that are not medically certified, many different data sources and diagnostic approaches must be used from surveillance systems, demographic research sites, surveys, censuses, disease registries, and police records to construct a consolidated picture of causes of death in various populations. Because of the variety of data sources and their associated biases, causes of death assessments are inherently uncertain and subject to vigorous debate."

The agency responsible for overseeing this system in the United States is the National Center for Health Statistics, a division of Centers for Disease Control and Prevention (CDC). Vital statistics for the US can be found here.

The agency responsible for overseeing this system in the United Kingdom is the Office for National Statistics. Vital statistics for the UK can be found here.

CRVS (Civil Registration and Vital Statistic)

This article's use of external links may not follow Wikipedia's policies or guidelines. Please improve this article by removing excessive or inappropriate external links, and converting useful links where appropriate into footnote references. (July 2018) (Learn how and when to remove this template message)

The CRVS System is defined by World Health Organization as "A well-functioning civil registration and vital statistics (CRVS) system registers all births and deaths, issues birth and death certificates, and compiles and disseminates vital statistics, including cause of death information. It may also record marriages and divorces."

Originally, the civil status or vital record are registered at a local level in a civil registry. Most off the time at the city or county level. The main problem with this traditional method to proceed is that the vital statistics are stored in a decentralized database. The limitation of this kind of system is the lack of coherence between data and reality plus the impossibility to verify te veracity of such data.

In the era of big data veracity is a must. The increasing capability of technologies and the speed of telecommunication have led to the first initiatives of centralized system in the early 21st century.

Initiatives

MOVE-IT is a non-governmental program led by the World Health Organization that aimed to improve the monitoring of vital record. From 2008 until it was dissolved in 2013, the Health Metrics Network (HMN) started innovative projects using information technologies across the world (about 20 projects) with one common goal, improving CRVS systems.

Civil Africa

Civil Africa is a new technology start up created by Mr. Adama Sawadogo which purpose is to end the problem of "ghost" children. iCivil's target is to register all new born. The first pilot project have started in 2015 in Burkina Faso.

Civil CRVS System is the combination of a mobile based application that uses the SMS network and a unique bubble seal bracelet for newborn. "What makes this system so special is that uses a bubble tagging technology," stated Mr. Sawadogo to Mr. Rawlson King during ID4Africa forum. The bubble seal bracelet for new born is based on a chaosmetric technology that gives it physical properties of uniqueness, immutability and impossible to reproduce. This technology is called the bubble tag.

Governmental Initiatives

Rwanda CRVS Systems is in line with the program of development of the country which target is to define an action plan.

Oman: Civil Status Mobile Registration Unit

Civil Status Mobile Registration Unit in Oman is a centralized digital CRVS System that aim to improve the life of their citizen in facilitating access to information.

New Zealand: SmartStart program

The SmartStart program is an online platform of services that helps parents along the birth registration process

Census

A census is the procedure of systematically acquiring and recording information about the members of a given population. The term is used mostly in connection with national population and housing censuses; other common censuses include agriculture, business, and traffic censuses. The United Nations defines the essential features of population and housing censuses as "individual enumeration, universality within a defined territory, simultaneity and defined periodicity", and recommends that population censuses be taken at least every 10 years. United Nations recommendations also cover census topics to be collected, official definitions, classifications and other useful information to co-ordinate international practice.

The word is of Latin origin: during the Roman Republic, the census was a list that kept track of all adult males fit for military service. The modern census is essential to international comparisons of any kind of statistics, and censuses collect data on many attributes of a population, not just how many people there are. Censuses typically began as the only method of collecting national demographic data, and are now part of a larger system of different surveys. Although population estimates remain an important function of a census, including exactly the geographic distribution of the population, statistics can be produced about combinations of attributes e.g. education by age and sex in different regions. Current administrative data systems allow for other approaches to enumeration with the same level of detail but raise concerns about privacy and the possibility of biasing estimates.

A census can be contrasted with sampling in which information is obtained only from a subset of a population; typically main population estimates are updated by such intercensal estimates. Modern census data are commonly used for research, business marketing, and planning, and as a baseline for designing sample surveys by providing a sampling frame such as an address register. Census counts are necessary to adjust samples to be representative of a population by weighting them as is common in opinion polling. Similarly, stratification requires knowledge of the relative sizes of different population strata which can be derived from census enumerations. In some countries, the census provides the official counts used to apportion the number of elected representatives to regions (sometimes controversially - e.g., Utah v. Evans). In many cases, a carefully chosen random sample can provide more accurate information than attempts to get a population census.

Sampling

A census is often construed as the opposite of a sample as its intent is to count everyone in a population rather than a fraction. However, population censuses rely on a sampling frame to count the population. This is the only way to be sure that everyone has been included as otherwise those not responding would not be followed up on and individuals could be missed. The fundamental premise of a census is that the population is not known and a new estimate is to be made by the analysis of primary data. The use of a sampling frame is counterintuitive as it suggests that the population size is already known. However, a census is also used to collect attribute data on the individuals in the nation. This process of sampling marks the difference between historical census, which was a house to house process or the product of an imperial decree, and the modern statistical project. The sampling frame used by census is almost always an address register. Thus it is not known if there is anyone resident or how many people there are in each household. Depending on the mode of enumeration, a form is sent to the householder, an enumerator calls, or administrative records for the dwelling are accessed. As a preliminary to the dispatch of forms, census workers will check any address problems on the ground. While it may seem straightforward to use the postal service file for this purpose, this can be out of date and some dwellings may contain a number of independent households. A particular problem is what are termed 'communal establishments' which category includes student residences, religious orders, homes for the elderly, people in prisons etc. As these are not easily enumerated by a single householder, they are often treated differently and visited by special teams of census workers to ensure they are classified appropriately.

Residence definitions

Individuals are normally counted within households and information is typically collected about the household structure and the housing. For this reason international documents refer to censuses of population and housing. Normally the census response is made by a household, indicating details of individuals resident there. An important aspect of census enumerations is determining which individuals can be counted from which cannot be counted. Broadly, three definitions can be used: de facto residence; de jure residence; and, permanent residence. This is important to consider individuals who have multiple or temporary addresses. Every person should be identified uniquely as resident in one place but where they happen to be on Census Day, their de facto residence, may not be the best place to count them. Where an individual uses services may be more useful and this is at their usual, or de jure, residence. An individual may be represented at a permanent address, perhaps a family home for students or long term migrants. It is necessary to have a precise definition of residence to decide whether visitors to a country should be included in the population count. This is becoming more important as students travel abroad for education for a period of several years. Other groups causing problems of enumeration are new born babies, refugees, people away on holiday, people moving home around census day, and people without a fixed address. People having second homes because of working in another part of the country or retaining a holiday cottage are difficult to fix at a particular address sometimes causing double counting or houses being mistakenly identified as vacant. Another problem is where people use a different address at different times e.g. students living at their place of education in term time but returning to a family home during vacations or children whose parents have separated who effectively have two family homes. Census enumeration has always been based on finding people where they live as there is no systematic alternative - any list you could use to find people is derived from census activities in the first place. Recent UN guidelines provide recommendation on enumerating such complex households.

ENUMERATION STRATEGIES

Historical censuses used crude enumeration assuming absolute accuracy. Modern approaches take into account the problems of overcount and undercount, and the coherence of census enumerations with other official sources of data. This reflects a realist approach to measurement, acknowledging that under any definition of residence there is a true value of the population but this can never be measured with complete accuracy. An important aspect of the census process is to evaluate the quality of the data.

Many countries use a post-enumeration survey to adjust the raw census counts. This works in a similar manner to capture-recapture estimation for animal populations. In census circles this method is called dual system enumeration (DSE). A sample of households are visited by interviewers who record the details of the household as at census day. These data are then matched to census records and the number of people missed can be estimated by considering the number missed in the census or survey but counted in the other. This way counts can be adjusted for non-response varying between different demographic groups. An explanation using a fishing analogy can be found in "Trout, Catfish and Roach..." which won an award from the Royal Statistical Society for excellence in official statistics in 2011.

Triple system enumeration has been proposed as an improvement as it would allow evaluation of the statistical dependence of pairs of sources. However, as the matching process is the most difficult aspect of census estimation this has never been implemented for a national enumeration. It would also be difficult to identify three different sources that were sufficiently different to make the triple system effort worthwhile. The DSE approach has another weakness in that it assumes there is no person counted twice (over count). In de facto residence definitions this would not be a problem but in de jure definitions individuals risk being recorded on more than one form leading to double counting. A particular problem here are students who often have a term time and family address.

Several countries have used a system which is known as short form/long form. This is a sampling strategy which randomly chooses a proportion of people to send a more detailed questionnaire to (the long form). Everyone receives the short form questions. Thereby more data are collected but not imposing a burden on the whole population. This also reduces the burden on the statistical office. Indeed, in the UK all residents were required to fill in the whole form but only a 10% sample were coded and analysed in detail, until 2001. New technology means that all data are now scanned and processed. Recently there has been controversy in Canada about the cessation of the long form with the head, Munir Sheikh resigning.

The use of alternative enumeration strategies is increasing but these are not so simple as many people assume and only occur in developed countries. The Netherlands has been most advanced in adopting a census using administrative data. This allows a simulated census to be conducted by linking several different administrative databases at an agreed time. Data can be matched and an overall enumeration established accounting for where the different sources are discrepant. A validation survey is still conducted in a similar way to the post enumeration survey employed in a traditional census. Other countries which have a population register use this as a basis for all the census statistics needed by users. This is most common among Nordic countries but requires a large number of different registers to be combined including population, housing, employment and education. These registers are then combined and brought up to the standard of a statistical register by comparing the data in different sources and ensuring the quality is sufficient for official statistics to be produced. A recent innovation is the French instigation of a rolling census programme with different regions enumerated each year such that the whole country is completely enumerated every 5 to 10 years. In Europe, in connection with the 2010 census round, a large number of countries adopted alternative census methodologies, often based on the combination of data from registers, surveys and other sources.

Technology

Censuses have evolved in their use of technology with the latest censuses, the 2010 round, using many new types of computing. In Brazil, handheld devices were used by enumerators to locate residences on the ground. In many countries, census returns could be made via the Internet as well as in paper form. DSE is facilitated by computer matching techniques which can be automated, such as propensity score matching. In the UK, all census formats are scanned and stored electronically before being destroyed, replacing the need for physical archives. The record linking to perform an administrative census would not be possible without large databases being stored on computer systems.

New technology is not without problems in its introduction. The US census had intended to use the handheld computers but cost escalated and this was abandoned, with the contract being sold to Brazil. Online response is a good idea but one of the functions of census is to make sure everyone is counted accurately. A system which allowed people to enter their address without verification would be open to abuse. Therefore, households have to be verified on the ground, typically by an enumerator visit or post out. Paper forms are still necessary for those without access to Internet connections. It is also possible that the hidden nature of an administrative census means that users are not engaged with the importance of contributing their data to official statistics. Alternatively, population estimations may be carried out remotely with GIS and remote sensing technologies.

Census and development

According to UNFPA, "The information generated by a population and housing census - numbers of people, their distribution, their living conditions and other key data - is critical for development." This is because this type of data is essential for policymakers so that they know where to invest. Unfortunately, many countries have outdated or inaccurate data about their populations and therefore, without accurate data are unable to address the needs of their population.

UNFPA stated that,

"The unique advantage of the census is that it represents the entire statistical universe, down to the smallest geographical units, of a country or region. Planners need this information for all kinds of development work, including: assessing demographic trends; analysing socio-economic conditions; designing evidence-based poverty-reduction strategies; monitoring and evaluating the effectiveness of policies; and tracking progress toward national and internationally agreed development goals."

In addition to making policymakers aware about population issues, it is also an important tool for identifying forms of social, demographic or economic exclusions, such as inequalities relating to race, ethics and religion as well as disadvantaged groups such as those with disabilities and the poor.

An accurate census can empower local communities by providing them with the necessary information to participate in local decision-making and ensuring they are represented.

Uses of census data

In the nineteenth century, the first censuses collected paper enumerations that had to be collated by hand so the statistical uses were very basic. The government owned the data and were able to publish statistics themselves on the state of the nation. Uses were to measure changes in the population and apportion representation. Population estimates could be compared to those of other countries.

By the beginning of the twentieth century, censuses were recording households and some indications of their employment. In some countries, census archives are released for public examination after many decades, allowing genealogists to track the ancestry of interested people. Archives provide a substantial historical record which may challenge established notions of tradition. It is also possible to understand the societal history through job titles and arrangements for the destitute and sick.

There are a lot of politics that surround the census in many countries. In Canada in 2010 for example, the government under the leadership of Stephen Harper abolished the mandatory long-form census. The decision to cut the long-form census was a response to protests from some Canadians who resented the personal questions. The long-form census was reinstated by the Justin Trudeau government in 2016.

Census data and research

As governments assumed responsibility for schooling and welfare, large government research departments made extensive use of census data. Actuarial estimates could be made to project populations and plan for provision in local government and regions. It was also possible for central government to allocate funding on the basis of census data. Even into the mid twentieth century, census data was only directly accessible to large government departments. However, computers meant that tabulations could be used directly by university researchers, large businesses and local government offices. They could use the detail of the data to answer new questions and add to local and specialist knowledge.

Now, census data are published in a wide variety of formats to be accessible to business, all levels of governance, media, students and teachers, charities and any citizen who is interested; researchers in particular have an interest in the role of Census Field Officers (CFO) and their assistants. Data can be represented visually or analysed in complex statistical models, to show the difference between certain areas, or to understand the association between different personal characteristics. Census data offer a unique insight into small areas and small demographic groups which sample data would be unable to capture with precision.

Privacy

Although the census provides a useful way of obtaining statistical information about a population, such information can sometimes lead to abuses, political or otherwise, made possible by the linking of individuals' identities to anonymous census data. This consideration is particularly important when individuals' census responses are made available in microdata form, but even aggregate-level data can result in privacy breaches when dealing with small areas and/or rare subpopulations. For instance, when reporting data from a large city, it might be appropriate to give the average income for black males aged between 50 and 60. However, doing this for a town that only has two black males in this age group would be a breach of privacy because either of those persons, knowing his own income and the reported average, could determine the other man's income.

Typically, census data are processed to obscure such individual information. Some agencies do this by intentionally introducing small statistical errors to prevent the identification of individuals in marginal populations; others swap variables for similar respondents. Whatever measures have been taken to reduce the privacy risk in census data, new technology in the form of better electronic analysis of data poses increasing challenges to the protection of sensitive individual information. This is known as statistical disclosure control.

Another possibility is to present survey results by means of statistical models in the form of a multivariate distribution mixture. The statistical information in the form of conditional distributions (histograms) can be derived interactively from the estimated mixture model without any further access to the original database. As the final product does not contain any protected microdata, the model based interactive software can be distributed without any confidentiality concerns. Another method is simply to release no data at all, except very large scale data directly to the central government. Different release strategies between government have led to an international project (IPUMS) to co-ordinate access to microdata and corresponding metadata. Such projects also promote standardising metadata by projects such as SDMX so that best use can be made of the minimal data available.

Historical censuses

Censuses in Egypt first appear in the late Middle Kingdom and develops in the New Kingdom Pharaoh Amasis, according to Herodotus, require every Egyptian to declare annually to the nomarch, "whence he gained his living". Under the Ptolemies and the Romans several censuses were conducted in Egypt by governments officials

Ancient Greece

Censuses are mentioned in the Bible. God commands a per capita tax to be paid with the census in Exodus 30:11-16 for the upkeep of the Tabernacle. The Book of Numbers is named after the counting of the Israelite population (in Numbers 1-4) according to the house of the Fathers after the exodus from Egypt. A second census was taken while the Israelites were camped in the plains of Moab, in Numbers 26.

King David performed a census that produced disastrous results (in 2 Samuel 24 and 1 Chronicles 21). His son, King Solomon, had all of the foreigners in Israel counted in 2 Chronicles 2:17.

When the Romans took over Judea in AD 6, the legate Publius Sulpicius Quirinius organised a census for tax purposes. The Gospel of Luke links the birth of Jesus to this event. Luke 2.

China

One of the world's earliest preserved censuses was held in China in AD 2 during the Han Dynasty, and is still considered by scholars to be quite accurate. The population was registered as having 57,671,400 individuals in 12,366,470 households. Another census was held in AD 144.

India

The oldest recorded census in India is thought to have occurred around 300 BC during the reign of The Emperor Chandragupta Maurya under the leadership of Kautilya or Chanakya and Ashoka.

Rome

The word "census" originated in ancient Rome from the Latin word censere ("to estimate"). The census played a crucial role in the administration of the Roman Empire, as it was used to determine taxes. With few interruptions, it was usually carried out every five years. It provided a register of citizens and their property from which their duties and privileges could be listed. It is said to have been instituted by the Roman king Servius Tullius in the 6th century BC, at which time the number of arms-bearing citizens was supposedly counted at around 80,000. The 6 AD "census of Quirinius" undertaken following the imposition of direct Roman rule in Judea was partially responsible for the development of the Zealot movement and several failed rebellions against Rome that ended in the Diaspora. The 15-year indiction cycle established by Diocletian in AD 297 was based on quindecennial censuses and formed the basis for dating in late antiquity and under the Byzantine Empire.

Rashidun and Umayyad Caliphates

In the Middle Ages, the Caliphate began conducting regular censuses soon after its formation, beginning with the one ordered by the second Rashidun caliph, Umar. The Domesday Book was undertaken in AD 1086 by William I of England so that he could properly tax the land he had recently conquered in medieval Europe. In 1183, a census was taken of the crusader Kingdom of Jerusalem, to ascertain the number of men and amount of money that could possibly be raised against an invasion by Saladin, sultan of Egypt and Syria.

1328 : occurs in France the first census at the national level (" L'État des paroisses et des feux ") mostly done for fiscal reasons. French population estimated at that time at 16 to 17 millions inhabitants.

Inca Empire

In the 15th century, the Inca Empire had a unique way to record census information. The Incas did not have any written language but recorded information collected during censuses and other numeric information as well as non-numeric data on quipus, strings from llama or alpaca hair or cotton cords with numeric and other values encoded by knots in a base-10 positional system.

Spanish Empire

On May 25, 1577, King Philip II of Spain ordered by royal cédula the preparation of a general description of Spain's holdings in the Indies. Instructions and a questionnaire, issued in 1577 by the Office of the Cronista Mayor, were distributed to local officials in the Viceroyalties of New Spain and Peru to direct the gathering of information. The questionnaire, composed of fifty items, was designed to elicit basic information about the nature of the land and the life of its peoples. The replies, known as "relaciones geográficas," were written between 1579 and 1585 and were returned to the Cronista Mayor in Spain by the Council of the Indies.

World population estimates

The earliest estimate of the world population was made by Giovanni Battista Riccioli in 1661; the next by Johann Peter Süssmilch in 1741, revised in 1762; the third by Karl Friedrich Wilhelm Dieterici in 1859.

In 1931, Walter Willcox published a table in his book, International Migrations: Volume II Interpretations, that estimated the 1929 world population to be roughly 1.8 billion.

Social research

"Sociological methodology" redirects here. For the journal, see Sociological Methodology.

Social research is a research conducted by social scientists following a systematic plan. Social research methodologies can be classified as quantitative and qualitative.

- Quantitative designs approach social phenomena through quantifiable evidence, and often rely on statistical analysis of many cases (or across intentionally designed treatments in an experiment) to create valid and reliable general claims. Related to quantity.
- Qualitative designs emphasize understanding of social phenomena through direct observation, communication with participants, or analysis of texts, and may stress contextual subjective accuracy over generality. Related to quality.

While methods may be classified as quantitative or qualitative, most methods contain elements of both. For example, qualitative data analysis often involves a fairly structured approach to coding the raw data into systematic information, and quantifying intercoder reliability. Thus, there is often a more complex relationship between "qualitative" and "quantitative" approaches than would be suggested by drawing a simple distinction between them.

Social scientists employ a range of methods in order to analyse a vast breadth of social phenomena: from census survey data derived from millions of individuals, to the in-depth analysis of a single agent's social experiences; from monitoring what is happening on contemporary streets, to the investigation of ancient historical documents. Methods rooted in classical sociology and statistics have formed the basis for research in other disciplines, such as political science, media studies, program evaluation and market research.

Method

Social scientists are divided into camps of support for particular research techniques. These disputes relate to the historical core of social theory (positivism and antipositivism; structure and agency). While very different in many aspects, both qualitative and quantitative approaches involve a systematic interaction between theory and data. The choice of method often depends largely on what the researcher intends to investigate. For example, a researcher concerned with drawing a statistical generalization across an entire population may administer a survey questionnaire to a representative sample population. By contrast, a researcher who seeks full contextual understanding of an individuals' social actions may choose ethnographic participant observation or open-ended interviews. Studies will commonly combine, or triangulate, quantitative and qualitative methods as part of a multi-strategy design.

Barcode reader

A bar code reader (or bar code scanner) is an electronic device that can read and output printed barcodes to a computer. Like a flatbed scanner, it consists of a light source, a lens and a light sensor translating for optical impulses into electrical signals.Additionally, nearly all barcode readers contain decoder circuitry analyzing the bar code's image data provided by the sensor and sending the barcode's content to the scanner's output port.

PEN TYPE SCANNERS

Pen-type readers consist of a light source and photodiode that are placed next to each other in the tip of a pen. To read a bar code, the person holding the pen must move the tip of it across the bars at a relatively uniform speed. The photodiode measures the intensity of the light reflected back from the light source as the tip crosses each bar and space in the printed code. The photodiode generates a waveform that is used to measure the widths of the bars and spaces in the bar code. Dark bars in the bar code absorb light and white spaces reflect light so that the voltage waveform generated by the photodiode is a representation of the bar and space pattern in the bar code. This waveform is decoded by the scanner in a manner similar to the way Morse code dots and dashes are decoded.

Laser scanners

Laser scanners work the same way as pen type readers except that they use a laser beam as the light source and typically employ either a reciprocating mirror or a rotating prism to scan the laser beam back and forth across the bar code. As with the pen type reader, a photo-diode is used to measure the intensity of the light reflected back from the bar code. In both pen readers and laser scanners, the light emitted by the reader is rapidly varied in brightness with a data pattern and the photo-diode receive circuitry is designed to detect only signals with the same modulated pattern.

CCD readers (also known as LED scanners)

CCD readers use an array of hundreds of tiny light sensors lined up in a row in the head of the reader. Each sensor measures the intensity of the light immediately in front of it. Each individual light sensor in the CCD reader is extremely small and because there are hundreds of sensors lined up in a row, a voltage pattern identical to the pattern in a bar code is generated in the reader by sequentially measuring the voltages across each sensor in the row. The important difference between a CCD reader and a pen or laser scanner is that the CCD reader is measuring emitted ambient light from the bar code whereas pen or laser scanners are measuring reflected light of a specific frequency originating from the scanner itself.

Camera-based readers

Two-dimensional imaging scanners are a newer type of bar code reader. They use a camera and image processing techniques to decode the bar code.

Video camera readers use small video cameras with the same CCD technology as in a CCD bar code reader except that instead of having a single row of sensors, a video camera has hundreds of rows of sensors arranged in a two dimensional array so that they can generate an image.

Large field-of-view readers use high resolution industrial cameras to capture multiple bar codes simultaneously. All the bar codes appearing in the photo are decoded instantly (ImageID patents and code creation tools) or by use of plugins (e.g. the Barcodepedia used a flash application and some web cam for querying a database), have been realized options for resolving the given tasks.

Omnidirectional barcode scanners

Omnidirectional scanning uses "series of straight or curved scanning lines of varying directions in the form of a starburst, a Lissajous curve, or other multiangle arrangement are projected at the symbol and one or more of them will be able to cross all of the symbol's bars and spaces, no matter what the orientation. Almost all of them use a laser. Unlike the simpler single-line laser scanners, they produce a pattern of beams in varying orientations allowing them to read barcodes presented to it at different angles. Most of them use a single rotating polygonal mirror and an arrangement of several fixed mirrors to generate their complex scan patterns.

Omnidirectional scanners are most familiar through the horizontal scanners in supermarkets, where packages are slid over a glass or sapphire window. There are a range of different omnidirectional units available which can be used for differing scanning applications, ranging from retail type applications with the barcodes read only a few centimetres away from the scanner to industrial conveyor scanning where the unit can be a couple of metres away or more from the code. Omnidirectional scanners are also better at reading poorly printed, wrinkled, or even torn barcodes.

Cell phone cameras

While cell phone cameras without auto-focus are not ideal for reading some common barcode formats, there are 2D barcodes which are optimized for cell phones, as well as QR Codes (Quick Response) codes and Data Matrix codes which can be read quickly and accurately with or without auto-focus.

Cell phone cameras open up a number of applications for consumers.For example, -

- Movies: DVD/VHS movie catalogs.
- Music: CD catalogs - play MP3 when scanned.
- Book catalogs and device.
- Groceries, nutrition information, making shopping lists when the last of an item is used, etc.
- Personal Property inventory (for insurance and other purposes)code scanned into personal finance software when entering. Later, scanned receipt images can then be automatically associated with the appropriate entries. Later, the barcodes can be used to rapidly weed out paper copies not required to be retained for tax or asset inventory purposes.
- If retailers put barcodes on receipts that allowed downloading an electronic copy or encoded the entire receipt in a 2D barcode, consumers could easily import data into personal finance, property inventory, and grocery management software.

Receipts scanned on a scanner could be automatically identified and associated with the appropriate entries in finance and property inventory software.

- Consumer tracking from the retailer perspective (for example, loyalty card programs that track consumers purchases at the point of sale by having them scan a QR code).

A number of enterprise applications using cell phones are appearing:

- Access control (for example, ticket validation at venues), inventory reporting (for example, tracking deliveries), asset tracking (for example, anti-counterfeiting).

The Internal Revenue Service (IRS) is the revenue service of the United States federal government. The government agency is a bureau of the Department of the Treasury, and is under the immediate direction of the Commissioner of Internal Revenue, who is appointed to a five-year term by the President of the United States. The IRS is responsible for collecting taxes and administering the Internal Revenue Code, the main body of federal statutory tax law of the United States. The duties of the IRS include providing tax assistance to taxpayers and pursuing and resolving instances of erroneous or fraudulent tax filings. The IRS has also overseen various benefits programs, and enforces portions of the Affordable Care Act.

The IRS originated with the Commissioner of Internal Revenue, a federal office created in 1862 to assess the nation's first income tax, which was to raise funds for the American Civil War. The temporary measure provided over a fifth of the Union's war expenses and was allowed to expire a decade later. In 1913, the Sixteenth Amendment to the U.S. Constitution was ratified authorizing Congress to impose a tax on income, and the Bureau of Internal Revenue was established. In 1953, the agency was renamed the Internal Revenue Service.

Though the IRS brings in most of the revenue needed to fund the federal government, its resources have been cut year after year. In 2016 the American College of Tax Counsel wrote to the Congressional leadership stating, "We have watched the agency struggle with significant decreases in funding that have caused staffing and morale issues. In our practices, we have seen the negative impact this has had on our clients, the taxpayers."

In the 2017 fiscal year, the IRS processed more than 245 million returns and collected more than $3.4 trillion in gross revenue, spending 34¢ for every $100 it collected.

On June 28, 2018, Bloomberg News wrote, "The agency has been reeling from budget cuts. The current budget of $11.43 billion is less than in fiscal 2008, and the IRS pared about 15 percent of its workforce over the past five years. The enforcement staff has plunged by more than 25 percent since 2010."

In the 2018 fiscal year, the U.S. federal government spent $779 billion more than it brought in. It's estimated that in fiscal year 2019 the loss will be close to $1 trillion. In fiscal year 2019 the IRS plans to cut an additional 2,200 employees.

Smartphones

- Smartphones can be used in Google's mobile Android operating system via both their own Google Goggles application. Nokia's Symbian operating system features a barcode scanner which can scan barcodes, while mbarcode is a barcode reader for the Maemo operating system. In the Apple iOS, a barcode reader is not automatically included, but there are more than fifty free or paid apps available with both scanning capabilities and hard-linking to URI. With BlackBerry devices, the App World application can natively scan barcodes. Windows Phone 8 is able to scan barcodes through the Bing search app.

Housing

A large multifunction barcode scanner being used to monitor the transportation of packages of radioactive pharmaceuticals

- Barcode readers can be distinguished based on housing design as follows:

Handheld scanner

with a handle and typically a trigger button for switching on the light like this are used in factory and farm automation for quality management and shipping.

PDA scanner (or Auto-ID PDA)

- PDA with a built-in barcode reader or attached barcode scanner.
- Automatic reader
- back office equipment to read barcoded documents at high speed (50,000/hour).
- Cordless scanner (or Wireless scanner)
- cordless barcode scanner is operated by a battery fit inside it and is not connected to the electricity mains and transfer data to the connected device like PC.

Methods of connection

Early barcode scanners, of all formats, almost universally used the then-common RS-232 serial interface. This was an electrically simple means of connection and the software to access it is also relatively simple, although needing to be written for specific computers and their serial ports.

There are a few other less common interfaces. These were used in large EPOS systems with dedicated hardware, rather than attaching to existing commodity computers. In some of these interfaces, the scanning device returned a "raw" signal proportional to the intensities seen while scanning the barcode. This was then decoded by the host device. In some cases the scanning device would convert the symbology of the barcode to one that could be recognized by the host device, such as Code 39.

PS/2 keyboard and mouse ports

With the popularity of the PC and its standard keyboard interface, it became ever easier to connect physical hardware to a PC and so there was commercial demand similarly to reduce the complexity of the associated software. "Keyboard wedge" hardware plugged between the PS/2 port and the keyboard, with characters from the barcode scanner appearing exactly as if they had been typed at the keyboard. This made the addition of simple barcode reading abilities to existing programs very easy, without any need to change them, although it did require some care by the user and could be restrictive in the content of the barcodes that could be handled.

USB

Later barcode readers began to use USB connectors rather than the keyboard port, as this became a more convenient hardware option. To retain the easy integration with existing programs, a device driver called a "software wedge" could be used, to emulate the keyboard-impersonating behavior of the old "keyboard wedge" hardware.

In many cases, a choice of USB interface types (HID, CDC) are provided. Some have PoweredUSB.

Wireless networking

Some modern handheld barcode readers can be operated in wireless networks according to IEEE 802.11g (WLAN) or IEEE 802.15.1 (Bluetooth). Some barcode readers also support radio frequencies viz. 433 MHz or 910 MHz. Readers without external power sources require their batteries be recharged occasionally, which may make them unsuitable for some uses.

Resolution

The scanner resolution is measured by the size of the dot of light emitted by the reader. If this dot of light is wider than any bar or space in the bar code, then it will overlap two elements (two spaces or two bars) and it may produce wrong output. On the other hand, if a too small dot of light is used, then it can misinterpret any spot on the bar code making the final output wrong.

The most commonly used dimension is 13 thou (0.013 in or 0.33 mm), although some scanners can read codes with dimensions as small as 3 thou (0.003 in or 0.075 mm). Most manufacturers advertise bar code resolution in mil, which is interchangeable with thou. Smaller bar codes must be printed at high resolution to.

Methodological assumptions

Social research is based on logic and empirical observations. Charles C. Ragin writes in his Constructing Social Research book that "Social research involved the interaction between ideas and evidence. Ideas help social researchers make sense of evidence, and researchers use evidence to extend, revise and test ideas." Social research thus attempts to create or validate theories through data collection and data analysis, and its goal is exploration, description, explanation, and prediction. It should never lead or be mistaken with philosophy or belief. Social research aims to find social patterns of regularity in social life and usually deals with social groups (aggregates of individuals), not individuals themselves (although science of psychology is an exception here). Research can also be divided into pure research and applied research. Pure research has no application on real life, whereas applied research attempts to influence the real world.

There are no laws in social science that parallel the laws in natural science. A law in social science is a universal generalization about a class of facts. A fact is an observed phenomenon, and observation means it has been seen, heard or otherwise experienced by researcher. A theory is a systematic explanation for the observations that relate to a particular aspect of social life. Concepts are the basic building blocks of theory and are abstract elements representing classes of phenomena. Axioms or postulates are basic assertions assumed to be true. Propositions are conclusions drawn about the relationships among concepts, based on analysis of axioms. Hypotheses are specified expectations about empirical reality derived from propositions. Social research involves testing these hypotheses to see if they are true.

Social research involves creating a theory, operationalization (measurement of variables) and observation (actual collection of data to test hypothesized relationship). Social theories are written in the language of variables, in other words, theories describe logical relationships between variables. Variables are logical sets of attributes, with people being the "carriers" of those variables (for example, gender can be a variable with two attributes: male and female). Variables are also divided into independent variables (data) that influences the dependent variables (which scientists are trying to explain). For example, in a study of how different dosages of a drug are related to the severity of symptoms of a disease, a measure of the severity of the symptoms of the disease is a dependent variable and the administration of the drug in specified doses is the independent variable. Researchers will compare the different values of the dependent variable (severity of the symptoms) and attempt to draw conclusions.

ELECTRONIC RECORDS MANAGEMENT SYSTEMS

An Electronic Document and Records Management System is a computer program or set of programs used to track and store records. The term is distinguished from imaging and document management systems that specialize in paper capture and document management respectively. Electronic records management Systems commonly provide specialized security and auditing functionality tailored to the needs of records managers.

The National Archives and Records Administration (NARA) has endorsed the U.S. Department of Defense standard 5015.2 as an "adequate and appropriate basis for addressing the basic challenges of managing records in the automated environment that increasingly characterizes the creation and use of records." Records Management Vendors can be certified as compliant with the DoD 5015.2-STD after verification from the Joint Interoperability Test Command which builds test case procedures, writes detailed and summary final reports on 5015.2-certified products, and performs on-site inspection of software. The National Archives in the UK has published two sets of functional requirements to promote the development of the electronic records management software market (1999 and 2002). It ran a program to evaluate products against the 2002 requirements. While these requirements were initially formulated in collaboration with central government, they have been taken up with enthusiasm by many parts of the wider public sector in the UK and in other parts of the world. The testing program has now closed.

The European Commission has published "MoReq", the Model Requirements for Electronic Records and Document Management in 2001. Although not a formal standard, it is widely regarded and referred to as a standard. This was funded by the Commission's IDA program, and was developed at the instigation of the DLM Forum. A major update of MoReq, known as MoReq2, was published in February 2008. This too was initiated by the DLM Forum and funded by the European Commission, on this occasion by its IDABC program (the successor to IDA). A software testing framework and an XML schema accompany MoReq2; a software compliance testing regime was agreed at the DLM Forum conference in Toulouse in December 2008.

The National Archives of Australia (NAA) published the Functional Specifications for Electronic Records Management Systems Software (ERMS), and the associated Guidelines for Implementing the Functional Specifications for Electronic Records Management Systems Software, as exposure drafts in February 2006.

Archives New Zealand published a 'discretionary best practice' Electronic Recordkeeping Systems Standard (Standard 5) in June 2005, issued under the authority of Section 27 of the Public Records Act 2005.

Commercial records centers

Commercial records centers are facilities which provide services for the storage for paper records for organizations. In some cases, they also offer storage for records maintained in electronic formats. Commercial records centers provide high density storage for paper records and some offer climate controlled storage for sensitive non-paper and critical (vital) paper media. There is a trade organization for commercial records centers (for example, PRISM International), however, not all service providers are members. Privacy is the ability of an individual or group to seclude themselves, or information about themselves, and thereby express themselves selectively. The boundaries and content of what is considered private differ among cultures and individuals, but share common themes. When something is private to a person, it usually means that something is inherently special or sensitive to them. The domain of privacy partially overlaps with security (confidentiality), which can include the concepts of appropriate use, as well as protection of information. Privacy may also take the form of bodily integrity. The right not to be subjected to unsanctioned invasions of privacy by the government, corporations or individuals is part of many countries' privacy laws, and in some cases, constitutions. All countries have laws which in some way limit privacy. An example of this would be law concerning taxation, which normally requires the sharing of information about personal income or earnings. In some countries individual privacy may conflict with freedom of speech laws and some laws may require public disclosure of information which would be considered private in other countries and cultures. This was a major concern in the United States, with the Supreme Court passage of Citizens United.

Privacy may be voluntarily sacrificed, normally in exchange for perceived benefits and very often with specific dangers and losses, although this is a very strategic view of human relationships. For example, people may be ready to reveal their name, if that allows them to promote trust by others and thus build meaningful social relations. Research shows that people are more willing to voluntarily sacrifice privacy if the data gatherer is seen to be transparent as to what information is gathered and how it is used. In the business world, a person may volunteer personal details (often for advertising purposes) in order to gamble on winning a prize. A person may also disclose personal information as part of being an executive for a publicly traded company in the USA pursuant to federal securities law. Personal information which is voluntarily shared but subsequently stolen or misused can lead to identity theft.

The concept of universal individual privacy is a modern construct primarily associated with Western culture, British and North American in particular, and remained virtually unknown in some cultures until recent times. According to some researchers, this concept sets Anglo-American culture apart even from Western European cultures such as French or Italian. Most cultures, however, recognize the ability of individuals to withhold certain parts of their personal information from wider society-closing the door to one's home, for example.

The distinction or overlap between secrecy and privacy is ontologically subtle, which is why the word "privacy" is an example of an untranslatable lexeme, and many languages do not have a specific word for "privacy". Such languages either use a complex description to translate the term or borrow from English "privacy" (as Indonesian privasi or Italian la privacy). The distinction hinges on the discreteness of interests of parties (persons or groups), which can have emic variation depending on cultural mores of individualism, collectivism, and the negotiation between individual and group rights. The difference is sometimes expressed humorously as, "when I withhold information, it is privacy; when you withhold information, it is secrecy."

Concepts

A broad multicultural literary tradition going to the beginnings of recorded history discusses the concept of privacy. One way of categorizing all concepts of privacy is by considering all discussions as one of these concepts:

1. the right to be let alone
2. the option to limit the access others have to one's personal information
3. secrecy, or the option to conceal any information from others
4. control over others' use of information about oneself
5. states of privacy
6. personhood and autonomy
7. self-identity and personal growth
8. protection of intimate relationships

Right to be let alone

In 1890 the United States jurists Samuel D. Warren and Louis Brandeis wrote The Right to Privacy, an article in which they argued for the "right to be let alone", using that phrase as a definition of privacy. There is extensive commentary over the meaning of being "let alone", and among other ways, it has been interpreted to mean the right of a person to choose seclusion from the attention of others if they wish to do so, and the right to be immune from scrutiny or being observed in private settings, such as one's own home. Although this early vague legal concept did not describe privacy in a way that made it easy to design broad legal protections of privacy, it strengthened the notion of privacy rights for individuals and began a legacy of discussion on those rights.

Limited access

Limited access refers to a person's ability to participate in society without having other individuals and organizations collect information about them.

Various theorists have imagined privacy as a system for limiting access to one's personal information. Edwin Lawrence Godkin wrote in the late 19th century that "nothing is better worthy of legal protection than private life, or, in other words, the right of every man to keep his affairs to himself, and to decide for himself to what extent they shall be the subject of public observation and discussion." Adopting an approach similar to the one presented by Ruth Gavison 9 years earlier, Sissela Bok said that privacy is "the condition of being protected from unwanted access by others-either physical access, personal information, or attention."

Control over information

Control over one's personal information is the concept that "privacy is the claim of individuals, groups, or institutions to determine for themselves when, how, and to what extent information about them is communicated to others." Charles Fried said that "Privacy is not simply an absence of information about us in the minds of others; rather it is the control we have over information about ourselves. Nevertheless, in the era of big data, control over information is under pressure.

States of privacy

Alan Westin defined four states-or experiences-of privacy: solitude, intimacy, anonymity, and reserve. Solitude is a physical separation from others. Intimacy is a "close, relaxed, and frank relationship between two or more individuals" that results from the seclusion of a pair or small group of individuals. Anonymity is the "desire of individuals for times of 'public privacy.'" Lastly, reserve is the "creation of a psychological barrier against unwanted intrusion"; this creation of a psychological barrier requires others to respect an individual's need or desire to restrict communication of information concerning himself or herself.

In addition to the psychological barrier of reserve, Kirsty Hughes identified three more kinds of privacy barriers: physical, behavioral, and normative. Physical barriers, such as walls and doors, prevent others from accessing and experiencing the individual. (In this sense, "accessing" an individual includes accessing personal information about him or her.) Behavioral barriers communicate to others-verbally, through language, or non-verbally, through personal space, body language, or clothing-that an individual does not want them to access or experience him or her. Lastly, normative barriers, such as laws and social norms, restrain others from attempting to access or experience an individual.

Secrecy

Privacy is sometimes defined as an option to have secrecy. Richard Posner said that privacy is the right of people to "conceal information about themselves that others might use to their disadvantage". In various legal contexts, when privacy is described as secrecy, a conclusion if privacy is secrecy then rights to privacy do not apply for any information which is already publicly disclosed. When privacy-as-secrecy is discussed, it is usually imagined to be a selective kind of secrecy in which individuals keep some information secret and private while they choose to make other information public and not private.

Personhood and autonomy

Privacy may be understood as a necessary precondition for the development and preservation of personhood. Jeffrey Reiman defined privacy in terms of a recognition of one's ownership of his or her physical and mental reality and a moral right to his or her self-determination. Through the "social ritual" of privacy, or the social practice of respecting an individual's privacy barriers, the social group communicates to the developing child that he or she has exclusive moral rights to his or her body-in other words, he or she has moral ownership of his or her body. This entails control over both active (physical) and cognitive appropriation, the former being control over one's movements and actions and the latter being control over who can experience one's physical existence and when.

Alternatively, Stanley Benn defined privacy in terms of a recognition of oneself as a subject with agency-as an individual with the capacity to choose. Privacy is required to exercise choice. Overt observation makes the individual aware of himself or herself as an object with a "determinate character" and "limited probabilities." Covert observation, on the other hand, changes the conditions in which the individual is exercising choice without his or her knowledge and consent.

In addition, privacy may be viewed as a state that enables autonomy, a concept closely connected to that of personhood. According to Joseph Kufer, an autonomous self-concept entails a conception of oneself as a "purposeful, self-determining, responsible agent" and an awareness of one's capacity to control the boundary between self and other-that is, to control who can access and experience him or her and to what extent. Furthermore, others must acknowledge and respect the self's boundaries-in other words, they must respect the individual's privacy.

The studies of psychologists such as Jean Piaget and Victor Tausk show that, as children learn that they can control who can access and experience them and to what extent, they develop an autonomous self-concept. In addition, studies of adults in particular institutions, such as Erving Goffman's study of "total institutions" such as prisons and mental institutions, suggest that systemic and routinized deprivations or violations of privacy deteriorate one's sense of autonomy over time.

Self-identity and personal growth

Privacy may be understood as a prerequisite for the development of a sense of self-identity. Privacy barriers, in particular, are instrumental in this process. According to Irwin Altman, such barriers "define and limit the boundaries of the self" and thus "serve to help define [the self]." This control primarily entails the ability to regulate contact with others. Control over the "permeability" of the self's boundaries enables one to control what constitutes the self and thus to define what is the self.

In addition, privacy may be seen as a state that fosters personal growth, a process integral to the development of self-identity. Hyman Gross suggested that, without privacy-solitude, anonymity, and temporary releases from social roles-individuals would be unable to freely express themselves and to engage in self-discovery and self-criticism. Such self-discovery and self-criticism contributes to one's understanding of oneself and shapes one's sense of identity.

9

POPULAR MEDIA & PRIVACY WAYS

Privacy can mean different things in different contexts; different people, cultures, and nations have different expectations about how much privacy a person is entitled to or what constitutes an invasion of privacy.

PERSONAL PRIVACY

Most people have a strong sense of privacy in relation to the exposure of their body to others. This is an aspect of personal modesty. A person will go to extreme lengths to protect this personal modesty, the main way being the wearing of clothes. Other ways include erection of walls, fences, screens, use of cathedral glass, partitions, by maintaining a distance, beside other ways. People who go to those lengths expect that their privacy will be respected by others. At the same time, people are prepared to expose themselves in acts of physical intimacy, but these are confined to exposure in circumstances and of persons of their choosing. Even a discussion of those circumstances is regarded as intrusive and typically unwelcome.

Physical privacy could be defined as preventing "intrusions into one's physical space or solitude." This would include concerns such as:

- Preventing intimate acts or hiding one's body from others for the purpose of modesty; apart from being dressed this can be achieved by walls, fences, privacy screens, cathedral glass, partitions between urinals, by being far away from others, on a bed by a bed sheet or a blanket, when changing clothes by a towel, etc.; to what extent these measures also prevent acts being heard varies

- Video, of aptly named graphic, or intimate, acts, behaviors or body parts
- Preventing searching of one's personal possessions
- Preventing unauthorized access to one's home or vehicle
- Medical privacy, the right to make fundamental medical decisions without governmental coercion or third-party review, most widely applied to questions of contraception

An example of the legal basis for the right to physical privacy is the U.S. Fourth Amendment, which guarantees "the right of the people to be secure in their persons, houses, papers, and effects, against unreasonable searches and seizures". Most countries have laws regarding trespassing and property rights also determine the right of physical privacy.

Physical privacy may be a matter of cultural sensitivity, personal dignity, and/or shyness. There may also be concerns about safety, if for example one is wary of becoming the victim of crime or stalking. Civil inattention is a process whereby individuals are able to maintain their privacy within a crowd.

INFORMATIONAL

Information or data privacy refers to the evolving relationship between technology and the legal right to, or public expectation of, privacy in the collection and sharing of data about one's self. Privacy concerns exist wherever uniquely identifiable data relating to a person or persons are collected and stored, in digital form or otherwise. In some cases these concerns refer to how data are collected, stored, and associated. In other cases the issue is who is given access to information. Other issues include whether an individual has any ownership rights to data about them, and/or the right to view, verify, and challenge that information.

Various types of personal information are often associated with privacy concerns. Information plays an important role in the decision-action process, which can lead to problems in terms of privacy and availability. First, it allows people to see all the options and alternatives available. Secondly, it allows people to choose which of the options would be best for a certain situation. An information landscape consists of the information, its location in the so-called network, as well as its availability, awareness, and usability. Yet the set-up of the information landscape means that information that is available in one place may not be available somewhere else. This can lead to a privacy situation that leads to questions regarding which people have the power to access and use certain information, who should have that power, and what provisions govern it. For various reasons, individuals may object to personal information such as their religion, sexual orientation, political affiliations, or personal activities being revealed, perhaps to avoid discrimination, personal embarrassment, or damage to their professional reputations.

Financial privacy, in which information about a person's financial transactions is guarded, is important for the avoidance of fraud including identity theft. Information about a person's purchases, for instance, can reveal a great deal about their preferences, places they have visited, their contacts, products (such as medications) they use, their activities and habits, etc. In addition to this, financial privacy also includes privacy over the bank accounts opened by individuals. Information about the bank where the individual has an account with, and whether or not this is in a country that does not share this information with other countries can help countries in fighting tax avoidance.

Internet privacy is the ability to determine what information one reveals or withholds about oneself over the Internet, who has access to such information, and for what purposes one's information may or may not be used. For example, web users may be concerned to discover that many of the web sites which they visit collect, store, and possibly share personally identifiable information about them. Similarly, Internet email users generally consider their emails to be private and hence would be concerned if their email was being accessed, read, stored or forwarded by third parties without their consent. Tools used to protect privacy on the Internet include encryption tools and anonymizing services like I2P and Tor.

Medical privacy Protected Health Information OCR/HIPAA (Health Insurance Portability and Accountability Act of 1996) allows a person to withhold their medical records and other information from others, perhaps because of fears that it might affect their insurance coverage or employment, or to avoid the embarrassment caused by revealing medical conditions or treatments. Medical information could also reveal other aspects of one's personal life, such as sexual preferences or proclivity. A right to sexual privacy enables individuals to acquire and use contraceptives without family, community or legal sanctions.

Political privacy has been a concern since voting systems emerged in ancient times. The secret ballot helps to ensure that voters cannot be coerced into voting in certain ways, since they can allocate their vote as they wish in the privacy and security of the voting booth while maintaining the anonymity of the vote. Secret ballots are nearly universal in modern democracy, and considered a basic right of citizenship, despite the difficulties that they cause (for example the inability to trace votes back to the corresponding voters increases the risk of someone stuffing additional fraudulent votes into the system: additional security controls are needed to minimize such risks). Corporate privacy refers to the privacy rights of corporate actors like senior executives of large, publicly traded corporations. Desires for corporate privacy can frequently raise issues with obligations for public disclosures under securities and corporate law.

Organizational

Government agencies, corporations, groups/societies and other organizations may desire to keep their activities or secrets from being revealed to other organizations or individuals, adopting various security practices and controls in order to keep private information confidential. Organizations may seek legal protection for their secrets. For example, a government administration may be able to invoke executive privilege or declare certain information to be classified, or a corporation might attempt to protect valuable proprietary information as trade secrets.

Spiritual and intellectual

The earliest legislative development of privacy rights began under British common law, which protected "only the physical interference of life and property." Its development from then on became "one of the most significant chapters in the history of privacy law." Privacy rights gradually expanded to include a "recognition of man's spiritual nature, of his feelings and his intellect." Eventually, the scope of those rights broadened even further to include a basic "right to be let alone", and the former definition of "property" would then comprise "every form of possession-intangible, as well as tangible." By the late 19th century, interest in a "right to privacy" grew as a response to the growth of print media, especially newspapers.

History

Privacy has historical roots in philosophical discussions, the most well-known being Aristotle's distinction between two spheres of life: the public sphere of the polis, associated with political life, and the private sphere of the oikos, associated with domestic life. More systematic treatises of privacy in the United States did not appear until the 1890s, with the development of privacy law in America.

Technology

Advertisement for dial telephone service available to delegates to the 1912 Republican convention in Chicago. A major selling point of dial telephone service was that it was "secret", in that no operator was required to connect the call.

As technology has advanced, the way in which privacy is protected and violated has changed with it. In the case of some technologies, such as the printing press or the Internet, the increased ability to share information can lead to new ways in which privacy can be breached. It is generally agreed that the first publication advocating privacy in the United States was the article by Samuel Warren and Louis Brandeis, "The Right to Privacy", 4 Harvard Law Review 193 (1890), that was written largely in response to the increase in newspapers and photographs made possible by printing technologies.

New technologies can also create new ways to gather private information. For example, in the United States it was thought that heat sensors intended to be used to find marijuana-growing operations would be acceptable. However, in 2001 in Kyllo v. United States (533 U.S. 27) it was decided that the use of thermal imaging devices that can reveal previously unknown information without a warrant does indeed constitute a violation of privacy.

Generally the increased ability to gather and send information has had negative implications for retaining privacy. As large-scale information systems become more common, there is so much information stored in many databases worldwide that an individual has no practical means of knowing of or controlling all of the information about themselves that others may have hold or access. Such information could potentially be sold to others for profit and/or be used for purposes not known to or sanctioned by the individual concerned. The concept of information privacy has become more significant as more systems controlling more information appear. Also the consequences of privacy violations can be more severe. Privacy law in many countries has had to adapt to changes in technology in order to address these issues and, to some extent, maintain privacy rights. But the existing global privacy rights framework has also been criticized as incoherent and inefficient. Proposals such as the APEC Privacy Framework have emerged which set out to provide the first comprehensive legal framework on the issue of global data privacy.

There are various theories about privacy and privacy control. The Invasion Paradigm defines privacy violation as the hostile actions of a wrongdoer who causes direct harm to an individual. This is a reactive view of privacy protection as it waits until there is a violation before acting to protect the violated individual, sometimes through criminal punishments for those who invaded the privacy of others. In the Invasion Paradigm this threat of criminal punishment that is supposed to work as deterrent. The Secrecy paradigm defines a privacy invasion as someone's concealed information or hidden world being revealed through surveillance. The Negative Freedom Paradigm views privacy as freedom from invasion rather than a right, going against the more popular view of a "right to privacy." Finally, the Inaccessibility Paradigm states that privacy is the state where something is completely inaccessible to others. Daniel Solove, a law professor at George Washington University also has a theory of privacy. He believes that a conceptualized view of privacy will not work because there is no one core element. There are many different, interconnected elements involved in privacy and privacy protection. Therefore, Solove proposes looking at these issues from the bottom up, focusing on privacy problems. People may often overlook the fact that certain elements of privacy problems are due to the structure of privacy itself. Therefore, the architecture must change wherein people must learn to view privacy as a social and legal structure. He also states that people have to redefine the relationship between privacy and businesses and the government. Participation in certain privacy elements of the government and businesses should allow people to choose whether they want to be a part of certain aspects of their work that could be considered privacy invasion.

Another trend is the design of privacy aware algorithms and sensors by designers. These include the use of privacy preserving sensors, privacy policies regarding data-sharing in a collaborative and distributive environment and data ownership itself for visual privacy. For example, face detection algorithms are used by Google Streetview to blur out the faces detected while collecting data for Google maps. There has also been an emergence of context-aware visual privacy and sensors that only use depth or thermal imaging data to obfuscate the user and redact sensitive information.

Internet

The Internet has brought new concerns about privacy in an age where computers can permanently store records of everything: "where every online photo, status update, Twitter post and blog entry by and about us can be stored forever", writes law professor and author Jeffrey Rosen.

This currently has an effect on employment. Microsoft reports that 75 percent of U.S. recruiters and human-resource professionals now do online research about candidates, often using information provided by search engines, social-networking sites, photo/video-sharing sites, personal web sites and blogs, and Twitter. They also report that 70 percent of U.S. recruiters have rejected candidates based on internet information. This has created a need by many to control various online privacy settings in addition to controlling their online reputations, both of which have led to legal suits against various sites and employers.

The ability to do online inquiries about individuals has expanded dramatically over the last decade. Facebook for example, as of August 2015, was the largest social-networking site, with nearly 1,490 million members, who upload over 4.75 billion pieces of content daily. Over 83.09 million accounts were fake. Twitter has more than 316 million registered users and over 20 million are fake users. The Library of Congress recently announced that it will be acquiring-and permanently storing-the entire archive of public Twitter posts since 2006, reports Rosen.

Importantly, directly observed behaviour, such as browsing logs, search queries, or contents of the Facebook profile can be automatically processed to infer secondary information about an individual, such as sexual orientation, political and religious views, race, substance use, intelligence, and personality. Effectively, individual views and preferences can be revealed even if they were not directly expressed or indicated (e.g. by stating their political views on their Facebook profile, or visiting a gay community website).

According to some experts, many commonly used communication devices may be mapping every move of their users. Senator Al Franken has noted the seriousness of iPhones and iPads having the ability to record and store users' locations in unencrypted files, although Apple denied doing so.

Andrew Grove, co-founder and former CEO of Intel Corporation, offered his thoughts on internet privacy in an interview published in May 2000:

Privacy is one of the biggest problems in this new electronic age. At the heart of the Internet culture is a force that wants to find out everything about you. And once it has found out everything about you and two hundred million others, that's a very valuable asset, and people will be tempted to trade and do commerce with that asset. This wasn't the information that people were thinking of when they called this the information age.

Actions which reduce privacy

As with other concepts about privacy, there are various ways to discuss what kinds of processes or actions remove, challenge, lessen, or attack privacy. In 1960 legal scholar William Prosser created the following list of activities which can be remedied with privacy protection:

1. Intrusion into a person's private space, own affairs, or wish for solitude
2. Public disclosure of personal information about a person which could be embarrassing for them to have revealed
3. Promoting access to information about a person which could lead the public to have incorrect beliefs about them
4. Encroaching someone's personality rights, and using their likeness to advance interests which are not their own

Building from this and other historical precedents, Daniel J. Solove presented another classification of actions which are harmful to privacy, including collection of information which is already somewhat public, processing of information, sharing information, and invading personal space to get private information.

Collecting information

In the context of harming privacy, information collection means gathering whatever information can be obtained by doing something to obtain it. Surveillance is an example of this, when someone decides to begin watching and recording someone or something, and interrogation is another example of this, when someone uses another person as a source of information. Examples of information collection agencies include the NSA and the participants in the Five Eyes program.

Aggregating information

It can happen that privacy is not harmed when information is available, but that the harm can come when that information is collected as a set then processed in a way that the collective reporting of pieces of information encroaches on privacy. Actions in this category which can lessen privacy include the following:

- data aggregation, which is connecting many related but unconnected pieces of information
- identification, which can mean breaking the de-identification of items of data by putting it through a de-anonymization process, thus making facts which were intended to not name particular people to become associated with those people
- insecurity, such as lack of data security, which includes when an organization is supposed to be responsible for protecting data instead suffers a data breach which harms the people whose data it held
- secondary use, which is when people agree to share their data for a certain purpose, but then the data is used in ways without the data donors' informed consent
- exclusion is the use of a person's data without any attempt to give the person an opportunity to manage the data or participate in its usage

INFORMATION DISSEMINATION

Information dissemination is an attack on privacy when information which was shared in confidence is shared or threatened to be shared in a way that harms the subject of the information. There are various examples of this. Breach of confidentiality is when one entity promises to keep a person's information private, then breaks that promise. Disclosure is making information about a person more accessible in a way that harms the subject of the information, regardless of how the information was collected or the intent of making it available. Exposure is a special type of disclosure in which the information disclosed is emotional to the subject or taboo to share, such as revealing their private life experiences, their nudity, or perhaps private body functions. Increased accessibility means advertising the availability of information without actually distributing it, as in the case of doxxing. Blackmail is making a threat to share information, perhaps as part of an effort to coerce someone. Appropriation is an attack on the personhood of someone, and can include using the value of someone's reputation or likeness to advance interests which are not those of the person being appropriated. Distortion is the creation of misleading information or lies about a person.

Invasions

Invasion of privacy, a subset of expectation of privacy, is a different concept from the collecting, aggregating, and disseminating information because those three are a misuse of available data, whereas invasion is an attack on the right of individuals to keep personal secrets. An invasion is an attack in which information, whether intended to be public or not, is captured in a way that insults the personal dignity and right to private space of the person whose data is taken. An intrusion is any unwanted entry into a person's private personal space and solitude for any reason, regardless of whether data is taken during that breach of space. "Decisional interference" is when an entity somehow injects itself into the personal decision making process of another person, perhaps to influence that person's private decisions but in any case doing so in a way that disrupts the private personal thoughts that a person has.

Right to privacy

Privacy uses the theory of natural rights, and generally responds to new information and communication technologies. In North America, Samuel D. Warren and Louis D. Brandeis wrote that privacy is the "right to be let alone" (Warren & Brandeis, 1890) focuses on protecting individuals. This citation was a response to recent technological developments, such as photography, and sensationalist journalism, also known as yellow journalism.

Privacy rights are inherently intertwined with information technology. In his widely cited dissenting opinion in Olmstead v. United States (1928), Brandeis relied on thoughts he developed in his Harvard Law Review article in 1890. But in his dissent, he now changed the focus whereby he urged making personal privacy matters more relevant to constitutional law, going so far as saying "the government [was] identified .... as a potential privacy invader." He writes, "Discovery and invention have made it possible for the Government, by means far more effective than stretching upon the rack, to obtain disclosure in court of what is whispered in the closet." At that time, telephones were often community assets, with shared party lines and the potentially nosey human operators. By the time of Katz, in 1967, telephones had become personal devices with lines not shared across homes and switching was electro-mechanical. In the 1970s, new computing and recording technologies began to raise concerns about privacy, resulting in the Fair Information Practice Principles.

Definitions

In recent years there have been only few attempts to clearly and precisely define a "right to privacy." Some experts assert that in fact the right to privacy "should not be defined as a separate legal right" at all. By their reasoning, existing laws relating to privacy in general should be sufficient. Other experts, such as Dean Prosser, have attempted, but failed, to find a "common ground" between the leading kinds of privacy cases in the court system, at least to formulate a definition. One law school treatise from Israel, however, on the subject of "privacy in the digital environment", suggests that the "right to privacy should be seen as an independent right that deserves legal protection in itself." It has therefore proposed a working definition for a "right to privacy":

The right to privacy is our right to keep a domain around us, which includes all those things that are part of us, such as our body, home, property, thoughts, feelings, secrets and identity. The right to privacy gives us the ability to choose which parts in this domain can be accessed by others, and to control the extent, manner and timing of the use of those parts we choose to disclose.

An individual right

Alan Westin believes that new technologies alter the balance between privacy and disclosure, and that privacy rights may limit government surveillance to protect democratic processes. Westin defines privacy as "the claim of individuals, groups, or institutions to determine for themselves when, how, and to what extent information about them is communicated to others". Westin describes four states of privacy: solitude, intimacy, anonymity, and reserve. These states must balance participation against norms:

Each individual is continually engaged in a personal adjustment process in which he balances the desire for privacy with the desire for disclosure and communication of himself to others, in light of the environmental conditions and social norms set by the society in which he lives. - Alan Westin, Privacy and Freedom, 1968

Under liberal democratic systems, privacy creates a space separate from political life, and allows personal autonomy, while ensuring democratic freedoms of association and expression.

David Flaherty believes networked computer databases pose threats to privacy. He develops 'data protection' as an aspect of privacy, which involves "the collection, use, and dissemination of personal information". This concept forms the foundation for fair information practices used by governments globally. Flaherty forwards an idea of privacy as information control, "[i]ndividuals want to be left alone and to exercise some control over how information about them is used".

Richard Posner and Lawrence Lessig focus on the economic aspects of personal information control. Posner criticizes privacy for concealing information, which reduces market efficiency. For Posner, employment is selling oneself in the labour market, which he believes is like selling a product. Any 'defect' in the 'product' that is not reported is fraud. For Lessig, privacy breaches online can be regulated through code and law. Lessig claims "the protection of privacy would be stronger if people conceived of the right as a property right", and that "individuals should be able to control information about themselves". Economic approaches to privacy make communal conceptions of privacy difficult to maintain.

A collective "value" and a "human right"

There have been attempts to reframe privacy as a fundamental human right, whose social value is an essential component in the functioning of democratic societies. Amitai

Etzioni suggests a communitarian approach to privacy. This requires a shared moral culture for establishing social order. Etzioni believes that "[p]rivacy is merely one good among many others", and that technological effects depend on community accountability and oversight (ibid). He claims that privacy laws only increase government surveillance by weakening informal social controls. Furthermore, the government is no longer the only or even principle threat to people's privacy. Etzioni notes that corporate data miners, or "Privacy Merchants," stand to profit by selling massive dossiers personal information, including purchasing decisions and Internet traffic, to the highest bidder. And while some might not find collection of private information objectionable when it is only used commercially by the private sector, the information these corporations amass and process is also available to the government, so that it is no longer possible to protect privacy by only curbing the State.

Priscilla Regan believes that individual concepts of privacy have failed philosophically and in policy. She supports a social value of privacy with three dimensions: shared perceptions, public values, and collective components. Shared ideas about privacy allows freedom of conscience and diversity in thought. Public values guarantee democratic participation, including freedoms of speech and association, and limits government power. Collective elements describe privacy as collective good that cannot be divided. Regan's goal is to strengthen privacy claims in policy making: "if we did recognize the collective or public-good value of privacy, as well as the common and public value of privacy, those advocating privacy protections would have a stronger basis upon which to argue for its protection".

Leslie Regan Shade argues that the human right to privacy is necessary for meaningful democratic participation, and ensures human dignity and autonomy. Privacy depends on norms for how information is distributed, and if this is appropriate. Violations of privacy depend on context. The human right to privacy has precedent in the United Nations Declaration of Human Rights: "Everyone has the right to freedom of opinion and expression; this right includes freedom to hold opinions without interference and to seek, receive and impart information and ideas through any media and regardless of frontiers." Shade believes that privacy must be approached from a people-centered perspective, and not through the marketplace.

Protection

Privacy International 2007 privacy ranking

Most countries give citizen rights to privacy in their constitutions. Representative examples of this include the Constitution of Brazil, which says "the privacy, private life, honor and image of people are inviolable"; the Constitution of South Africa says that "everyone has a right to privacy"; and the Constitution of the Republic of Korea says "the privacy of no citizen shall be infringed." Among most countries whose constitutions do not explicitly describe privacy rights, court decisions have interpreted their constitutions to intend to give privacy rights.

Many countries have broad privacy laws outside their constitutions, including Australia's Privacy Act 1988, Argentina's Law for the Protection of Personal Data of 2000, Canada's 2000 Personal Information Protection and Electronic Documents Act, and Japan's 2003 Personal Information Protection Law. Beyond national privacy laws, there are international privacy agreements. The United Nations Universal Declaration of Human Rights says "No one shall be subjected to arbitrary interference with his privacy, family, home or correspondence, nor to attacks upon his honor and reputation." The Organisation for Economic Co-operation and Development published its Privacy Guidelines in 1980. The European Union's 1995 Data Protection Directive guides privacy protection in Europe. The 2004 Privacy Framework by the Asia-Pacific Economic Cooperation is a privacy protection agreement for the members of that organization. In the 1960s people began to consider how changes in technology were bringing changes in the concept of privacy. Vance Packard's The Naked Society was a popular book on privacy from that era and led discourse on privacy at that time.

Free market versus consumer protection approaches

Approaches to privacy can, broadly, be divided into two categories: free market, and consumer protection. In a free market approach, commercial entities are largely allowed to do what they wish, with the expectation that consumers will choose to do business with corporations that respect their privacy to a desired degree. If some companies are not sufficiently respectful of privacy, they will lose market share. Such an approach may be limited by lack of competition in a market, by enterprises not offering privacy options favorable to the user, or by lack of information about actual privacy practices.

Claims of privacy protection made by companies may be difficult for consumers to verify, except when they have already been violated. One example of the free market approach is to be found in the voluntary OECD Guidelines on the Protection of Privacy and Transborder Flows of Personal Data. The principles reflected in the guidelines are analysed in an article putting them into perspective with concepts of the GDPR put into law later in the European Union. In a consumer protection approach, in contrast, it is claimed that individuals may not have the time or knowledge to make informed choices, or may not have reasonable alternatives available. In support of this view, Jensen and Potts showed that most privacy policies are above the reading level of the average person. Therefore, this approach advocates greater government definition and enforcement of privacy standards.

Privacy law

Privacy law is the area of law concerning the protecting and preserving of privacy rights of individuals. While there is no universally accepted privacy law among all countries, some organizations promote certain concepts be enforced by individual countries. For example, the Universal Declaration of Human Rights, article 12, states:

No one shall be subjected to arbitrary interference with his privacy, family, home or correspondence, nor to attacks upon his honor and reputation. Everyone has the right to the protection of the law against such interference or attacks.

Australia

The Privacy Act 1988 is administered by the Office of the Australian Information Commissioner. Privacy law has been evolving in Australia for a number of years. The initial introduction of privacy law in 1998 extended to the public sector, specifically to Federal government departments, under the Information Privacy Principles. State government agencies can also be subject to state based privacy legislation. This built upon the already existing privacy requirements that applied to telecommunications providers (under Part 13 of the Telecommunications Act 1997), and confidentiality requirements that already applied to banking, legal and patient / doctor relationships.

The Privacy Act 1988 was then extended to include the private sector in 2000 with the introduction of the National Privacy Principles. These took effect in 2001. Small businesses with an annual turnover of $3 million were excluded from meeting the obligations specified in the National Privacy Principles with some exceptions such as those whose primary business was dealing in personal information.

In 2008 the Australian Law Reform Commission (ALRC) conducted a review of Australian Privacy Law. The resulting report "For Your Information". was one of the largest reports ever released by the ALRC. Amongst its many recommendations were the consolidation of both the Information Privacy Principles and the National Privacy Principles to form what is now known as the Australian Privacy Principles. This recommendation, and many others, were taken up and implemented by the Australian Government via the Privacy Amendment (Enhancing Privacy Protection) Bill 2012

The Australian Privacy Principles, along with other key changes to the overall Act, took effect on 12 March 2014. The new structure of the privacy principles follow the information cycle and incorporate key emerging privacy concepts including privacy by design.

There are currently 14 Australian Privacy Principles:

1. open and transparent management of personal information
2. anonymity and pseudonymity

3. collection of solicited personal information
4. dealing with unsolicited personal information
5. notification of the collection of personal information
6. use or disclosure of personal information
7. direct marketing
8. cross-border disclosure of personal information
9. adoption, use or disclosure of government related identifiers
10. quality of personal information
11. security of personal information
12. access to personal information
13. correction of personal information

As of 22 February 2018, the Privacy Amendment (Notifiable Data Breaches) Act 2017 will introduce a mandatory data breach notification obligations for all organisations that are subject to Australia's Privacy Act 1988 (Cth). This includes all Australian-registered companies and foreign-registered companies that carry on business in Australia or that interact with Australian data subjects.

Other Australian Privacy Laws

There are a range of other laws that provide privacy protection in Australia. These include, but are not limited to, the Telecommunications Act 1997, Spam Act 2006, the Do Not Call Register Act 2009, general confidentiality obligations arising from certain professional relationships including with doctors, lawyers and other health providers, state based legislation including NSW workplace surveillance laws, state based laws that apply in NSW, Queensland and other states for the handling of health information and the handling of information by state government agencies.

Brazil

The Constitution of Brazil sets privacy as a major fundamental right. Even the State is not allowed to violate personal data, intimacy, private life, honor and image (article 5, incise X). In extreme situations, a judicial order can authorize some level of disclosure. But some data, such as correspondence, are absolutely inviolable, and not even judicial order can authorize the disclosure.

China

Article 245 Whoever unlawfully subjects another person to a body search or a search of his residence or unlawfully intrudes into another person's residence shall be sentenced to fixed-term imprisonment of not more than three years or criminal detention. Any judicial officer who abuses his power and commits the crime mentioned in the preceding paragraph shall be given a heavier punishment.

Article 246 Whoever, by violence or other methods, publicly humiliates another person or invent stories to defame him, if the circumstances are serious, shall be sentenced to fixed-term imprisonment of not more than three years, criminal detention, public surveillance or deprivation of political rights. The crime mentioned in the preceding paragraph shall be handled only upon complaint, except where serious harm is done to public order or to the interests of the State.

Article 252 Whoever conceals, destroys or unlawfully opens another person's letter, thereby infringing upon the citizen's right to freedom of correspondence, if the circumstances are serious, shall be sentenced to fixed-term imprisonment of not more than one year or criminal detention.

Article 253 Any postal worker who opens without authorization or conceals or destroys mail or telegrams shall be sentenced to fixed-term imprisonment of not more than two years or criminal detention. Whoever steals money or property by committing the crime mentioned in the preceding paragraph shall be convicted and given a heavier punishment in accordance with the provisions of Article 264 of this Law.

Canada

Canadian privacy law is governed federally by multiple acts, including the Canadian Charter of Rights and Freedoms, and the Privacy Act (Canada). Mostly this legislation concerns privacy infringement by government organizations. Data privacy was first addressed with the Personal Information Protection and Electronic Documents Act, and provincial-level legislation also exists to account for more specific cases personal privacy protection against commercial organizations.

European Union

For Europe, Article 8 of the European Convention on Human Rights guarantees the right to respect for private and family life, one's home and correspondence. The European Court of Human Rights in Strasbourg has developed a large body of jurisprudence defining this fundamental right to privacy. The European Union requires all member states to legislate to ensure that citizens have a right to privacy, through directives such as the 1995 Directive 95/46/EC on the protection of personal data. It is regulated in the United Kingdom by the Data Protection Act 1998 and in France data protection is also monitored by the CNIL, a governmental body which must authorize legislation concerning privacy before it can be enacted. In civil law jurisdictions, the right to privacy fell within the ambit of the right to a private life (droit a la vie privee) from which the tort could be claimed. Personality rights and the broader tort based interpretation of the right to privacy protected correspondence, personal information and dignity. These rights gave rise to causes for damages in most civil law jurisdictions and common law jurisdictions prior to the sui generis development of Data Protection. Although there are comprehensive regulations for data protection, some studies show that despite the laws, there is a lack of enforcement in that no institution feels responsible to control the parties involved and enforce their laws. The European Union is also championing for the 'Right to be Forgotten' concept (which allows individuals to ask that links leading to information about themselves be removed from internet search engine results) to be adopted by other countries.

India

Due to the introduction of the Aadhaar project inhabitants of India were afraid that their privacy could be invaded. The project was also met with mistrust regarding the safety of the social protection infrastructures. To tackle the fear amongst the people, India's supreme court put a new ruling into action that stated that privacy from then on was seen as a fundamental right. On 24 August 2017 this new law was established.

Italy

In Italy the right to privacy is enshrined in Article 15 of the Constitution, which states:

"Freedom and confidentiality of correspondence and of every other form of communication is inviolable. Limitations may only be imposed by judicial decision stating the reasons and in accordance with the guarantees provided by the law."

United Kingdom

In the United Kingdom, it is not possible to bring an action for invasion of privacy. An action may be brought under another tort (usually breach of confidence) and privacy must then be considered under EC law. In the UK, it is sometimes a defence that disclosure of private information was in the public interest. There is, however, the Information Commissioner's Office (ICO), an independent public body set up to promote access to official information and protect personal information. They do this by promoting good practice, ruling on eligible complaints, giving information to individuals and organisations, and taking action when the law is broken. The relevant UK laws include: Data Protection Act 1998; Freedom of Information Act 2000; Environmental Information Regulations 2004; Privacy and Electronic Communications Regulations 2003. The ICO has also provided a "Personal Information Toolkit" online which explains in more detail the various ways of protecting privacy online.

United States

Although the US Constitution does not explicitly include the right to privacy, individual as well as locational privacy are implicitly granted by the Constitution under the

4th Amendment. The Supreme Court of the United States has found that other guarantees have "penumbras" that implicitly grant a right to privacy against government intrusion, for example in Griswold v. Connecticut (1965). In the United States, the right of freedom of speech granted in the First Amendment has limited the effects of lawsuits for breach of privacy. Privacy is regulated in the US by the Privacy Act of 1974, and various state laws. The Privacy Act of 1974 only applies to Federal agencies in the executive branch of the Federal government. Certain privacy rights have been established in the United States via legislation such as the Children's Online Privacy Protection Act (COPPA), the Gramm-Leach-Bliley Act (GLB), and the Health Insurance Portability and Accountability Act (HIPAA).

Privacy Index

The Electronic Privacy Information Center's Privacy Index puts Brazil, Australia, Japan and South Africa in the higher level of privacy (around 2.2). On the bottom of the list are the United States and United Kingdom (around 1.4).

Privacy on the Internet

There are many means to protect one's privacy on the internet. For example, e-mails can be encrypted (via S/MIME or PGP) and anonymizing proxies or anonymizing networks like I2P and Tor can be used to prevent the internet service providers from knowing which sites one visits and with whom one communicates. Covert collection of personally identifiable information has been identified as a primary concern by the U.S. Federal Trade Commission. Although some privacy advocates recommend the deletion of original and third-party HTTP cookies, Anthony Miyazaki, marketing professor at Florida International University and privacy scholar, warns that the "elimination of third-party cookie use by Web sites can be circumvented by cooperative strategies with third parties in which information is transferred after the Web site's use of original domain cookies." As of December 2010, the Federal Trade Commission is reviewing policy regarding this issue as it relates to behavioral advertising. Another aspect of privacy on the Internet relates to online social networking. Several online social network sites (OSNs) are among the top 10 most visited websites globally. A review and evaluation of scholarly work regarding the current state of the value of individuals' privacy of online social networking show the following results: "first, adults seem to be more concerned about potential privacy threats than younger users; second, policy makers should be alarmed by a large part of users who underestimate risks of their information privacy on OSNs; third, in the case of using OSNs and its services, traditional one-dimensional privacy approaches fall short". This is exacerbated by the research indicating that personal traits such as sexual orientation, race, religious and political views, personality, or intelligence can be inferred based on the wide variety of digital footprint, such as samples of text, browsing logs, or Facebook Likes.

Privacy and location-based services

Increasingly, mobile devices facilitate location tracking. This creates user privacy problems. A user's location and preferences constitute personal information. Their improper use violates that user's privacy. A recent MIT study by de Montjoye et al. showed that 4 spatio-temporal points, approximate places and times, are enough to uniquely identify 95% of 1.5M people in a mobility database. The study further shows that these constraints hold even when the resolution of the dataset is low. Therefore, even coarse or blurred datasets provide little anonymity.

Several methods to protect user privacy in location-based services have been proposed, including the use of anonymizing servers, blurring of information e.a. Methods to quantify privacy have also been proposed, to calculate the equilibrium between the benefit of providing accurate location information and the drawbacks of risking personal privacy. Users of such services may also choose to display more generic location information (i.e. "In the City" or "Philadelphia" or "Work") to some of their more casual acquaintances while only displaying specific location information, such as their exact address, to closer contacts like spouse, relatives, and good friends.

In recent years, seen with the increasing importance of mobile devices and paired with the National Do Not Call Registry, telemarketers have turned attention to mobiles. The efforts of telemarketers to use mobile devices have been met with both Federal Trade Commission and companies like PrivacyStar. Each year, thousands of complaints are filed to the FTC database with the help of companies and consumers.

Privacy by design

The principle of privacy by design states that privacy and data protection are embedded throughout the entire life cycle of technologies, from the early design stage to their deployment, use and ultimate disposal.

Privacy engineering

The practice of constructing, ostensibly, software or information systems that adhere to given privacy policies and relevant compliances is a developing area and is known as Privacy engineering

Privacy self-synchronization

Privacy self-synchronization is the mode by which the stakeholders of an enterprise privacy program spontaneously contribute collaboratively to the program's maximum success. The stakeholders may be customers, employees, managers, executives, suppliers, partners or investors. When self-synchronization is reached, the model states that the personal interests of individuals toward their privacy is in balance with the business interests of enterprises who collect and use the personal information of those individuals.

Privacy paradox

The privacy paradox is a phenomenon in which online users state that they are concerned about their privacy but behave as if they were not. While this term was coined as early as 1998, it wasn't used in its current popular sense until the year 2000. In his article titled "'Opting In': A Privacy Paradox," John Schwartz wrote that "It's one of the more puzzling conundrums of online life. While companies that capitalize on the Internet's powerful potential to invade privacy are denounced as villains of the information age, millions of people type out highly personal data and send it off to Web sites they've barely heard of, with no strong legal protection against misuse of the information. ...The paradox helps illustrate the complexity of the debate over privacy."

Susan B. Barnes similarly used the term "privacy paradox" to refer to the ambiguous boundary between private and public space on social media. When compared to adults, young people tend to disclose more information on social media. However, this does not mean that they are not concerned about their privacy. Susan B. Barnes gave a case in her article: in a television interview about Facebook, a student addressed her concerns about disclosing personal information online. However, when the reporter asked to see her Facebook page, she put her home address, phone numbers, and pictures of her young son on the page.

Privacy paradox has been studied and scripted in different research settings. Although several studies have shown this inconsistency between privacy attitudes and behavior among online users, the reason for the paradox still remains unclear. A main explanation for the privacy paradox is that users lack awareness of the risks and the degree of protection. Users may underestimate the harm of disclosing information online. On the other hand, some researchers argue the privacy paradox comes from lack of technology literacy and from the design of sites. For example, users may not know how to change their default settings even though they care about their privacy. Psychologists particularly pointed out that the privacy paradox occurs because users must trade-off between their privacy concerns and impression management. Other individual factors such as gender, age, trust and personality, may also account for the paradox.

The right to privacy in popular culture

The 1993 film The Pelican Brief, based on the novel of the same name, touches on privacy. In one scene, a law professor discusses the Constitutional right to privacy. One of his students, played by Julia Roberts, argues that the majority opinion in Bowers v Hardwick was wrongly decided.

In "Short List", 1999 episode of the TV series The West Wing, the right to privacy arises during the appointment of a Supreme Court judge. Sam Seabourne ventures the opinion that Internet privacy will be a major social issue in the next two decades.

Selfie culture

Selfies are popular today. A search for photos with the hashtag #selfie retrieves over 23 million results on Instagram and "a whopping 51 million with the hashtag #me" However, due to modern corporate and governmental surveillance, this may pose a risk to privacy. In a research which takes a sample size of 3763, researchers found that for selfies, females generally have greater concerns than male social media users. Users who have greater concerns inversely predict their selfie behavior and activity.

Electronic document and records management system

Electronic document and records management system (EDRMS) is a type of content management system and refers to the combined technologies of document management and records management systems as an integrated system.

Electronic document and records management is used by organizations to manage documents and records throughout the document life-cycle, from creation to destruction.

Typically, systems consider a document or file to be a work-in-progress until it has undergone review, approval, lock-down, and (potentially) publication, where it will wait to be used. The version of the form that is saved containing user content will become a formal record within the organization.

Once a document achieves the status of a record, the organization may apply best-practice or legally enforced retention policies which state how the second half of the record life-cycle will progress. This typically involves retention (and protection from change), until some events occur which relate to the record and which trigger the final disposition schedule to apply to the record. Eventually, typically at a set time after these events, the record undergoes destruction.

EDRMS software

A range of software vendors offer these systems at an enterprise level (i.e. targeted at managing all documents and records within an enterprise).

These vendors have historically provided electronic document management systems and have acquired smaller records management system companies. The seamlessness of the integration and the original intention of the records-management component to manage electronic records typically sets the complexity of deploying and potentially of using the final system.

Information and Records Management Society

The IRMS (Information and Records Management Society) (formerly known as the Records Management Society) was founded in 1983 as the main professional body for records managers in Great Britain and Ireland. Its objectives are to strive to further knowledge of good governance in the management of information and records created during the course of the business activities of any organisation, whatever their media, and to promote fellowship and co-operation amongst individuals working in the field.

All those in any country concerned with records and information, regardless of their professional or organisational status or qualifications, can join the society, which currently has over 1100 members from 30 countries. There are specific interest groups for the public sector, third sector, SharePoint, property, financial and higher and further education, as well as geographical groups in Ireland, Scotland and Wales and the North, Midlands, London, and South West of England.

The society organises meetings and an annual conference, publishes the bi-monthly Record Management Bulletin containing comment, analysis, case studies and news from the UK and international information and records management scene, produces information guides on issues such as records retention and information technology, and runs training courses for members and non-members. The society changed its name to the Information and Records Management Society in 2010. The society changed its name to the IRMS in 2014 along with its strap line from "The Home of Information and Records Management" to The Interactive Hub of the Information World.

National Archives and Records Administration

The National Archives and Records Administration (NARA) is an independent agency of the United States government charged with preserving and documenting government and historical records and with increasing public access to those documents, which comprise the National Archives. NARA is officially responsible for maintaining and publishing the legally authentic and authoritative copies of acts of Congress, presidential directives, and federal regulations. The NARA also transmits votes of the Electoral College to Congress.

Organization

The Archivist of the United States is the chief official overseeing the operation of the National Archives and Records Administration. The Archivist not only maintains the official documentation of the passage of amendments to the U.S. Constitution by state legislatures, but has the authority to declare when the constitutional threshold for passage has been reached, and therefore when an act has become an amendment.

The Office of the Federal Register publishes the Federal Register, Code of Federal Regulations, and United States Statutes at Large, among others. It also administers the Electoral College.

The National Historical Publications and Records Commission (NHPRC)-the agency's grant-making arm-awards funds to state and local governments, public and private archives, colleges and universities, and other nonprofit organizations to preserve and publish historical records. Since 1964, the NHPRC has awarded some 4,500 grants.

The Office of Government Information Services (OGIS) is a Freedom of Information Act (FOIA) resource for the public and the government. Congress has charged NARA with reviewing FOIA policies, procedures and compliance of Federal agencies and to recommend changes to FOIA. NARA's mission also includes resolving FOIA disputes between Federal agencies and requesters.

History

Originally, each branch and agency of the U.S. government was responsible for maintaining its own documents, which often resulted in the loss and destruction of records. Congress established the National Archives Establishment in 1934 to centralize federal record keeping, with the Archivist of the United States as chief administrator. The National Archives was incorporated with GSA in 1949; in 1985 it became an independent agency as NARA (National Archives and Records Administration).

The first Archivist, R.D.W. Connor, began serving in 1934, when the National Archives was established by Congress. As a result of a first Hoover Commission recommendation, in 1949 the National Archives was placed within the newly formed General Services Administration (GSA). The Archivist served as a subordinate official to the GSA Administrator until the National Archives and Records Administration became an independent agency on April 1, 1985.

In March 2006, it was revealed by the Archivist of the United States in a public hearing that a memorandum of understanding between NARA and various government agencies existed to "reclassify", i.e., withdraw from public access, certain documents in the name of national security, and to do so in a manner such that researchers would not be likely to discover the process (the U.S. reclassification program). An audit indicated that more than one third withdrawn since 1999 did not contain sensitive information. The program was originally scheduled to end in 2007.

In 2010, Executive Order 13526 created the National Declassification Center to coordinate declassification practices across agencies, provide secure document services to other agencies, and review records in NARA custody for declassification.

Records

NARA's holdings are classed into "record groups" reflecting the governmental department or agency from which they originated. Records include paper documents, microfilm, still pictures, motion pictures, and electronic media.

Archival descriptions of the permanent holdings of the federal government in the custody of NARA are stored in the National Archives Catalog. The archival descriptions include information on traditional paper holdings, electronic records, and artifacts. As of December 2012, the catalog consisted of about 10 billion logical data records describing 527,000 artifacts and encompassing 81% of NARA's records. There are also 922,000 digital copies of already digitized materials.

Most records at NARA are in the public domain, as works of the federal government are excluded from copyright protection. However, records from other sources may still be protected by copyright or donor agreements. Executive Order 13526 directs originating agencies to declassify documents if possible before shipment to NARA for long-term storage, but NARA also stores some classified documents until they can be declassified. Its Information Security Oversight Office monitors and sets policy for the U.S. government's security classification system. Many of NARA's most requested records are frequently used for genealogy research. This includes census records from 1790 to 1940, ships' passenger lists, and naturalization records.

Facilities and exhibition spaces

The most well known facility of the National Archives and Records Administration is the National Archives Building (informally known as "Archives I"), located north of the National Mall on Constitution Avenue in Washington, D.C.. A sister facility, known as the National Archives at College Park ("Archives II") was opened 1994 near the University of Maryland, College Park. The Washington National Records Center (WNRC), also located in the Washington, D.C., metropolitan area, is a large warehouse facility where federal records that are still under the control of the creating agency are stored. Federal government agencies pay a yearly fee for storage at the facility. In accordance with federal records schedules, documents at WNRC are transferred to the legal custody of the National Archives after a certain time; this usually involves a relocation of the records to College Park. Temporary records at WNRC are either retained for a fee or destroyed after retention times have elapsed. WNRC also offers research services and maintains a small research room.

Across the United States, the National Archives maintains both research facilities and additional federal records centers (FRCs). In many cases, the research rooms of regional archives are located at the same site as the federal records center, which are inaccessible to the public.

Public-private partnerships

In an effort to make its holdings more widely available and more easily accessible, the National Archives began entering into public-private partnerships in 2006. A joint venture with Google will digitize and offer NARA video online. When announcing the agreement, Archivist Allen Weinstein said that this pilot program is

"... an important step for the National Archives to achieve its goal of becoming an archive without walls. Our new strategic plan emphasizes the importance of providing access to records anytime, anywhere. This is one of many initiatives that we are launching to make our goal a reality. For the first time, the public will be able to view this collection of rare and unusual films on the Internet."

On January 10, 2007, the National Archives and Fold3.com (formerly Footnote) launched a pilot project to digitize historic documents from the National Archives holdings. Allen Weinstein explained that this partnership would "allow much greater access to approximately 4.5 million pages of important documents that are currently available only in their original format or on microfilm" and "would also enhance NARA's efforts to preserve its original records."

In July 2007, the National Archives announced it would make copies of its collection of Universal Newsreels from 1929 to 1967 available for purchase through CreateSpace, an Amazon.com subsidiary. During the announcement, Weinstein noted that the agreement would "... reap major benefits for the public-at-large and for the National Archives." Adding, "While the public can come to our College Park, Maryland, research room to view films and even copy them at no charge, this new program will make our holdings much more accessible to millions of people who cannot travel to the Washington, D.C. area." The agreement also calls for CreateSpace partnership to provide the National Archives with digital reference and preservation copies of the films as part of NARA's preservation program.

In May 2008, the National Archives announced a five-year agreement to digitize selected records including the complete U.S. Federal Census Collection, 1790-1930, passenger lists from 1820 to 1960 and World War I and World War II draft registration cards. The partnership agreement allows for exclusive use of the digitized records by Ancestry.com for a 5-year embargo period whereupon the digital records will be turned over to the National Archives.

Social media

The National Archives currently utilizes social media and Web 2.0 technologies in an attempt to communicate better with the public.

On June 18, 2009, the National Archives announced the launching of a YouTube channel "to showcase popular archived films, inform the public about upcoming events around the country, and bring National Archives exhibits to the people." Also in 2009, the National Archives launched a Flickr photostream to share portions of its photographic holdings with the general public. A new teaching-with-documents Web site premiered in 2010 and was developed by the education team. The site features 3,000 documents, images, and recordings from the holdings of the Archives. It also features lesson plans and tools for creating new classroom activities and lessons.

In 2011, the National Archives initiated a WikiProject on the English Wikipedia to expand collaboration in making its holdings widely available through Wikimedia.

Notable crimes

- In 1963, Robert Bradford Murphy and his wife, Elizabeth Irene Murphy were arrested and sentenced to ten years in prison for stealing documents from several federal depositories, including the National Archives.
- In 1987, Charles Merrill Mount was arrested and sentenced to five years in prison for stealing 400 documents from the National Archives.
- In 2002, Shawn Aubitz was arrested for stealing hundreds of documents and photographs from the National Archives; served 21 months in prison and paid $73,000 in restitution.
- In 2005, Sandy Berger was charged with an unauthorized removal of documents from the National Archives; sentenced to 100 hours of community service and fined $50,000.
- In 2005, Howard Harner was sentenced to two years in prison and fined $10,000 after stealing 100 documents from the National Archives.
- In 2006, Denning McTague was sentenced to 15 months in prison and fined $3,000 after stealing 164 documents from the National Archives.
- In 2011, Leslie Waffen was sentenced to 18 months in prison after stealing 955 recordings from the National Archives.
- In 2011, Thomas Lowry was permanently banned from the National Archives after he confessed to altering the date on a presidential pardon signed by Abraham Lincoln.
- In 2011, Barry Landau and Jason Savedoff were arrested and sentenced to seven-and-a-half years in prison for stealing ten thousand documents from the National Archives.

Records management taxonomy is the representation of data, upon which the classification of unstructured content is based, within an organization. It may manifest itself as metadata in structured database fields or in folder structures represented to end users from a user interface within a system. It is created to facilitate the correct records management policies within the organization, fulfilment of regulatory compliance, integration to operational and knowledge management systems and the search for information within the organization. It can be applied to physical and or electronic records.

Disciplines and or professions may create template taxonomies which are commonly used such as for Engineering and or Pharmaceutical Research. However, most organizations and or business functions within an organization may define taxonomies based on organizational requirements.

A records manager is the professional responsible for records management in an organization. This role has evolved over time and takes many forms, with many related areas of knowledge required for professional competency.

Records managers are found in all types of organizations, including business, government, and nonprofit sectors. Generally, dedicated (i.e., full-time) records managers are found in larger organizations.

Records management evolved from the development of archives in the United States government following World War II. With the explosion of paper records during that war, better systems of management were needed to retain and make the records available for current use. Records managers became specialists that bridged the gap between file clerks and archivists. The profession expanded into the corporate world in the 1950s.

BIBLIOGRAPHY

- ARMA International. "Glossary of Records and Information Management Terms, 3rd Edition". ARMA International. Archived from the original on 2013-09-28.
- International Organization for Standardization - ISO (2001). "ISO 15489-1:2001 - Information and Documentation - Records Management - Part 1: General". International Organization for Standardization - ISO. Archived from the original on 2014-04-02.
- Megill, Kenneth (2005). Corporate Memory: Records and Information Management in the Knowledge Age (2nd ed.). Munich: K.G. Saur/Thomson.
- Anthony Tarantino (2008-02-25). Governance, Risk, and Compliance to the Handbook. ISBN 978-0-470-09589-8.
- Yeo, Geoffrey (2007). "Concepts of Record (1): Evidence, Information, and Persistent Representations". American Archivist. 70 (2): 315-343. doi:10.17723/aarc.70.2.u327764v1036756q.
- Schellenberg, T. R. (October 1956). "The Appraisal of Modern Records". Bulletins of the National Archives (8). Archived from the original on 2016-11-24.
- "Glossary of Records and Information Management Terms, 3rd Edition". ARMA International. Archived from the original on September 27, 2013. Retrieved September 3, 2016.
- Pearce-Moses, Richard. "Record". Glossary of Archival and Records Terminology. Society of American Archivists. Archived from the original on 24 November 2016. Retrieved 23 November 2016.

- Muller, S.; Feith, J. A.; Fruin, R (1968). Arthur H. Leavitt, ed. Manual for the Arrangement and Description of Archives (1898) (2nd ed.). New York.
- Cook, Terry (1997). "What Is Past Is Prologue: A History of Archival Ideas Since 1898, and the Future Paradigm Shift". Archivaria. 43: 17-63. Archived from the original on 24 November 2016. Retrieved 23 November 2016.
- Assistant Secretary of Defence for Networks and Information Integration, Department of Defence Chief Information Officer (April 25, 2007). "United States Department of Defense Standard 5015.02 (DoD Std 5012.02), Electronic Records Management Software Applications Design Criteria Standard" (PDF). United States Department of Defense - US DOD. Archived from the original (PDF) on 2013-02-22.
- Hale, Judith (December 2011). Performance-Based Certification: How to Design a Valid, Defensible, Cost-Effective Program. John Wiley & Sons, Inc. ISBN 978-1-118-02724-0. Archived from the original on 2013-09-27.
- Hulme, Tony (June 2012). "Information Governance: Sharing the IBM approach". Business Information Review. 29 (vol. 29 no. 2): 99-104. doi:10.1177/0266382112449221. Archived from the original on 2013-09-25.
- Jeremy C. Maxwell; Annie I. Antón; Peter Swire; Maria Riaz; Christopher M. McCraw (June 2012). "A legal cross-references taxonomy for reasoning about compliance requirements". Requirements Engineering. 17 (Volume 17, Issue 2): 99-115. doi:10.1007/s00766-012-0152-5.
- European Commission (2011). MoReq2010, modular requirements for records systems, Core services & plug-in modules, version 1.1, Volume 1. European Commission. doi:10.2792/2045. ISBN 978-92-79-18519-9.
- "Records management code". The National Archives. Archived from the original on 2016-02-02.
- COMP7420: Electronic Document and Records Management, Tom Worthington, Australian National University, from February 2011 Archived February 19, 2011, at the Wayback Machine
- https://www.archives.gov/records_management/policy_and_guidance/automated_recordkeeping_requirements.html Archived April 9, 2005, at the Wayback Machine

INDEX

9 789390 013739

Printed at Repro India Ltd.